MW00446159

W. G. SEBALD –
IMAGE, ARCHIVE, MODERNITY

W. G. SEBALD –
IMAGE, ARCHIVE, MODERNITY

J. J. Long

COLUMBIA UNIVERSITY PRESS
NEW YORK

Columbia University Press
Publishers Since 1893
New York

Copyright © 2007 J. J. Long
All rights reserved

First published in the United Kingdom by Edinburgh University Press

Library of Congress Cataloging-in-Publication Data

Long, J. J. (Jonathan James), 1969–
  W. G. Sebald : image, archive, modernity / J. J. Long.
    p. cm.
  Includes bibliographical references and index.
  ISBN 978-0-231-14512-1 (cloth : alk. paper)-ISBN 978-0-231-14513-8 (pbk. : alk. paper)
  1. Sebald, Winfried Georg, 1944–2001—Criticism and interpretation. I. Title.

PT2681.E18Z68 2007
833′914—dc22

2007036216

CONTENTS

ACKNOWLEDGEMENTS

In writing this book, I have benefited immensely from an ongoing dialogue with a large international community of Sebald scholars. In particular, I would like to thank Anne Fuchs for numerous stimulating exchanges of ideas, and for the invitation to participate in a Sebald symposium at University College, Dublin. I have also welcomed the opportunity to present tentative versions of this material at conferences in Davidson, Munich, and Sydney, and thank Scott Denham, Claudia Öhlschläger, Michael Niehaus, and Gerhard Fischer for the invitations. Thanks are also due to Silke Arnold-de Simine, who generously provided a pre-publication copy of her essay on the museum in *Austerlitz*. My colleagues at Durham have been a constant source of support, encouragement, and expertise. I wish especially to thank Ed Welch and Andrea Noble for their detailed comments on parts of the draft manuscript, and Nick Saul for conversations about everything from Romanticism to gypsies.

The University of Durham granted me a term of leave when I needed it most, and a second term of leave was funded by the Arts and Humanities Research Council of Great Britain. I am pleased to acknowledge their support here.

Working with Edinburgh University Press has been a pleasure. I am grateful to Jackie Jones for her enthusiasm for this project, and to James Dale for guiding the book through the press with wonderful efficiency.

Portions of Chapters 3 and 6 were previously published in an article entitled 'History, Narrative and Photography in W. G. Sebald's *Die Ausgewanderten*', *Modern Language Review* 98 (2003), 118–37, and are reproduced with the permission of the Modern Humanities Research Association. I wish to thank Theo Collier of the Wylie Agency for his help and advice in securing permission to reprint copyright material from Sebald's works. The sources of quotations and images are as follows:

Quotations from *Austerlitz*
From *Austerlitz* by W. G. Sebald, translated by Anthea Bell (Hamish Hamilton, 2001). Copyright © the Estate of W. G. Sebald. Translation copyright © Anthea Bell.

Excerpted from *Austerlitz* by W. G. Sebald. Copyright © W. G. Sebald 2001. Reprinted by permission of Knopf Canada.

From *Austerlitz* by W. G. Sebald, translated by Anthea Bell, copyright © 2001 by Anthea Bell. Used by permission of Random House, Inc.

Figures 3.2, 3.3, 3.5 and 6.1
© W.G. Sebald, from *Die Ausgewanderten*, first published in Germany by Eichborn AG, Frankfurt/Main 1993.

Figures 3.1, 3.4, 3.6, 3.7, 4.1, 5.1, 5.2
© W.G. Sebald, from *Schwindel. Gefühle*, first published in Germany by Eichborn AG, Frankfurt/Main 1990.

Finally, I owe more gratitude than I can express to Marita who is a wonderful companion, and to Jacob who is a delightful distraction. It is to them that this book is lovingly dedicated.

A NOTE ON REFERENCES AND TRANSLATIONS

Wherever possible in this study, I have quoted from the published English translations of Sebald's work, but page references to the German editions have been provided for those wishing to consult the original texts. The table below lists the abbreviations used. Full publication details are given in the bibliography at the end of the volume.

Abbreviation	English Title	German Title
A	*Austerlitz*	*Austerlitz*
BU		*Die Beschreibung des Unglücks*
CS	*Campo Santo*	*Campo Santo*
E	*The Emigrants*	*Die Ausgewanderten*
LL		*Logis in einem Landhaus*
NHD	*On the Natural History of Destruction*	*Luftkrieg und Literatur*
AN	*After Nature*	*Nach der Natur*
RS	*The Rings of Saturn*	*Die Ringe des Saturn*
U	*Unrecounted*	*Unerzählt*
UH		*Unheimliche Heimat*
V	*Vertigo*	*Schwindel.Gefühle*

All page references to the English translation will be given first, then those to the German edition. So, for example, the reference 'E 15/24' means that the quotation can be found on page 15 of *The Emigrants* and page 24 of *Die Ausgewanderten*.

For other works, published translations have been used wherever possible. All other translations are my own.

I

INTRODUCTION

Since his death in a road accident in December 2001, W. G. Sebald has become one of the most written-about contemporary German authors. Conferences devoted to his work have been held in Davidson (North Carolina), Munich, Paris, Sydney, Marbach am Neckar and elsewhere, and the secondary literature devoted to his work is now extensive – to say nothing of interviews, reviews, obituaries and further publications in press. While these scholarly writings discuss a wide range of thematic and formal aspects of Sebald's work, it is possible to identify a limited number of topoi that recur in almost all the criticism so far published: the Holocaust, trauma and memory, melancholy, photography, travel and flânerie, intertextuality and *Heimat*.[1] It is my contention that these individual topoi can in fact be seen as epiphenomena of a much wider 'meta-problem' in Sebald's work, one to which only a small number of critics have drawn explicit attention, but which dominates his work from start to finish. That is the problem of modernity.

By modernity, I understand the seismic social, economic, political and cultural transformations that took place in European societies from the eighteenth century onwards.[2] These changes have their roots in a longer history that goes back to developments that occurred in the decades around 1500 (the 'discovery' of the New World, the Renaissance, the Reformation and the emergence of mercantilism). These moments conventionally represent the threshold between the medieval and early modern periods. But the eighteenth century witnesses accelerated change in economic, political and social organisation as a result of three related factors: Enlightenment thought, the Industrial Revolution and the French Revolution. The changes that characterise modernity are both numerous and varied, but one might single out the following as especially salient features: the industrialisation of production and the transformation of knowledge into technology on which industry depended; the unprecedented exploitation of natural resources; increasing standardisation and rationalisation in both the production and consumption of serially produced goods; rapid urban growth and concomitant demographic shifts as societies moved from being largely rural and agrarian to being predominantly industrial and urban; a series of developments in communications technology, including the telegraph, telephone and steam press, that facilitated the binding together of diverse and geographically dispersed audiences; the spread of new transport networks through railways, motorised road travel and aviation; and an increasingly rapid circulation of goods within an ever-expanding world market. Within the context of this study, of particular significance is the expansion of the nation state sustained by a proliferation of bureaucratic apparatuses and a range of civic institutions whose intended function was the regulation, discipline and control of populations.

The ways in which modernity is thematised in Sebald's writings can best be illustrated by surveying the various topics that have come to dominate Sebald research. One of the most widespread but also most problematic readings of Sebald is as a writer of 'Holocaust literature'. Journalistic reception of his work in Britain and the United States frequently portrayed Sebald in this light, and referred to his living 'in exile' in such a way as to imply expulsion or inner compulsion rather than economic migration, thereby implicitly establishing parallels between Sebald and the protagonists of *The Emigrants* and *Austerlitz*.[3] The emphasis on the Holocaust as the central concern of Sebald's work has been particularly prominent among anglophone critics. This is not to say that German critics have ignored the Holocaust, but in quantitative terms it remains the province of anglophone criticism.[4] It is effectively impossible to discuss the Holocaust without touching on the question of modernity. The 'Final Solution' has been conceived of as a pathological reaction to the experience of modernity, or as a kind of negation of modernity, a regression from the rational processes of civilisation to an archaic state of barbarism. Other scholars, such as Zygmunt Bauman (2000) and Tzvetan Todorov (1999), have countered this view, arguing that the Holocaust was an event whose very conditions of possibility lay in the technological rationality and bureaucracy characteristic of modernity itself. A third way is suggested by Dominick LaCapra, who advocates elucidation of:

> the intricate conjunction of [the Holocaust's] distinctively modern features (such as the seemingly dominant role of instrumental rationality,

bureaucratization, and massive technical resources) with the recurrence of often repressed forces, such as scapegoating with 'sacrificial' dimensions. (1994: 94)

However one seeks to understand the Holocaust, though, an examination of its relationship to modernity is inescapable.

Sebald scholars have in recent years – notably since the publication of *Austerlitz* in 2001 – begun to notice that the thematisation of the Holocaust in his work goes hand in hand with a profound concern with the longer history of modernity. In an article by Arthur Williams, for example, the 'metanarrative' of the Holocaust slips over into another metanarrative according to which the beginnings of the catastrophes of twentieth-century history are located firstly (and somewhat arbitrarily) 'around 1905' (2001: 80), and then in the seventeenth century (83). Thus even within the work of a critic who insists more than most on the centrality of the Holocaust, there is an acknowledgment, however fleeting, that Sebald is actually concerned with what Mark Anderson calls the *longue durée* of European modernity (2003: 104). To quote Anderson once more, '[T]he roads in Sebald's work do not all lead to Theresienstadt. The view of human devastation and darkness is much larger, at once geophysical and metaphysical, though their roots lie in a profound meditation on the violence of European modernity' (120).[5] This 'profound meditation' has yet to be explored in detail, even though it haunts other areas of Sebald research.

The question of memory, for example, is generally addressed with reference to the remembrance of the victims of Nazism in Sebald's work.[6] The so-called 'memory boom' has been identified as a feature of the past quarter-century of Western cultural life, and is seen by Andreas Huyssen as a response to specific late-twentieth-century technical processes – such as fast-speed information networks, Baudrillardian simulacra, and a threatening sense of non-synchronicity and heterogeneity – that are transforming our *Lebenswelt* (1995: 7). Yet memory has long formed an integral part of the way in which European societies sought to come to terms with the nature of modernity. In his book *Stranded in the Present: Modern Time and the Melancholy of History*, Peter Fritzsche locates the beginnings of this trend in the French Revolution and the European wars that followed it, which, he argues, produced major shifts in historical consciousness and a heightened awareness of the need to preserve the past. The experience of exile, for example, led to French aristocrats' conserving the artifacts of both exile and the *Ancien Régime*, thereby establishing loss and remembrance as fundamental components of identity (2004: 79). One might, with Richard Terdiman, locate the origins of the memory crisis at an even earlier point, in the changes wrought by shifts in production brought about by machines and the capitalisation of European economies (1993: 29). The continual production of the new in capitalism has as its concomitant the continual destruction of the old, and the acceleration of obsolescence itself. In this light, modernity was, from quite an early stage, understood as something that perpetually generated loss. Two effects can be seen to emerge from this. The first was to establish remembrance of loss as an imperative and thereby to link European identities to the recollected past. The second was to induce a crisis of memory at both individual and collective levels, engendered by a profound sense of historical rupture, a sense that the world had decisively changed, and consequently also a 'massive disruption of traditional forms of memory' (Terdiman 1993: 5). The expanding institutions of preservation and collection detailed by Fritzsche (2004), Susan Crane (2000) and Wolfgang Ernst (2003), the emergence of history as a distinct academic discipline, and ultimately also the hypertrophied historical consciousness lambasted by Nietzsche in *Vom Nutzen und Nachteil der Historie für das Leben* (1988) [*On the Use and Abuse of History for Life*] can all be seen as symptoms of the memory crisis at a collective level. In the sphere of individual life, it was primarily psychoanalysis, for which memory is both the source of the problem and the resource of the cure, that established the determining role of the past for a subject's present life.

One characteristic of the memory crisis is that memory ceases to be a pure matter of consciousness, and comes to reside instead in the very material of our social or psychic life. This is clear in the role that the institutions of memory – museums, archives, historiography, newspapers, photography – came to play in the course of the nineteenth century. Even in psychoanalysis, though, the unconscious exists within us but functions without our participation or our explicit allegiance (Terdiman 1993: 34). Furthermore, Freud's attempts to find suitable metaphors for the functioning of the unconscious led him repeatedly to material metaphors: archaeology, the 'mystic writing pad', and, most tellingly photography, which was a metaphor that Freud repeatedly invoked, rejected and reinstated, from 'A Note on the Unconscious in Psychoanalysis' (Freud 1958a) to *Moses and Monotheism* (Freud 1964). These metaphors imply that consciousness is always already infected by external mnemotechnical supplements; the artifacts of modernity are permanently lodged in the psyche as a kind of internal prosthesis. Memory and modernity are indissolubly linked.

Of the various media of memory, photography is the one most obviously present in Sebald's work.[7] Photography is in many ways the emblematic medium of modernity. Roland Barthes implied that the history of the world can be divided up into 'before' and 'after' photography (1977: 44), and Vilém Flusser sees the development of photography as a revolutionary moment on a par with the invention of linear writing in the second millennium BC (2000: 10). Jonathan Crary, on the other hand, sees photography as one part of a reorganisation of the 'ways in which vision was discussed, controlled, and incarnated in cultural and scientific practices' (1990: 7). For Crary, then, the visual regime of modernity begins not with photography, but with a 'radical abstraction and reconstruction of optical experience' (9) whose origins lay in the emergence of physiological optics in the late eighteenth and early nineteenth century. Furthermore, as a technical mode of representation that allows for potentially infinite mechanical reproduction, photography embodies the principles of technological rationality and seriality that govern capitalist production. Beyond that, however, photography also participates in numerous institutions, practices and discourses that lie at the heart of the modern European nation state: the discourses of criminology, anthropology, ethnography and race; the politics of colonialism; the implementation of 'scientific management'; the institutions of discipline and surveillance, and of the nuclear and extended family, to name just a few. In the context of Sebald's work, photography is most often discussed in relation to the crisis of memory, with particular focus on Sebald's questioning of photography's referentiality and mnemonic capacity. As we will see, however, the function of photography in Sebald's work exceeds by far the question of memory and touches on many of the discourses and practices of modernity that I have briefly outlined above.

Writings on photography frequently dwell on the inherent melancholy of the medium,[8] and melancholy is also one of the more obvious features of Sebald's prose.[9] Mary Cosgrove argues that Sebald's texts are dominated by an understanding of history as melancholy, which maroons the subject in the ruins of the immediate post-war years (Cosgrove 2006a: 218–20). In this light, the title of Peter Fritzsche's book *Stranded in the Present* aptly conveys the state of Sebald and his narrators. Fritzsche argues, furthermore, that this sense of history is a specifically modern phenomenon: 'Part of modern experience was a deepening sense of loss, a feeling of disconnection with the past, and a growing dread of the future' (2004: 49).[10]

But this is not the only link between melancholy and modernity. Wolf Lepenies' seminal work *Melancholie und Gesellschaft* (1998) [*Melancholy and Society*] offers an historical sociology of melancholy. In the foreword to the 1998 edition, Lepenies argues that the melancholy of the intellectual becomes a topos in Europe at the point when capitalism and the protestant work ethic instal the *vita activa* as the behavioural norm within bourgeois society, and marginalise the *vita contemplativa* (XXI). Whereas melancholy in the seventeenth century was worldly and internal to the social system that it served to stabilise (74), the melancholic of the eighteenth century – particularly but not solely in Germany – was excluded from political power (83). Though his melancholy was a reaction to this political disenfranchisement, it strove to conceal its own origins by positing the individual psyche as the cause of the melancholy (84–5). Lepenies points to the recurrence of a melancholy response to political setbacks in German history. He draws explicit parallels between the melancholy of the eighteenth-century German bourgeoisie, for whom political power failed to keep pace with economic emancipation, and the post-war Federal Republic's reaction to the moral and political catastrophe of Nazism (83–4). This tradition has been extended by Peter Morgan to encompass the left's response to the failures of 1968, and he sees Sebald as a belated and extreme example of this defining *linke Melancholie* or leftist melancholy (2005: 89). There are numerous other correspondences between Lepenies' bourgeois melancholic and the Sebaldian narrator, foremost among them being the tendency to flânerie as a way of protesting (albeit vainly) against commodification, and the elevation of nature to the status not only of a refuge (1998: 135), but of a mute recipient of the melancholic's emotional investments and projections (108). Like memory, then, melancholy is an aspect of Sebald's texts that might appear to be irreducibly individual or psychological, but once historicised emerges as one more element in a wider exploration of modernity.

Intimately related to the question of nature is that of *Heimat*, that untranslatable German word that basically means home, the place in which one is born and grows up and to which one feels a particular affinity. As most commentators note, the discourse of *Heimat* as it developed in the late nineteenth and early twentieth centuries was structured around a series of binary oppositions that:

> set country against city, province against metropolis, tradition against modernity, nature against artificiality, organic culture against civilization, fixed, familiar, rooted identity against cosmopolitanism, hybridity, alien otherness, or the faceless mass. (Boa and Palfreyman 2000: 2)

Indeed, the tradition-modernity binary actually subsumes the other pairings; *Heimat*-discourse is a product of modernity.[11] The notion of *Heimat* is, of course, dependant on its opposite and other, namely 'die Fremde' – the strange, foreign, geographically removed.[12] Sebald's peripatetic narrators repeatedly encounter new places, people and things. Their penchant for walking links them with the flâneur, that emblematic figure of urban modernity who, in his Benjaminian incarnation, responds to the rise of early commodity culture exemplified by the Parisian arcades, and to other features of urban life: the mass, alienation, the need to develop a shorthand form of making sense of fleeting urban encounters.[13] But Sebald's walkers are not tied exclusively to the urban environment. Eluned Summers-Bremner (2004), for example, suggests that Sebald's narrators' rural wanderings are an attempt to re-appropriate the legacy of the *Wandervogel* movement from its ideological debasement in Nazism. This movement originated in 1896, and its celebration of nature and of the human body's own locomotion, together with its revival of folk-song, can, like *Heimat*-discourse, be seen as a response to the forces of industrialisation, urbanisation and mechanisation. As such, the *Wandervögel* were a late manifestation of a longer history of walking as leisure pursuit that had begun with the Romantics in the late eighteenth century and stemmed from precisely the same motives (Solnit 2000: 83–4 and 104–17). Thus the modes of walking thematised in Sebald's works – urban flânerie and Romantic rural wandering – are products of modernity. Sebald's travelogues can be linked to modernity in other ways as well. Bianca Theisen, for example, sees Sebald's work as following a distinctively modern tradition of travel writing. She argues that the travel genre shifts in the eighteenth century from being an object-orientated account providing information about foreign countries and journeys to being a more clearly 'fictional', subject-orientated genre. This was facilitated by improved transport infrastructure, improved safety, and the greater accessibility of travel. Travel literature no longer needed to communicate information; rather, it couched travel experiences in personal reflections and awareness of a world that was already mediated by literature (2004: 166).

This implies, of course, that eighteenth-century travel writing was deeply intertextual, and intertextuality is the final major field of Sebald research.[14] If, as Gabriella Rovagnati (2005b: 146) claims, the practice of intertextuality is as old as literature itself and only the term is of recent provenance, intertextuality is clearly one area of investigation that ostensibly eludes the modernity problematic. And yet it is possible to historicise intertextuality. One of the problems addressed by W. K. Wimsatt and Monroe Beardsley in their famous article 'The Intentional Fallacy' (1970) was the high degree of allusiveness demonstrated by modernist poetry. This points to the emergence of a form of intertextuality in the work of Eliot and Pound – but also Joyce, Roussel, Kafka, Borges and numerous others – that was perceived as something new. Writing of painting, Foucault remarks that modernism was the first form of 'museum art' because it entertained a self-reflexive relationship to the tradition of painting and the institutions of art. Indeed, paintings such as Manet's *Olympia* acknowledge 'the new and substantial relationship of painting to itself, as a manifestation of the existence of museums and the particular reality and interdependence that paintings acquire in museums' (1977: 92). By thus thematising tradition in their paintings, the impressionists demonstrated their profound allegiance to one of modernity's central institutions. The same may be said of modernist writing: 'Flaubert produced the first literary work whose exclusive domain is that of books' (92). The institutions of literature are, of course, different, but in an age that saw the widespread opening of public libraries, the professionalisation of criticism, and the emergence of vernacular literatures as university disciplines that were deeply bound up with the constitution of national identity,[15] allusion in literature was a way of building into the text one's own relationship to the canon in a way that could be appreciated only by those professionals in possession of sufficient knowledge to notice the allusions and of the power to grant access to the canon. Such, I would argue, is the intertextuality of Sebald. It is an allusiveness aimed at academics and designed to ensure the works' canonicity.

There is more to the question of intertextuality than this. A further development characteristic of modernity is the realisation that the self is constituted of discourses that lie beyond the confines of consciousness. This is articulated by the German Romantics and finds its programmatic expression in Novalis' laconic dictum 'Das Ich ist eine Kunst, ein Kunstwerck' ['The self is an art, a work of art']. This is tantamount to the insight that literary subjectivity is a construct, a notion that is foregrounded time and time again in the literature of the nineteenth and, more conspicuously, the twentieth century. The deployment of intertextuality in Sebald's works is clearly indebted to this Romantic tradition, beginning with *Vertigo* and *The Emigrants*, whose narrators and protagonists 'must continuously confront the "truth" that [their] consciousness is inseparable from the endlessly reiterated narrative patterns of Western literature' (Kilbourn 2006: 63), and reaching an apotheosis in the figure of Jacques Austerlitz, the fabric of whose entire existence consists of references and allusions to other writers, philosophers and historians. In its use as both a guarantee of canonicity and a mode of subject-formation, intertextuality can be seen as a further continuation of the engagement with modernity that exists elsewhere in Sebald's work.

Wherever one looks in the literature on Sebald, then, one is confronted with topoi that are ineluctably and inextricably connected to the problems of modernity. In saying this, I do not wish to suggest that existing criticism on Sebald is misguided or irrelevant. My point is rather that modernity is a concern that permeates Sebald's writings, and the various themes that dominate Sebald scholarship testify, in symptomatic fashion, to this wider problematic.

This book offers an account of Sebald's relationship to modernity. My central focus is the (photographic) image and the archive. As I argue in more detail below, these are so central both to modernity and to Sebald's narrative project that they facilitate a wide-ranging exploration of modernity in Sebald's work and allow me to touch – sometimes directly, sometimes tangentially – on all the critical concerns mentioned above. Furthermore, it will emerge that the very structural and formal properties of Sebald's writing are themselves governed by an archival logic that can be understood only in relation to the problem of modernity.

MODERNITY AND THE ARCHIVE

One of the most striking and memorable moments in W. G. Sebald's oeuvre occurs towards the end of *Austerlitz*, when the protagonist launches an attack, simultaneously vituperative and comic, on the new Bibliothèque Nationale in Paris. He comes to the conclusion that the more perfect a system of information storage and retrieval is designed to be, the more likely this perfection is to flip over into chronic dysfunction and constitutional susceptibility to collapse (A 392–3/395). And yet the new Bibliothèque Nationale is built on the site of a Nazi facility for the cataloguing and 'redistribution' of goods confiscated from Parisian Jews. This was itself a vast archival enterprise, and foregrounds the close connection between archives and power.

For Sebald, who spent much of his professional life reading and writing about Austrian literature, the theme of the archive as a site of both power and malfunction will have been intimately familiar. The supreme example comes from an episode in Kafka's *The Castle*, in which the protagonist K. visits an official of the castle bureaucracy in order to find out more about his duties as a land surveyor.[16] The gouty and bed-ridden official orders his wife Mizzi to help:

> The woman opened the cabinet at once. K and the Superintendant looked on. The cabinet was crammed full of papers. When it was opened two large packages of papers rolled out, tied round in bundles, as one usually binds firewood; the woman sprang back in alarm. 'It must be down below, at the bottom', said the Superintendant, directing operations from the bed. Gathering the papers in both arms the woman obediently threw them all out of the cabinet so as to read those at the bottom. The papers now covered half the floor. 'A great deal of work is got through here,' said the Superintendant nodding his head, 'and that's only a small fraction of it. I've put away the most important pile in the shed, but the great mass of it has simply gone astray'. (1992: 62)

Sylvio Vietta, who begins his book on modern German literature by quoting this passage, sees the image of administrative and epistemological chaos as an image of the modern, *ein Bild der Moderne*. Vietta notes that in Kafka, all attempts at transmitting information and attaining knowledge tend to degenerate into the chaotic and labyrinthine. The representation of cognitive situations that become increasingly confused is, he argues, typical of the literature of the modern age, from the late eighteenth century to the present. It is a literature dominated by a profound sense of epistemological and linguistic crisis, in which the apprehension of any kind of totality is impossible, and the fragment or detail all that remains (1992: 7–8).

Yet in its concentration on collapse and confusion, Vietta's reading of Kafka remains one-dimensional, for the episode he analyses attests, too, to another aspect of modernity, namely the assumption that contingency and uncertainty can be managed through the error-free functioning of the administrative apparatus. The Superintendant tells K. the 'unpleasant truth' that the community has no need of a land surveyor, but denies that his being summoned was in any way down to bureaucratic malfunction. The files themselves provide proof: ' "[I]t was only certain auxiliary circumstances that entered and confused the matter, I'll prove it to you from the official papers," ' states the Superintendant (64). ' "It is a working principle of the Head Bureau that the very possibility of error must be ruled out of account. This ground principle is justified by the consummate organization of the whole authority, and it is necessary if the maximum speed in transacting business is to be attained" ' (66). The self-understanding of modernity itself is based not on a pervasive sense of epistemological chaos, but on an unbroken faith in the rationality of the archive.

A third facet of modernity also emerges from K.'s experiences in the house of the Superintendant, and that is the tendency of the apparatus to take on a life of its own and to function without human agency. If, for example, a case has dragged on for a long time, it sometimes happens that an arbitrary decision is suddenly reached. ' "It's as if the administrative apparatus were unable any longer to bear the tension, the year-long irritation caused by the same affair – probably trivial in itself – and had hit upon the decision by itself, without the assistance of the officials," ' explains the Superintendant (70). In Sebald's example, the ludicrous lengths to which a visitor has to go in order to gain entrance to the Bibliothèque Nationale (A 386–91/388–95) partly involve transfer from one level of the library to another by means of a moving walkway, the German *Förderband* (conveyor belt) demonstrating by its proximity to *Fließband* (production line) (and by the fact that in *Duden*'s definition a *Förderband* is designed to carry goods, not people) the similarity of the library to processes of industrial production. This inversion, according to which humans become subservient to the demands of the apparatus, dramatises an aspect of modernity that theorists from Marx to Foucault and beyond have sought to comprehend, namely the role of the apparatus in the constitution of the modern subject.

What we encounter in both the inhuman monumentality of Sebald's Bibliothèque Nationale and the shambolic amateurishness of Kafka's filing cupboard is a series of ambivalences that lie at the heart of cultural responses to modernity. On the one hand, there is an acknowledgment of modernity's drive towards rationalisation, bureaucratisation and documentation across a large and expanding range of human activity. On the other hand, there is a sense that these processes tend to subject individuals to the exigencies of the apparatus, which in turn produces effects of subjectivity that may be more or less negatively evaluated. Furthermore, the archival apparatus has in both cases expanded to such an extent that it exceeds the cognitive capacity of any single individual fully to apprehend it. Increasing rationalisation thus paradoxically gives rise to a perception of precisely the confusion and epistemological chaos to which Vietta refers. One of the recurring thematic emphases in accounts of modernity, from Baudelaire and Marx to David Harvey, is that processes of rationalisation are *experienced* as flux, ephemerality, instability, disorientation and fragmentation. Though it may be a lousy translation of Marx's dictum 'alles Ständische und Stehende verdampft', the title of Marshall Berman's book (1988) neatly sums up the sentiment: *All that is Solid Melts into Air*.[17]

In this book, I trace the ways in which these ambivalences manifest themselves in Sebald's work. Following Sebald (who is himself following Kafka), I explore these problems with reference to the archive. As a political technology, an epistemological technology, and a technology of representation, the archive is one of modernity's signature artifacts. Mary Ann Doane (2002) argues that modernity is characterised by a generalised 'archival desire', a desire to which a large range of institutions and recording technologies responded. Michel Foucault, too, identifies the archival idea as a distinctly modern phenomenon, noting that:

> the idea of accumulating everything, the idea of constituting a sort of general archive, the desire to contain all times, all ages, all forms, all tastes in one place, the idea of constituting a place of all times that is itself outside of time and protected from its erosion, the project of thus organising a sort of perpetual and indefinite accumulation of time in a place that will not move – well, in fact, all of this belongs to our modernity. (Foucault 2000: 182)[18]

The archive also lies at the very heart of Sebald's narrative project. His work is profoundly concerned with the material and infrastructural basis of knowledge systems, and his narrators spend an inordinate amount of time in museums and galleries, libraries and archives, zoos and menageries. They betray a fascination with timetables, inventories, ledgers, albums, ships' logs, atlases, newspapers, diaries, letters and photographs. In short, they are obsessed with processes of archivisation and with the places where the past has deposited traces and fragments that have been preserved and in many cases systematised, catalogued, or indexed.

My use of the word 'archive' is deliberately broad. Media theorist Wolfgang Ernst is at pains to distinguish the archive proper from the museum and library on the one hand, and, on the other, from the metaphorical extension of the term such as one finds in recent French philosophy. For Ernst, who is deeply indebted to a specifically German form of *Archivwissenschaft*, the archive is first and foremost a juridico-political instrument of state administration. He sees it as non-narrative (and at times even non-discursive), and opposes it to the use of archives by historians which, he argues, constitutes a misreading and misuse of the archive proper (2002: 8). Ernst repeatedly makes the point that archives become available to the historian once their immediate political functionality is lost: 'It is precisely at the point where there is no longer a connection between the documents and power that the archive is opened and the work of the historian begins, retroactively' (8). While his later book *Im Namen von Geschichte* traces the encroaching influence of the idea of the nation and the demands of historiography on archival practice (2003: 594–615), Ernst discusses the archive almost exclusively on the level of the state. There are two fundamental problems with this approach. The first is that it is narrow and normative, and proves incapable of accounting either for archival practices and institutions that exist below the level of the state or for other modes of storage and taxonomy that share in an archival epistemology. The second is that Ernst's conception of power is monolithic and naïve. The notion that the relationship between archives and power disappears the moment archival material is no longer of instrumental use to a particular state neglects the fact that, as Foucault has shown, modes of knowledge are implicated in power relationships that cannot be reduced to a top-down model of state prohibition. What is needed is a concept of the archive that acknowledges the vast plurality of archival practices that emerge in modernity, and an understanding of power that might account for their biopolitical functioning.

The term 'archive' as used here thus encompasses a wide range of institutions and practices that are linked by several fundamental defining qualities. Jacques Derrida's *Archive Fever*, while not without its problems (as we shall see at several points throughout this study), begins with a meditation on what constitutes an archive by linking the word to its etymology in the *archeion*, the office of the *archons* or chief magistrates of ancient Athens. Derrida posits an 'archontic function', which unites the right to interpret archival documents ('to speak the law') with a place of domiciliation and the provision of a stable substrate for the archive (1995: 2). But he goes on to note that this archontic power 'also gathers the functions of unification, of identification, of classification' and what he calls 'consignation' or gathering together (3). Derrida's concern with Freud in *Archive Fever* saddles him with a psychoanalytic conception of power as prohibition or patriarchal law. This is again excessively monolithic. The other aspects of Derrida's definition of the archontic function, however, respond precisely to the need for a more inclusive notion of the archive. If the archive is defined not by immediate etatist functionality but by the principles of unification, identification, classification and gathering, then clearly museums, libraries, and all kinds of collection fall within its purview.

It is true that the modern public archive came into being in order to 'solidify and memorialise first monarchical and then state power' (Steedman 2001: 69). More importantly, archives emerged as part of the *modernising* state: the House of Savoy instituted an archive in Turin in the early eighteenth century, followed by Peter the Great in St Petersburg in 1720 and Maria Theresia in Vienna in 1749. The 1760s and 1770s saw the establishment of princely and civic archives in Warsaw, Venice and Florence, while the National Archives in France were founded in 1790, and the British Public Records Office in 1838 (69). And yet state archives represent just one of numerous institutions, practices and technologies that characterise modernity's obsession with collecting, preserving and classifying. Many (though by no means all) of these ended up serving the interests of the expanding nineteenth-century state, but they did so not on the basis of a global or unitary strategic co-ordination, but as a result of myriad localised, tactical deployments of power.

This terminology is, of course, borrowed from Foucault (1980: 142),[19] whose account of the relationship between power and knowledge provides, I believe, the most powerful approach to the study of practices and institutions of collection, taxonomy, archivisation and display in modernity.[20] In his later work, Foucault develops what he calls an 'analytic of power', a term designed to distinguish his mode of descriptive analysis from theory as such. In *Discipline and Punish* (1979), volume one of *The History of Sexuality* (1990), and a series of shorter writings and interviews, he traces the ways in which traditional forms of sovereignty, based on centralised juridical (i.e. monarchical or princely) power, become dispersed in the later eighteenth and early nineteenth centuries, proliferating along new pathways and entering into new relationships. In a discussion of Machiavellian notions of the art of governing, Foucault argues that in the case of juridical power the prince represents a transcendent principle, and that the state functions in circular fashion to maintain and extend the power of the prince. Governmental power, on the other hand, takes as its object individuals and populations, and seeks to control and harness them to a variety of ends whose legitimacy derives from sources external to the self-serving calculation of juridical power (2002b). Foucault sums up these differences as follows:

> From the idea that the state has its own nature and its own finality, to the idea that man is the true object of the state's power, as far as he produces a surplus strength, as far as he is a living, working, speaking being, as far as he constitutes a society, and as far as he belongs to a population and an environment, we can see the increasing intervention of the state in the life of the individual.[21]

However, this kind of state intervention differs in fundamental ways from the operation of juridical power. While the latter functioned through edicts, laws and promulgations supported by whatever means of coercion and enforcement the prince could command, governmental power works through highly differentiated tactics for manipulating behaviour in specific desired directions. 'The eighteenth century', writes Foucault, 'invented . . . a synaptic regime of power, a regime of its exercise *within* the social body, rather than *from above*' (1980: 39). Foucault labels this specifically modern form of power 'power/knowledge', 'disciplinary power', or 'biopower', terms that designate a reorganisation of relations between knowledge, power and the body. His account thus concerns itself with 'the point where power reaches into the very grain of individuals, touches their bodies and inserts itself into their actions and attitudes' (39). For an example of such a transformation in the techniques of power, we need look no further than the work of Sebald himself. In the final chapter on sericulture in *The Rings of Saturn*, the narrator juxtaposes, in good Foucauldean fashion, a monarchical and a governmental approach to the development of a German silk industry. He notes that in the eighteenth century, orchestrated attempts by the rulers of the German states to establish such an industry by decree were doomed to failure. Writing in 1826, just a few years after the final collapse of this enterprise, one Josef von Hazzi published a treatise on sericulture in which he attributes this failure to 'authoritarian management, endeavours to create state monopolies, and an administrative system that buried any entrepreneurial spirit under a quite risible pile of regulations' (RS 290/343). Von Hazzi goes on to advocate the quasi-organic development of sericulture in the domestic sphere as a way of rendering economically productive all those normally excluded from labour: children and women, domestic servants, the elderly and the poor. This, he added, would not only increase Germany's international competitiveness, but would contribute to the moral improvement of the population by disciplining those not used to work (RS 290/343). One could hardly wish for a better illustration of power exercised '*within* the social body, rather than *from above* it'.

As Foucault makes clear, the exercise of disciplinary power depends on several interrelated factors. Bodies can be rendered docile by voluntary submission to explicit regulations, but in disciplinary power, such regulations are bolstered by a series of other techniques that include the distribution of bodies in space; constant surveillance, observation, registration and examination; and the consequent accumulation of a vast documentary apparatus bearing information about individuals. Power thus conceived is not purely repressive; it is also productive. In the first instance, clearly, it serves to produce a 'docile [body] that may be subjected, used, transformed and improved' (1979: 136) – a means of extending the body's economic utility while reducing its capacity for disobedience (138). Beyond this, however, disciplinary power produces certain 'subjectivity effects'. These are related to two fundamental technologies that take centre stage in Foucault's work: panopticism and confession.

In *Discipline and Punish*, Foucault adduces the example of Jeremy Bentham's panopticon. The panopticon consists of a central tower encircled by an annular building divided into cells that extend the entire depth of the building and have windows facing inwards towards the tower and outwards to allow light to cross the cell from one side to the other. The consequent effect of backlighting allows an observer installed in the central tower to observe those shut up in the cells. The cells 'are like so many cages, so many small theatres, in which each actor is alone, perfectly individualized and constantly visible' (1979: 200). The effect of the panopticon is:

> to induce in the inmate a sense of conscious and permanent visibility that assures the automatic functioning of power. So to arrange things that the

surveillance is permanent in its effects even if it is discontinuous in its action; that the perfection of power should tend to render its actual exercise unnecessary; that this architectural apparatus should be a machine for creating and sustaining a power relation independent of the person who exercises it; in short that the inmates should be caught up in a power situation of which they themselves are the bearers. (201)

In order to achieve this, the inmate must know that he is observed even though there is no need that he actually *is* observed; indeed, the inmate must never know whether or not he is being observed, but must always be aware that he may always be so. This is the essence of panopticism, a disciplinary regime that is illustrated in paradigmatic fashion by the panopticon. Power becomes both individualised and automatised, embodied not in a person but in 'a certain concerted distribution of bodies, surfaces, lights, gazes; in an arrangement whose internal mechanisms produce the relation in which individuals are caught up' (202).

Panopticism thus forces the subject to internalise relations of power, leading to a level of self-surveillance and self-policing that renders the use of overt coercion largely unnecessary.[22] Furthermore, it allows knowledge to be gathered about individuals through the process of observation. Commenting on this aspect of Foucault's work, Dreyfus and Rabinow write:

> Not only has power introduced individuality in the field of observation, but power fixes that objective individuality in the field of writing. A vast, meticulous documentary apparatus becomes an essential component of the growth of power . . . The modern individual – objectified, analyzed, fixed – is a historical achievement. There is no universal person on whom power has performed its operations and knowledge, its inquiries. Rather, the individual is the effect and object of a certain crossing of power and knowledge. He is the product of complex strategic developments in the field of power and the multiple developments in the human sciences. (1983: 160)

Foucault's primary examples are drawn for the most part from French military, educational, medical and penal establishments of the eighteenth and nineteenth centuries, and their related disciplines: psychiatry, criminology, clinical medicine. But the salient disciplinary techniques he identifies, and the configuration of power within which they operate, provide a highly fruitful framework for the study of a wide variety of other practices and institutions that bear directly on the subject of this study, namely modernity, the image and the archive in the work of W. G. Sebald.

In the first volume of the *History of Sexuality*, Foucault extends his investigation of power to the sphere of sexuality. He denies that it is a realm of authentic and natural expression that is external to and threatened by power, and reconfigures it in terms of what he calls the *dispositif* of sexuality.[23] The more one seeks sexual emancipation and proclaims the 'truth' about sexuality, he argues, the more one becomes involved in the discourse of sexuality. This discourse is supported by the technology of confession, which Foucault sees as a central component in the expanding apparatuses for the discipline and control of bodies and populations that emerge in modernity:

> The confession has spread its effects far and wide. It plays a part in justice, medicine, education, family relationships, and love relations, in the most ordinary affairs of everyday life, and in the most solemn rites; one confesses one's crimes, one's sins, one's thoughts and desires, one's illnesses and troubles . . . One confesses in public and in private, to one's parents, one's educators, one's doctor, to those one loves; one admits to oneself, in pleasure and in pain, things it would be impossible to tell anyone else, the things people write books about. One confesses – or is forced to confess. (1990: 59)

It is not, however, merely the act of confession that enmeshes the subject within relations of power; it is that self-examination is tied to myriad institutions and practices of social control. Specifically, a range of medical, psychiatric and legal institutions and moral doctrines support the notion that self-examination and confession of one's (primarily sexual) thoughts lead to the discovery of the truth about the self. Thus the confession inscribes selfhood within a network of power relations with those whose possession of the keys to interpretation endows them with the authority to articulate the truth of these confessions. Like panopticism, confession entails a massive *mise en discours* and a set of procedures for recording the intimate impulses of the self. The quantity of diaries, memoirs and agendas that frequently furnish the material of Sebald's narratives show that confession is not only a central aspect of Sebald's work, but is inseparable from archival technologies.

And yet despite the discursive overlaps between Sebald and Foucault, and despite the numerous allusions to Foucault in Sebald's work, the representation of the archive in Sebald is not reducible to an illustration of Foucault's theses on power/knowledge. Indeed, Sebald's reception of Foucault is characterised by a thoroughgoing ambivalence that emerges clearly in his critical writings.[24] These demonstrate a sustained engagement with Foucault at a point when French theory had yet to make any significant impact on German studies in Britain, but evince also a desire to escape the totalising account of power that Foucault offers.[25] The following quotations come from Sebald's first collection of essays on Austrian literature, *Die Beschreibung des Unglücks*:

> Whoever fails to accommodate himself to the system feels persecuted and surrounded by rules and prohibitions. 'The world is a single, monstrous

jurisprudence. The world is a prison!' says a so-called madman in Thomas Bernhard. He knows what he's talking about. The prison is a panoptic construction. The guard in the tower always has the inmates within his field of view without having to leave his seat. Beyond its control function, prison architecture embodies the system of the order of surveillance. Those who are hunted feel nothing so painfully as permanent observation . . . In Kafka's *Trial* verbs like to glance, see, be seen, look up, look at, look around, observe, attract the gaze of others, follow with one's eyes and similar occur with remarkable frequency. Josef K. knows that he is everywhere exposed. The eye of God has proliferated. The eye of the law sends its agents through the streets, and in the totalitarian regime that Kafka saw on the horizon everyone is called upon to spy on his neighbour. The system of power is thus not only one of hierarchisation but of contiguity. It proliferates downwards, conquers the foundations, spreads laterally, so that escape becomes impossible. (BU 96–7)

Foucault set out the fundamental ambivalence in the discourse on sex, which in the verbal elaboration of sentiment not only enables the emancipation of sexuality, but, in the very same process, brings it under more precise social control through the claims of pastoral, psychological, juridical, and psychiatric interests. (BU 39–40)

In the first quotation, Sebald might initially appear to appropriate Foucault's analytic of power wholesale. And yet closer inspection reveals that Sebald's reading of Foucault significantly reduces the radical force of the latter's theses. Firstly, Sebald reinstals the law, as a secular representative of the divine, as a source of prohibition and the organising authority behind all systems of surveillance. Secondly, human subjectivity is clearly conceived as something that exists outside the disciplinary apparatus, rather than being constituted by it. Finally, Sebald understands the lateral extension of power through panopticism as a feature of totalitarian regimes, whereas Foucault expends considerable energy demonstrating that democratic government operates precisely through these mechanisms. The second quotation, too, betrays a somewhat tendentious reading of Foucault. In the first volume of the *History of Sexuality*, Foucault seeks to counter the thesis of sexual emancipation that Sebald puts forward here. As we have seen, Foucault argues that the notion of sexuality as an authentic realm of expression that power seeks to restrict and control is an illusion that is fostered by the *dispositif* of sexuality itself. The more one seeks sexual emancipation and proclaims the 'truth' about sexuality, he argues, the more one implicates the self within institutional structures of power/knowledge. The quasi-dialectical relationship between sexual emancipation and social control that emerges from Sebald's gloss turns out to be precisely the 'repressive hypothesis' that Foucault rejects.

These essays from *Die Beschreibung des Unglücks* testify to a remarkable degree of intellectual coherence on Sebald's part, for in a 1975 essay on Peter Handke's play *Kaspar*, he articulates similar views on the relationship between discipline and subjectivity.[26] The essay is preceded by an epigraph from Foucault's *Madness and Civilisation* that deals with the problem of reconstructing the history of madness in the light of the fact that the images and fantasies of the mad have never been recorded for posterity. The tenor of much of the essay, however, is more closely related to *Discipline and Punish*, even though it is unlikely that Sebald would have read that work before writing his piece on *Kaspar*, since both appeared in the same year. Nevertheless, it is clear that from this relatively early stage in his career, Sebald was concerned with the way in which power is written on the body. So, for example, he notes that the figure of Kaspar in Handke's play appears to perform the actions of a clown, but whereas clowning is the intentional performance of incompetence and therefore funny, Kaspar's clownish antics are unwilled, and he soon learns to avoid mishaps (which the clown, of course, does not). Sebald goes on to argue that Kaspar internalises this clownish behaviour, with the result that what appears to be progress – namely his increasing ability to function as a competent social being – is in fact 'nothing but the gradual humiliation of a trained creature' (CS 60/61). The final word in the German is 'der Dressierte', one who has been fully trained to perform certain tasks or actions. It is frequently used in the German translation of *Discipline and Punish* to refer to the production of docile bodies. The big difference between Sebald and Foucault is that the former can conceive of 'Dressur' only in terms of humiliation. For Sebald, discipline merely distorts subjectivity; it possesses no productive aspect.

The concern with power, subjectivity and the body that emerges in the *Kaspar* essay suggests one reason for Sebald's eager reception of Foucault's late work. But the notion of the pristine subject not yet distorted by socially imposed models of behaviour, which emerges clearly in this essay, might also account for the profound ambivalence towards Foucault's work that we find elsewhere in Sebald's critical writings. On the one hand, he adopts Foucauldean terminology and appears to align himself with Foucault's analysis of power. On the other, he nevertheless continues to operate with an implied notion of subjective autonomy that Foucault's work sought to invalidate. It is this ambivalence that determines the structure of this book. In Part I, I pursue a largely Foucauldean agenda in investigating the ways in which the image and the archive in Sebald's work are implicated in structures of power/knowledge and produce the corresponding subjectivity effects, though I am also attentive to the ways in which such structures are critiqued, undermined or circumvented. Looking first at museums and collections, then at photography, and finally at various disciplinary images and archives, I explore the contribution of these disciplinary structures to the construction of the subject within Sebald's four main prose narratives: *Vertigo*, *The Emigrants*, *The Rings of Saturn* and *Austerlitz*. The analysis in Part I is primarily thematic, and offers an overview of the archive as a constant focus of Sebald's texts in order to do justice to the high degree of thematic coherence evinced by his work. In Part II, I offer differentiated analyses of each of Sebald's major prose works in turn. The focus remains on the image, the archive and their relationship to power in modernity, but I expand the terms of reference to include the narratological dimension of Sebald's work. In so doing, I examine the extent to which Sebald's narratives offer possibilities for resisting modernity's disciplinary imperatives.

In Chapter 5, on *Vertigo*, I examine the ways in which the text thematises a specifically modern abdication of subjective interiority to a series of mnemotechnical supplements. The effect of this is to fragment experience and problematise the relationship between individual episodes and the narrative totality. The task faced by the narrator is to discover or construct a narrative and epistemological model that will allow the disparate elements of experience to coalesce into a more meaningful whole. The hidden correspondences that he establishes between ostensibly isolated events represent the moment when the rationality of archival epistemology flips over into magic, constituting the topography of the text in terms of wonder and thereby promoting an anti-disciplinary perception of modernity. In my reading of *The Emigrants* (Chapter 6), I turn my attention to the family archive and in particular the family album. In Foucault-inspired writings on family photography, the emphasis is on the production of bourgeois subjectivity and the reproduction of the ideology of the nuclear and extended family. Critical studies of domestic photography have thus tended to dwell on the disciplinary aspects of the practice and its participation in a fundamentally panoptic process of self-surveillance. While never fully denying the disciplinary aspects of photography, *The Emigrants* undertakes a rehabilitation of the family album and domestic photography. Furthermore, in its very structure – which relies extensively on metaphorical similarity – it constitutes the text itself as an archival space of preservation and stability amid historical flux and subjective trauma.

In Chapter 7, on *The Rings of Saturn*, I continue this investigation into the archival nature of the text. By wandering without maps, and exploring the empty spaces that the map deems functionally irrelevant, Sebald's narrator demonstrates a desire to escape the biopolitical effects of modernity's archives, of which the map is emblematic. This wandering goes hand in hand with a poetics of digression. The rejection of modern modes of transport in favour of walking and the rejection of an easily consumable text in favour of digression can be seen as complementary components in Sebald's critique of modernity. And yet this critique can take place only from within the very structures against which it seeks to rebel. The only way in which dilatoriness can be prevented from degenerating into complete incoherence in *The Rings of Saturn* is through the adoption of an archival structure for the text itself, as episodes follow on from each other not on the basis of causality or narrative logic, but on the basis of similarity. The archive, then, can be seen to contain the possibility of meaninglessness or incoherence, and yet it also represents the intrusion of a technology of modernity into the very fabric of a text that seeks to resist it.

Austerlitz forms the subject of Chapter 8, and involves in many respects the most complex treatment of the archive. The protagonist spends his academic career amassing compendious architectural knowledge as a form of compensation for his own lost memories of his past. The archive here thus replaces 'authentic' memory as a kind of 'prosthesis of the inside' (Derrida). And yet the putatively authentic memory that Austerlitz seeks to retrieve also emerges as external to the self, for its retrieval depends on the archives that he discovers in Theresienstadt and Prague. The archive is both a symptom of Austerlitz's lack of memory *and*, at the moment of discovery that constitutes the provisional *telos* of the narrative, the resource of the cure. There is thus no escape: Austerlitz seems to represent an extreme example of a subject constituted entirely by the archive. At the same time, however, the archive remains always incomplete. At the end of the text, Austerlitz sets off in search of his father, following traces that he finds in a Parisian archive. The epistemological promise of the archive is never fulfilled, which is why it leaves the end of this particular text open and the subjectivity of Austerlitz in a permanent state of incompletion.

In conclusion, I address the question of why the archives of modernity thematised in Sebald's work originate largely not in the late twentieth, but in the late nineteenth and early twentieth centuries. I argue that Sebald's narrative project borrows from the method of Foucault himself. Just as Foucault saw the keys to understanding modern society in the developments of the eighteenth and nineteenth century, so Sebald sees the key to the contemporary world in structures and technologies developed a century ago but whose effects – *pace* those who argue that Sebald posits 1945 as the end of history – continue to be felt. This in turn leads to a re-evaluation of Sebald's view of history, and position within literary history.

NOTES

1. This list is not, of course, exhaustive, but it does account for the vast majority of writings on Sebald.
2. The literature on modernity is multi-disciplinary and truly vast, with the inevitable consequence that attempts to define it are bound to be partial and incomplete. In writing this brief synthesis, I have drawn on Harvey 1990, Berman 1988, Kern 1983, Hansen 1995, and Habermas 1988 and 1990.
3. See, for example, Alvarez 2001, and the obituaries quoted in Fuchs 2004a: 11. Significantly, Sebald himself explicitly rejected the epithet 'exile' in an interview with Löffler 1997b: 131.
4. See, for example, Crownshaw 2004, Duncker 2003, Duttlinger 2004, Garloff 2004, Gunther 2006, Hall 2000, Pane 2005, Anne Parry 1997, Taberner 2004, Whitehead 2004.

5. As my argument in this study shows, I would add 'historical' to 'geophysical and metaphysical'.

6. Anne Fuchs' book *Die Schmerzensspuren der Geschichte* contains the most extensive and nuanced discussion of Sebald and memory (2004a). See also, for example, Atze 2005b, Bere 2001, Chandler 2003, Denneler 2000, Horstkotte 2005b, Kilbourn 2004, Loquai 1995, Reineke 2003, Weber 1993, Witthaus 2006.

7. In addition to works already cited, see Barzilai 2006, Boehncke 2003, Chaplin 2006, Harris 2001, Horstkotte 2005a, Long 2003, Tischel 2006.

8. Melancholy and loss constitute a dominant topos of photography studies. Siegfried Kracauer's essay 'Die Photographie' (Kracauer 1963), a foundational text of modern photographic theory, opens with a meditation on the ability of photography to communicate a sense of irrevocably past time and bring about a melancholy realisation of loss. Benjamin's *Kunstwerk* essay is, as Ariella Azoulay notes, a melancholy anticipation of the loss of aura of the artwork (2001: 18). More recent critics, from Barthes to Marianne Hirsch, have persistently drawn on this aspect of the photograph in their theoretical work.

9. On Sebald and melancholy, see Bond 2004, Heidelberger-Leonard 2001, Löffler 2003 and Santner 2006: 43–5 and 62–3.

10. It should be noted, however, that Fritzsche is decidedly more optimistic about the possibilities of melancholy and nostalgia as historiographical modalities.

11. On Sebald and *Heimat*, see Ecker 2006, Fuchs 2006a and 2004a: 109–63, Lobsien 2004.

12. In addition to the essays cited below, see the following on Sebald and travel: Bales 2003, Beck 2004, Gregory-Guider 2005, Kastura 1996, Sill 1997b, and Zilcosky 2004.

13. See the section on the flâneur in Benjamin 1973: 35–66. Keith Tester's volume *The Flâneur* (1994) offers interesting contemporary perspectives on the phenomenon. Especially valuable are the essays by Shields (1994) and Bauman (1994).

14. Intertextual approaches to Sebald are offered by Atze 1997b, Kilbourn 2006, Klebes 2004, Prager 2006, Schedel 2004, Sill 1997a, Steinmann 2006, Theisen 2006. Since Sebald's *Arbeitsbibliothek* has been made available to scholars, there has been a proliferation of studies examining 'Sebald and *x*'. See, for example, Atze 2004, 2005a and 2005b, Rovagnati 2005a, Loquai 2005a. For a more traditional piece of 'source criticism', see Gasseleder 2005.

15. The first chairs of German philology were established in Göttingen (1805) and Berlin (1807), in other words either side of the defeat and reorganisation of the German lands by Napoleon in 1806. These professorial posts can thus be seen as part of the massive effort to mobilise history and historical consciousness, particularly that of the Middle Ages, in order to reconstitute symbolically the lost Holy Roman Empire, and foster a specifically German national consciousness. Central to this enterprise was the *Monumenta Germaniae historica*, a collection of sources pertaining to Germany in the Middle Ages (see Ernst 2003: 91–270). The first chairs of modern German literature were established in 1874 and 1877 in Berlin – once again immediately after a major war with France, and once again as a form of symbolically bolstering the German nation. Similar developments can be witnessed, belatedly, in Britain (see Eagleton 1981: 17–53).

16. Sebald devoted two critical essays to *The Castle*, and as many critics have shown, his works are saturated with explicit and implicit intertextual references to Kafka. In addition to the Kafka episode discussed here, examples of malfunctioning archives can be found in Thomas Bernhard's *The Lime Works* and *Extinction*, Musil's *The Man without Qualities*, Norbert Gstrein's *Das Register*, and many other works.

17. Cf. Marx and Engels 1989: 23. See also Berman 1988: 16; Harvey 1990: 20–30; Benjamin 1973.
18. My understanding of the archive is unrelated to Foucault's eccentric definition of the word in *The Archaeology of Knowledge*. Foucault's concept of the archive turns out to have nothing to do with preservation, ordering and storage. On the contrary, it is the '*system of enunciability*' that underlies and enables any given statement-event. This concept of the archive, as the general system for the formation and trans-formation of statements, oscillates between language and corpus, between the latency of what can be said, and the actuality of what is (2002a: 146). Foucault thus 'dematerialises' the archive, and turns it into an abstract system. By contrast, I see archives as fundamentally material practices and institutions that participate in the power/knowledge nexus explored by Foucault in his later work.
19. In an interview with Jacques-Alain Miller and others, Foucault was repeatedly chal-lenged to clarify his ostensibly paradoxical thesis of a strategy without a subject. Foucault's answers are not always entirely convincing or satisfactory (1980: 202–4). However, the history of ethnographic collections offers one illustration of precisely the mechanisms Foucault describes. A point that emerges forcefully from Glenn Penny's book *Objects of Culture: Ethnology and Ethnographic Museums in Imperial Germany* (2002) is that the science of ethnology, which came to be seen as the colonial discipline par excellence, in fact emerged from a set of diverse factors and interest groups that included scientists, civic associations, private patrons, col-lectors, dealers and museum visitors. Elizabeth Edwards' analysis of archives and anthropological photography in *Raw Histories: Photographs, Anthropology and Museums* (2001) concentrates on the 'social biography' of photographs. Edwards shows that rather than embodying a monolithic 'colonial gaze', collections of anthropological photographs often came together on an ad hoc basis, a serendipi-tous result of diverse networks of exchange whose purpose was often sociable rather than scientific or commercial. Any strategy underlying colonial representa-tion and display thus has to be seen as an 'effect of finalisation' (Foucault 1980: 204), not as an origin.
20. For Foucauldean accounts of museums, see, for example, Bennett 1995 and Hooper-Greenhill 1992. On photographic archives, see Sekula 1992, Gunning 1995, Tagg 1988, Maxwell 1999, and Lalvani 1996. On disciplinarity and vision generally see also Crary 1990 and 1999. On medical cultures of archiving and display see McGrath 2002 and Cartwright 1995.
21. Foucault, lecture delivered at Stanford University, Palo Alto, California, 1979, quoted in Dreyfus and Rabinow 1983: 138.
22. One might think in this context of the CCTV cameras installed everywhere in Britain's cities, on the roads, in public buildings of all kinds and even in private households. The startling proliferation of surveillance techniques in the UK has made Foucault's work more relevant than ever for an understanding of the func-tioning of social power.
23. The French term *dispositif* designates what Dreyfus and Rabinow term a 'grid of intelligibility' (1983: 121). The English translation uses the word 'deployment', which is highly problematic in that it implies a degree of conscious agency from a higher authority, rather than the emergence within the social body of an intelligible relation between discourse and power.
24. Though various critics have drawn attention to the potential importance of Foucault for an understanding of Sebald's work, there has as yet been no sustained attempt to evaluate the relationship between the two writers. I offer an initial approach to this issue in Long 2006a. See also Santner 2006: 115, 181–4; Albes 2002: 296; Jackman 2004: 461; Theisen 2004: 175; Öhlschläger 2006a: 111–26, 133–7.

25. The totalising aspects of Foucault's later thought have been criticised in particular from within feminism and Marxism. See, for example, Butler 1990, Hayles 1998, Habermas 1988, Jameson 1983 and 1991.
26. Handke's play is one of several *Sprachstücke* or 'language plays' that he wrote in the 1960s. It concerns the protagonist's acquisition of language and social integration. The title is, of course, a reference to Kaspar Hauser, the foundling and 'child of nature' who turned up in Nuremburg in 1828. Though apparently a teenager, he had no memory and the behaviour of a young child.

PART I

2

THE COLLECTION

Museums and Modernity

Collections of various kinds are everywhere in Sebald's work: zoos, menageries and aviaries; museums and exhibitions; archives and libraries; cabinets of curiosities, and a whole host of ad hoc, less formal modes of collecting, from the entomological, ornithological and botanical specimens in Andromeda Lodge in *Austerlitz* to the piles of used envelopes clogging Michael Hamburger's house in *The Rings of Saturn*.

Anthropologist James Clifford notes that some form of collecting or gathering 'around the self and the group – the assemblage of a material "world", the marking-off of a subjective domain that is not "other" – is probably universal' (1988: 218). He also notes, however, that gathering as an accumulation of possessions and the related idea that identity is a kind of wealth (of objects, knowledge, memories, experience) is a predominantly Western phenomenon. In particular, it is linked to the political theory of possessive individualism, according to which the seventeenth century saw the emergence of an ideal of selfhood that was conceptualised in terms of ownership: 'the individual surrounded by accumulated property and goods' (217).[1] The history of widespread and systematic collecting in Europe extends beyond the seventeenth century to the dawn of the early modern era, with a series of developments that facilitated accelerated and increasingly efficient exchange of goods. Among these were improvements in ship-building and navigation, the expansion of trading empires (notably the Dutch and Venetian), and an appreciably more sophisticated European banking system (Blom 2003: 20–1). These developments in turn generated the surplus wealth that is necessary in order to perform the archetypal act of the collector, which involves removing the object from the regime of use value and recontextualising it in the collection.

This process of decontextualisation and recontextualisation is the means by which, as Susan Stewart argues, collections in general and museums in particular construct the illusion of adequate representation.[2] The object is first removed from its cultural, historical or intersubjective context and made to stand, in metonymic fashion, for a larger abstract whole. It is then subjected to a system of classification so that the ordering of the collection itself overrides the specific histories of the object and its conditions of production and use. The collection erases the labour involved in both producing the object and acquiring it for classification and display (1993: 161–5). In addition, the collection has the capacity to assign new value to objects that fall within its system.

Such processes can be seen at work in a wide diversity of collections characteristic of the modern era, including art history museums, ethnographic museums, museums of natural history, botanical gardens and zoos. The question is how these institutions came to function within the power/knowledge complex that, as we have seen, has been a characteristic of Western societies for the past two centuries or more. The answer to this question lies in the epistemic shifts that took place in the course of the transition from what Foucault terms the 'classical age' to the modern era, in the reconfiguration of the relationship between the collector, the collection and the spectator, and in the new spatial relationships that these developments entailed.

The museum in its modern form came into being in the late eighteenth and early nineteenth centuries. 'The process of its formation,' writes Tony Bennett:

> was as complex as it was protracted, involving, most obviously and immediately, a transformation of the practices of earlier collecting institutions and the creative adaptation of aspects of other new institutions – the international exhibition and the department store, for example – which developed alongside the museum. (1995: 19)

Among the transformations in the institutions and practices of collection is the organisation of collections according to what Foucault terms the modern *episteme*. In *The Archaeology of Knowledge*, Foucault offers a definition of the concept of the *episteme* as a set of relations uniting the discursive practices that give rise, at a given period, to 'epistemological figures, sciences, and possibly formalized systems' (2002a: 211). In *The Order of Things*, Foucault had already provided a historicised account of 'truth' as a product of precisely these relations as they undergo a series of transformations from the Renaissance to the modern era. The Renaissance *episteme* relied on a hermeneutics of resemblance (1989b: 30). Things were read for their hidden relationships to each other, the assumption being that the signs visible on the surface of objects pointed to the hidden similitude of all things. Collections were organised to demonstrate the hierarchies of the world and the analogies that bound the world together (Hooper-Greenhill 1992: 78–132). But because there was no established method of verification, these relationships could be endlessly rewritten: the Renaissance *episteme* was 'a thing of sand' (Foucault 1989b: 30). The force of the Renaissance *episteme* was shattered by the classical *episteme* with its concern with taxonomy. Collections came to be governed by new forms of scientific classification that were based on the visible and measurable differences between things (rather than their occult similitude), and the setting out of these differences in tabulated order (Hooper-Greenhill 1992: 133–6). It is in this kind of collection that we first witness the tendency for ordinary objects to be accorded a representative status, and to function metonymically in the way described above by Stewart. Furthermore, such classification privileges the typical over the bizarre, the series over the unique object.

For an understanding of the modern collection, however, it is the shift from the classical to the modern *episteme* that is of central importance. The modern *episteme* organises things not by entering them into taxonomic tables, but by inserting them into the flow of time: a 'temporalisation of taxonomy' as Andrea Hauser puts it (2001: 35). Tony Bennett has sketched out the importance of this for the development of the nineteenth-century museum:

> The birth of the museum is coincident with and supplied a primary institutional condition for the emergence of a new set of knowledges – geology, biology, archaeology, anthropology, history and art history – each of which, in its museological deployment, arranged objects as parts of evolutionary sequences (the history of the earth, of life, of man, and of civilization) which, in their interrelations, formed a totalizing order of things and peoples that was historicised through and through. (1995: 96)

While Bennett notes that this 'totalizing order' did not materialise instantly and fully-formed, he argues that by the mid-nineteenth century most specimens and artifacts were in the process of being removed from earlier forms of representation and inserted into one of various evolutionary series (97).

These epistemic shifts went hand in hand with changes in the relationships between knowledge and power. The Renaissance collection had recreated the world in miniature with the figure of the prince at its centre, who thereby claimed dominion over the world symbolically as well as in reality. The classical period and the Enlightenment saw a slow transformation of the collection from a private space to a site of public instruction (Hauser 2001: 34–7), a process that culminated in the large civic museums that have adorned virtually every Western capital since about 1825 (Prior 2002: 37). The archetype and paradigmatic example of this development is the Louvre, which embodies all the changes that cultural historians have identified as the fundamental features of the modern museum. In particular, the Louvre was a national, state-managed, public institution.

The relationship between the modern *episteme*, the notion of the national gallery, the role of the state, and the museum's mode of address emerges in the way the discipline of art history reconfigured the collection from the mid-eighteenth century. Rather then being displays of wealth, power and status, art objects were transformed by modern (i.e. evolutionary) taxonomic practice into 'material evidence for the elaboration of a universalist language of description and classification', as Donald Preziosi puts it. All differences, he continues, could be reduced to 'differential and time-factored qualitative manifestations of some panhuman capacity'. Artisanry, in other words, becomes posited as the essence of the human, and the greater the skill of the maker the greater the insight into the maker's mentality and the essence of humanness (2003: 35–6). At the heart of art history, then, lay a paradox: on the one hand, it was an instrument of a universalist Enlightenment vision, while on the other, it was a tool for making qualitative distinctions between individuals and societies. This is what facilitated its appropriation by the nation state, for such distinctions could be enlisted to justify narratives of social, national, racial, cultural or ethnic origins, identity and development (37). The museum organised according to art-historical principles thus helped foster a sense of national unity in three ways: it posited the host nation as the culmination of earlier states in the development of human civilisation; it facilitated comparison with the culture of other nations; and it constructed a public and standardised fantasy narrative of an organic national history. This in turn allowed the state to instal itself as the guardian of past glories and benefactor of the people.[3] The state constitutes the museum as a fully democratic realm that celebrates national glory, while the visitor is addressed as a citizen, a participant in and recipient of the nation's highest cultural achievements.

It almost goes without saying that the evolutionary ordering of ethnographic museums and technological exhibitions had similar (though not identical) implications. The function of such displays was to instantiate ideologies of progress and to insert the visitor into such a narrative. Moreover, the evolutionary time implied by the layout of nineteenth-century exhibitions is generally seen as an ideological tool for producing consent to bourgeois hegemony by projecting contemporary capitalism as the *telos* of evolution (Bennett 1995: 178, 214). Since the subject of capitalism is the white, Western, bourgeois male, it is clear that the exhibitionary practices of modernity worked to establish this subject as the end-point and pinnacle of the evolutionary development. This went hand in hand with the normalising and racialised discourse that established the white male body as the norm against which deviations could be measured. Such a normalising approach to anatomical display brought with it an increased tendency to display pathologised departures alongside the norm (Bennett 1995: 201–3). When mapped onto an evolutionary schema, the notion of norm and deviation produced a strictly hierarchised view of humanity in which a series of racial and gendered others was seen as occupying lower points on the evolutionary scale and therefore as being essentially inferior.

The reordering of collections that produced the modern museum also entailed a reorganisation of space, which itself formed part of the power/knowledge complex. As institutions of high culture came to be seen as a means of improving or reforming the population, museums were identified as one of many cultural resources that could be mobilised as instruments of liberal government. Indeed, the history of museum administration reveals a pervasive concern for the improvement of the labouring classes by luring them away from sites of raucous assembly such as fairs and pubs and into the civilised and civilising space of the museum, with its educational objectives and its attendant models of good conduct (Bennett 1995). The spatial arrangement of early museums, with a central exhibition space surrounded by an elevated gallery, provides a particularly transparent illustration of the implication of the museum in the regime of surveillance, and transforms the museum-going public into both surveyor and surveyed (68–9), producing precisely that permanent exercise of power through self-regulation that Foucault identifies as the effect of panopticism.

These disciplinary intentions, however, were not uniformly realised. There was a marked tendency, for example, for the scientific principles according to which museum exhibits were ordered to be perpetually compromised. Thus German ethnographic museums were under pressure from a variety of stakeholders, such as patrons, local elites and comparatively uneducated visitors, all of whom sought to influence the shape and content of exhibitions (Penny 2002: 135–51). Furthermore, the principles developed by German ethnologists for the categorisation and display of ethnographic artifacts were undermined by increasingly rapid cycles of acquisition and accumulation; the growth of collections exceeded the capacity of ethnologists to catalogue them (180–7). Whether in response to non-specialist demand or as a consequence of the failure of the discipline to keep pace with acquisitions, museums frequently eschewed strict 'scientific' ordering in favour of spectacular or even plain chaotic exhibitions. Writing from a similar perspective, Elizabeth Edwards has noted that aesthetic considerations frequently overrode scientific taxonomy in anthropological collections (2001: 61). Like the disorderly exhibits of the travelling fair, then, museums also traded in the abstruse, the unique and the spectacular. This alerts us to the fact that the 'totalizing order of things' (to use Bennett's totalising formulation) does not operate consistently and continuously across all modern museums. In particular, it opens up the possibility of alternative modes of subjectivity that are not purely reducible to the operations of power/knowledge. The relationship between discipline and resistance, surveillance and spectacle, will structure our investigation of the numerous collections thematised in Sebald's work.

ARCHAEOLOGY OF THE COLLECTION: FROM THOMAS BROWNE TO *NATURE WATCH*

Museum spaces and the artifacts they contain are a preoccupation of Sebald's work, and his development of the theme is multi-faceted. The narrators of Sebald's texts, as Silke Arnold-de Simine (forthcoming) points out, frequently visit museums. She argues that most of Sebald's museums are in a state of decline, but like the arcades in the work of Walter Benjamin, this decline reveals their mythological quality and unrealised utopian potential. I see Sebald's thematisation of museums rather differently, as a way of addressing distinctly modern questions of power, knowledge and subject-formation.

Displays of colonial booty such as the moth-eaten polar bear gracing the entrance to Somerleyton Hall in *The Rings of Saturn* (RS 36/49) or the miscellaneous African trophies adorning the rooms of the Hotel by the Bois de la Cambre in Brussels (RS 123/149) appear as pathetic relics of a bygone age of colonial glory. They are, however, collections that represent forms of purely individual power that have largely disappeared. When the narrator comes to talk of the Mauritshuis in The Hague, though, he addresses the transformation of the collection from private display to state institution discussed above. The 1644 opening of the Mauritshuis, we learn, was accompanied by dances performed by Indians that Johann Maurits had brought back with him from Brazil. The house itself had been 'fitted out as a cosmographic residence reflecting the wonders of the remotest regions of the earth' (RS 83/102–3). The house was thus initially a private display of personal wealth and prestige, but one that also embedded this individual power in the geopolitical framework of national colonial interests. It constituted Maurits as both the centre of a cosmos in his own right and as a representative of the Dutch Republic. It is now, of course, a museum run by the Dutch state, and has thus come to fulfil a rather different function. The transformation of the relationship between exhibition and power can be seen in the painting that Sebald's narrator travels to The Hague to see: Rembrandt's *Anatomy Lesson*. While the painting was commissioned by the Guild of Surgeons as a sign of the prestige, power and corporate identity of an emerging professional class, it is now fully integrated into an art-historical narrative of national schools that characterises the modern museum. While the narrator's reading of Rembrandt's painting stresses its secret subversion of the very profession it was meant to aggrandise, the recontextualisation of the painting as a example not only of the individual genius of Rembrandt, but of a distinctively Dutch national genius brings it once more within the compass of power. Cornelis de Jong's comments on the use of art to legitimise the wealth gained through the slave economy by sugar plantation owners such as Maurits and Tate (RS 194/242), therefore, addresses only part of the problem. For a history of modernity, it is the absorption of these privately-resourced collections into the state apparatus that is more significant in terms of its ideological and biopolitical effects.

Throughout Sebald's work, however, the most interesting collections concern not artworks, but natural specimens. Uniting both epistemic and disciplinary shifts that characterise modernity, Sebald's work offers a wide-ranging archaeology of the collection that takes us from the Renaissance writer Thomas Browne to the age of the television nature documentary.

In *The Rings of Saturn*, the description of Thomas Browne's researches in *The Garden of Cyrus* provides a late and striking example of the Renaissance *episteme*. Browne, Sebald claims, discovers the structure of the quincunx everywhere, in matter both animate and inanimate: in crystalline formations and the roots and seeds of plants, in the patterns on snakes' skin and the bodies of lepidoptera, in the spinal columns of birds, fish and mammals, and in the works of man such as the Pyramids and the garden of Solomon (RS 19–21/31–2). This is the hermeneutics of resemblance, with observable similarities between objects providing 'proof' of the universal oneness of all things. 'Studious Observators,' as Browne wrote, 'may discover more analogies in the orderly book of nature' (1977b: 360). And yet, as Sebald's narrator notes, 'Thomas Browne too was often distracted from his investigations into the isomorphic line of the quincunx by singular phenomena that fired his curiosity, and by work on a comprehensive pathology' (RS 22/33). This, he claims, is also a characteristic of the modern-day biological sciences, which on the one hand seek to describe a perfectly regular and rule-governed system, but on the other pay particular attention to creatures noteworthy for their bizarre physical appearance or weird and crazy behaviour (RS 21/33). The fascination with the strange, aberrant or monstrous then percolates into forms of popular culture that have educational aspirations, such as *Brehms Thierleben*, a hugely popular nineteenth-century German zoological encyclopaedia whose six volumes were devoted, respectively, to the taxonomic categories of mammals, birds, reptiles, amphibians, fish and invertebrates, but which gave pride of place, the narrator claims, to the crocodile, kangaroo, anteater, armadillo, sea-horse and pelican. It endures into the present in the form of television programmes 'which are entitled *Nature Watch* or *Survival* and are considered particularly educational'. Such television programmes are more likely to show 'some monster coupling at the bottom of Lake Baikal than an ordinary blackbird' (RS 22/33).

This passage is one of many in Sebald's work that deal with the classification and display of natural phenomena. Earlier in *The Rings of Saturn* the narrator goes in search of Thomas Browne's skull in the museum of the Norfolk and Norwich Hospital. While the museum appears no longer to exist, the narrator notes that when civic hospitals were built as part of early attempts to reform public health,[4] they frequently included museums or *Gruselkabinette* (chambers of horrors) in which premature or hydrocephalic foetuses along with a wide variety of deformed organs were preserved in formaldehyde for instructional purposes and periodic exhibition. Browne's skull, it transpires, had been housed 'amidst various anatomical curiosities' until 1921 (RS 11/19–20). Sebald's account of this collection implies that its specimens were exclusively of the deviant and diseased.[5] A similar emphasis on deviance and deformity can be found in *Austerlitz*, whose protagonist visits the museum of the Ecole Vétérinaire at Maisons-Alfort, Paris. Austerlitz enumerates the holdings of the museum, paying particular attention to the exhibits of the pathological and teratological collections, the latter of which contains 'monstrosities of every imaginable and unimaginable kind' (A 373/374). He also dwells on the various ways of preserving organic matter from decay, and talks at length about the man on horseback, the most famous of the so-called *écorchés* or wax-preserved flayed corpses that were prepared by the professor of anatomy, Honoré Fragonard, in the late eighteenth century (A 373–4/374–6).[6]

In their accounts of zoological and medical collections, and of popular representations of science, then, Sebald's narrators and protagonists frequently dwell on the abstruse, the deviant and the monstrous. Why Sebald should reduce such highly diverse collections to the common denominator of the monstrous is a question that takes us to the heart of the meaning of anatomical display in his work.

The universal resemblance that Browne discovers in *The Garden of Cyrus* is sustained by an extended metaphorical complex uniting the quincunx, the chiasmus and the net as the *tertium comparationis* that facilitates the perception of similitude across an incredible diversity of natural phenomena and cultural products. Writing on the cusp of the scientific age, Browne repeatedly extols empirical observation as a method for 'erect[ing] generalities' and dealing 'mortal and dispatching blows unto errour' (1977b: 386). But his world-view remains fundamentally indebted to the epistemic assumptions of the Renaissance.[7] Nature is the 'universall and publick Manuscript' of God, whose finger 'hath left an inscription upon all his workes' (1977a: 78, 136). Reading nature is thus a means by which Browne 'collect[s his] Divinity' (1977a: 78), and the *Garden of Cyrus* has to be understood as an exercise in devotional hermeneutics whose analogical method ultimately seeks similitude among diverse singularities that remain irreducibly particular while participating in the oneness of divine creation. This is why the quincuncial scheme is not at all disrupted by the numerous exceptions that Browne adduces. Indeed, he notes in the dedication '*how few generalities and* U finita's *there are in nature . . . How Botanicall Maximes must have fair allowance, and are intolerably currant, if not intolerably over-balanced by exceptions*'

(1977b: 320). In other words, exception *is* the rule. In *Religio Medici*, furthermore, Browne reasons that since God declared all creation to be good, and since he abhors deformity, there can be no deformity in nature, except in monstrosity. Pursuing this train of thought to its logical conclusion, he then argues monstrosity out of existence as well, since in the monstrous, too, there is a kind of beauty deriving from the felicitous assemblage of irregular parts (1977a: 80–1).

The epistemic implications of *The Garden of Cyrus* are identical to those of Browne's own collection. In 1671, the diarist John Evelyn wrote that 'the whole house & Garden' of Sir Thomas Browne was 'a Paradise & Cabinet of rarities, & that of the best collection, especially Medails, books, Plants, and natural things . . . and amongst other curiosities, a collection of the eggs of all the foule and birds he could procure' (quoted in Patrides 1977: 36). The striking thing here is the non-differentiation of man-made and natural specimens. Whether *naturalia* or *artificialia*, all items in the collection are evidence of God's greatness: 'nature is not at variance with art, nor art with nature; they being both the servants of his providence' (1977a: 81). Browne's posthumously published 'Miscellany Tract' *Musaeum Clausum*, which Sebald's narrator discusses towards the end of *The Rings of Saturn* (RS 271–3/321–4), is a further example. We learn that this '*Bibliotheca abscondita*' or imaginary museum is on a par with the great collections of Europe, including the '*Musaeum Aldrovandi, Calceolarianum, Moscardi, Wormanium*' and collections of the Duke of Tuscany, the Duke of Saxony, and the Austrian Emperor (Browne 1946: 131).[8] Knowledge and power were inseparably intertwined in these collections, as the replication of the macrocosm in microcosmic form – which constituted the collections' epistemic principle – demonstrated the collector's power through his ostensible ability to sustain a cosmos. The *Musaeum Clausum* can be seen as an impossible archive that sustains a fantasy of princely power, while Browne's own collection constitutes an archive for the display of the bourgeois self in an emerging age of possessive individualism.

Browne's interest in the singular and the monstrous is vastly different from the view of monstrosity that obtained in the epistemic configurations of later centuries. If the Linnean scheme that Foucault identifies as part of the classical *episteme* saw the natural order as a synchronous logical arrangement, for example, then anything that fell outside the purview of the logical definition was, as Thomas Richards notes, 'a singularity and freak of nature, to be confined to the bottomless category for all the deviations from logic traversed by nature, the special category of the monstrous' (1996: 47). Richards argues that the nineteenth-century science of morphology imagined a unitary natural world in which there could be no place for monstrosity. The synchronic table was replaced by the diachronic reconstruction of lines of evolutionary development, reducing even the monstrous to a fixed and knowable position in a continuous line of serial descent (46–7). For Richards, the two epistemological modalities of taxonomy and morphology entail diametrically opposed assumptions about nature and knowledge. The purpose of taxonomy, he argues, 'is not to exert control over non-ordered areas of the world, but to infer a universal order from the evidence at hand'. Within such a scheme, the monster represents the moment at which categorisation has to admit its own inexactitude, 'a tacit acknowledgement that knowledge is neither comprehensive in scope nor logical in form' (52–3). Morphology, on the other hand, could, with the aid of the fossil record, equip biology with an historical evolutionary archive that would account for every form that had ever existed, and allow the rehabilitation of the monstrous. As such, it was fundamentally imperialist in its implications, a point to which we shall return below.

In *The Birth of the Clinic*, Foucault maps these epistemic shifts onto changes in the theory and practice of medicine. Classical medicine, he argues, viewed disease in terms of kinships constituted though formal resemblance. Like botanical species, diseases could be mapped out on 'the flat surface of perpetual simultaneity. Table and picture . . . It is a space in which analogies define essences' (1986: 6). The way in which diseases were localised in the body was accounted for in terms of sympathy (11), though the patient's temperament could affect the quality of the disease, and so to know the illness from which one was suffering, one first had to subtract the individual and his particular qualities (14). In eighteenth-century clinical teaching, Foucault notes, it is not the gaze that has the power of analysis and synthesis, but the synthetic truth of language, imposed from the outside. The density of the visible merely obscures the truth. Medical science was not a question of observation but of decipherment (60). While autopsies were often carried out to 'confirm' medical diagnoses, the chronicle of observations generated by posthumous dissections had no scientific status or truth-value (62). The morbid specimen thus possessed an uncertain status in late eighteenth-century medical collections. Lacking status as a bearer of truth, it was merely a curiosity. Hence the emphasis, in Austerlitz's description of the Maisons-Alfort museum, on examples of intact organic structures whose purpose was anatomical instruction, and on monstrosities that fall outside the order of nature as understood by the classical *episteme*.[9]

In the museum of the Norwich and Norfolk Hospital, founded in 1853, the way in which the specimens are described suggests a decidedly different way of conceptualising monstrosity. Among the typical specimens of these nineteenth-century museums, the narrator lists 'prematurely born, deformed or hydrocephalic foetuses, hypertrophied organs, and other items of a similar nature' (RS 10/20). The vocabulary here is instructive, since it draws much more explicitly on the lexicon of clinical medicine, particularly in the word 'hypertrophied', attested in English for the first time in 1835. Furthermore, the German word used to refer to a collection of such exhibits is *Absonderlichkeiten*, which Michael Hulse translates as 'medical curiosities', but which in German possesses more of a sense of deviance from an accepted norm. What we have here are archives of the monstrous that are the product of a certain medical gaze, a conception of the body that differentiates not between the healthy and the sick, but between the normal and the deviant. This reflects the fact that, as the nineteenth century progressed, medical discourse became profoundly normative, not only distributing advice as to healthy life, but dictating 'the standards for physical and model relations of the individual and of the society in which he lives'. Thus whereas eighteenth-century medicine had been concerned to restore the lost properties of health to the body, nineteenth-century medicine was 'regulated more in accordance with normality than health; it formed its concepts and prescribed its interventions in relation to a standard of functioning of organic structure' (Foucault 1986: 34–5).

The distinction between the normal and the deviant was a major aspect of nineteenth-century biopolitics and is inestimably important for an understanding of modernity. Foucault has identified the 'normalising gaze' as a central technique of disciplinary society (1979: 177–84).[10] It structured knowledge in such human sciences as criminology, anthropology, sexology and epidemiology, and as such was indispensable to the fixing, control and discipline of populations that characterise modernity. Furthermore, the normal-deviant binary produced specific subject positions. In the hierarchical ranking characteristic of disciplinary institutions, Foucault notes, individuation takes place by referencing each individual to an overall rule or model, an optimum norm, while also establishing the boundary that separates the normal from the abnormal (182–3). Foucault has in mind schools and penitentiaries, but museums, too, participate in this wider discourse. The *Gruselkabinette* of nineteenth-century hospitals were not only determined by a normalising medical gaze, but *produced* this gaze in the spectator, who was impelled to accept the distinction between the normal and the pathological, and hence to internalise the disciplinary gaze of the emergent clinical medicine. The passage about the Norwich and Norfolk Hospital in *The Rings of Saturn* illustrates this very process.

It is in this light that we can understand the passage that Sebald attributes to Thomas Browne, but which I cannot trace to any of Browne's works. After quoting almost verbatim from the final paragraphs of *The Garden of Cyrus*, the narrator adds, '[W]e are occupied above all with the abnormalities of creation, be they the deformities produced by sickness or the grotesqueries with which Nature, with an inventiveness scarcely less diseased, fills every vacant space in her atlas' (RS 21/32–3). The idea of a pathological nature that has become autonomous from God, combined with a lexicon that post-dates Browne by at least a century and a half ('abnormality' is first attested in English in 1854, the German *Abnormität* in 1805 in a psychiatric context and 1822 in a clinical one), suggests that this is an addition from Sebald's pen. It involves a reconfiguration of Browne's interest in 'singular phenomena' in terms of norm and deviation, thereby turning Browne into an avatar of a distinctly modern epistemology.[11] It also involves a transfiguration of Browne's cosmology into a negative secular metaphysics that is more in tune with the philosophy of history that emerges as Sebald's text proceeds.

The one thing that is not accounted for by the foregoing analysis, however, is the fact that the thematic recurrence of the deviant, monstrous and deformed goes hand in hand with a degree of textual excess. Sebald provides extensive lists of the creatures mentioned by Browne in *The Garden of Cyrus*,[12] vivid and slightly gruesome descriptions of the exhibits at Maisons-Alfort, and lengthy quotations from the *Musaeum Clausum*, and seems to delight in abstruse or quasi-technical vocabulary. This expenditure of textual energy is ostensibly unmotivated beyond the desire to communicate the narrator's or protagonist's own sense of wonder and fascination. In the light of these considerations, it might at first sight appear that Sebald's texts illustrate the persistence into the present of pre-modern forms of organising and representing nature. According to what Glenn Penny terms the Whiggish history of museums, delight in curiosities is progressively replaced by scientific mastery and control of the world's diversity (2002: 165). On this model, the return of wonder, spectacle and a focus on the abstruse in Sebald's descriptions of museums would represent the moment of collapse of the modern epistemic endeavour: the eruption of the cabinet of curiosities or the fairground side-show into the bastion of modern scientific education.

Such a view, however, neglects the crucial fact that spectacle as well as surveillance is a part of modernity and its disciplinary regimes. Foucault claims, in *Discipline and Punish*, that 'our society is not one of spectacle but of surveillance . . . We are neither in the amphitheatre, nor on the stage, but in the panoptic machine, invested by its effects of power' (1979: 217). However, the way in which spectatorship itself inserts the individual into relations of power, arranging bodies in space and fixing the observer within normative, codified regimes of visual consumption, suggests that Foucault's dismissal of the spectacle is premature.[13] If the development of medicine from the eighteenth into the nineteenth century was characterised by an increasing emphasis on the privileging of vision over language – a tendency that continues into our own day with the numerous modes of seeing *inside* the body, from gastroscopy and endoscopy to CAT, MRI and ultrasound scans, and the retinal photography used as a diagnostic tool in *Austerlitz* (A 52/55–6) – spectacle can be seen to take its place at the very heart of the power/knowledge nexus. The spectacle disciplines by delimiting what is given to be seen and determining how it is to be seen. In the case of museums, for example, attention is managed through the distribution of exhibits, and the removal of the haptic aspects of perception by placing objects under glass domes, as in the case of Thomas Browne's skull (RS 11/20), or in the glass cabinets whose reflection can be seen in the photograph of the horse's bronchia in *Austerlitz* (A 372/375). Thus the visual mastery that the viewer exercises over the objects on display is paralleled by further workings of power/knowledge that operate through spectacle on the observer himself.[14] Indeed, the disciplinary aspects of spectacle are nicely illustrated by the titles of the two television programmes mentioned by Sebald's narrator in *The Rings of Saturn*: *Nature Watch* and *Survival*. If the first of these constitutes nature as a spectacle available for visual consumption from one's own armchair, thereby implying a position of scopic mastery over the natural world, the second implies the Darwinian assumptions that structure such nature documentaries, either in the form of explicit commentary on the adaptive mutation of unusual creatures, or in endlessly repeated scenes of predation. Like other forms of spectacle, television emerges as a means of managing attention and response and imposing on the viewer a specific way of interpreting nature in its entirety, for which the events on screen are a synechdochic surrogate.

Sebald's thematisation of the classification and display of nature, from Thomas Browne to television, can be understood in terms of an archaeology of knowledge, as the various collections mentioned demonstrate different epistemic structures. At the same time, all are equally shown to be part of a modern visual economy in which the disciplinary aspects of spectacle work alongside the notion of surveillance to produce the viewer as both the object and the subject of knowledge. These considerations feed into two further kinds of collection in Sebald's work: the *Naturalienkabinette* in Andromeda Lodge, and the various zoos visited by Sebald's narrators and protagonists.

NATURALIENKABINETTE AND ZOOS

Andromeda Lodge in *Austerlitz* is represented as a haven from Austerlitz's oppressive methodist upbringing in North Wales and from Stower Grange, the chaotic public school that he attends along with Gerald Fitzpatrick.[15] And yet its status as a rural idyll is destabilised by the fact that its inhabitants are gripped by a mania for collecting dead things. Practically every room in the house contains a display case housing parrots' eggs, seashells, geological specimens, beetles, butterflies, various reptiles preserved in formaldehyde, snail shells, crustaceans, crabs, starfish and a range of leaves, flowers and grasses (A 118–19/122). This collection, we learn, is a direct result of the visits made to Andromeda Lodge by Darwin as he was completing *The Descent of Man* near the neighbouring town of Dolgellau (A 119/123). Thus the Andromeda Lodge collection is intimately linked with the young science of morphology.

As we have seen above, morphology was imperial in its implications in the sense that it claimed to be able to bring every natural form that had ever existed under its dominion. In *Austerlitz*, though, the imperial aspect of collecting is not merely metaphorical, for the various parrots, whose mortal remains now lie in a large chest of specially-designed drawers, were acquired by Gerald's great-grandfather and great-great-grandfather on their travels, or purchased from a dealer in Le Havre (A 117/120). The *pièce de résistance*, furthermore, is an African Grey Parrot that originated in the Congo – the location of some of colonialism's worst excesses and abuses, such as those thematised in *The Rings of Saturn*.[16] The collection is thus a product of colonial geopolitics in which global travel and extensive networks of trade in rare species sustained the exhibition 'at home' of souvenirs from the farthest and most exotic reaches of empire. The connection between power, knowledge and the production of subjectivity is in full evidence here. The collection is subjected to rigorous taxonomical ordering, as shown by both the photograph of the butterfly case (A 118/122) and the Latin label on Jaco the parrot's cardboard sarcophagus: '*Ps. erithacus L*' (A 117/121). The removal of animals from their natural habitat, their reduction to a (Western) system of classification, and their integration into spaces of exhibition are characteristic of a colonial subjectivity defined in terms not only of its power to acquire and to name, but of its ability to place this power on display. Whereas the Renaissance collection operated metaphorically to locate the prince at the centre of a divinely-ordained cosmos, the synechdochic relationship between the Andromeda Lodge collections and the territories from which they have been pilfered instals the provincial Welsh collectors at the centre of empire.

The subjectivity of the colonial collector, however, is not allowed to stand unchallenged in *Austerlitz*. The strange case of Jaco the deceased parrot, which Gerald frequently removes from its little cardboard case, testifies to a moment of ambivalence at the heart of the collector's enterprise. Austerlitz quotes from the bird's obituaries, which mention his tame and trusting nature, his ability to speak with both himself and others, to mimic children, and to be taught by them. His only bad habit was to gnaw at the furniture if he was not given enough nuts and apricot stones to crack (A 118/121). The first thing that stands out here is that the obituaries both embody and express an explicit anthropomorphism. In his study of zoos, Randy Malamud argues that the interaction between humans and captive live animals is governed at one level by a desire for reciprocity, a desire to have one's gaze returned by the animals, even though this desire is bound to be thwarted by the unequal power relationship between exhibit and visitor and the scopic regime that structures their encounter (1998: 235, 250). The representation of Jaco the parrot suggests that the animals collected at Andromeda Lodge allowed this impossible desire to be realised.[17] However, Gerald's repeated symbolic exhumation of the dead creature endows it with the quality of a fetish. In Freud's classic account of fetishism, the fetish object represents a compromise formation that allows the male child both to abandon and preserve the idea of sexual difference in a structure of disavowal.[18] In an analogous fashion, Jaco's exquisite corpse allows Gerald both to acknowledge the destruction inherent in the activities of his naturalist forebears – an acknowledgment that is inscribed in Jaco's posthumous facial expression of profound grief – while disavowing it by admiring the beauty of its plumage and reading the obituaries, which imply a happy coexistence of the bird and its human captors.

This ambivalence towards the practice of collecting animals is also manifested by Great Uncle Alphonso, who provides a kind of counter-discourse when he talks about the staggering biodiversity that could once be seen along the coastline of south-west England but which has disappeared within the intervening half a century (A 126–7/130–1). This, he claims, is due to 'our passion for collecting and [to] other imponderable disturbances and disruptions' (A 127/131), thereby acknowledging that the precondition of collecting and of much biological knowledge is the destruction of its own object. The oblique reference to 'imponderable disturbances and disruptions' seems to be an allusion to the environmental depredation that Sebald thematises so extensively in *After Nature* and elsewhere, thereby linking scientific endeavour to the broader environmental impact of modernity.[19] And yet the need to collect, to name and classify, is evident even in those passages that are ostensibly critical of collecting. When Alphonso takes Austerlitz and Gerald into the garden in order to observe the moths that visit the place by night, Austerlitz's attitude appears to be one of wonder. He relates that he and Gerald 'could not get over our amazement at the endless variety of these invertebrates, which are usually hidden from our sight'. His role is reduced to watching in wonder (A 128/132), and he claims no longer to know what varieties of moth they caught. And yet this claim to nescience is immediately undermined by a long list of possible species, as though the desire to take possession, which was not available to Austerlitz and Gerald at the time, can be retrospectively fulfilled at the level of the text, which itself comes to constitute a kind of collection.

The Andromeda Lodge episode, then, shows that the constitution of the subject through the collection and classification of exotic animals – be they domestic or colonial – is precarious, and is dependent on structures of disavowal or retrospective appropriation. The various visits to zoos and menageries undertaken by Sebald's narrators and protagonists are likewise governed by a profound ambivalence.

The link between collections of exotic animals and the colonial project is foregrounded in *Austerlitz* when the narrator notes that he cannot think of the Antwerp Nocturama without thinking of the station, and vice versa. He conjectures that this is because he went straight from the zoo to the station on the afternoon in question, but what he notices when he returns to the station is that the building is a monument to colonialism, with a bronze statue of an African boy and a dromedary adorning one of the building's corner towers as synechdochic representations of native African people and fauna (A 4–5/8–9). This leads to a strange fantasy that conflates station and zoo:

> When I entered the great hall of the Centraal Station with its dome arching sixty metres high above it, my first thought, perhaps triggered by my visit to the zoo and the sight of the dromedary, was that this magnificent although then severely dilapidated foyer ought to have cages for lions and leopards let into its marble niches, and aquaria for sharks, octopuses and crocodiles, just as some zoos, conversely, have little railway trains in which you can, so to speak, travel to the farthest corners of the earth. (A 5/9)

Like the collections at Andromeda Lodge, the Antwerp zoo episode explores a mode of colonial subjectivity. The narrator notes that the architecture of the station exceeds by far the merely functional, the implication being that it constitutes a spectacular display of power. This implication is borne out in Austerlitz's lengthy disquisition on the symbolic intentions of the station's eclectic medley of styles (A 9–14/13–18). In this sense, it resembles the Palais de Justice in Brussels, whose hastily-constructed interior contains stairways that lead nowhere and inaccessible rooms that harbour 'the innermost secret of all sanctioned authority' (A 39/43).[20] But in the case of the station, that power is colonial rather than juridical: the building and its ornaments address themselves to a subject who is invited to see himself as occupying a privileged position at the heart of an extensive empire. This is also precisely the function of zoos. While keeping live animals has been a practice associated with the display of wealth and power for three-and-a-half millennia, the zoo in its modern incarnation came into being in the nineteenth century as a direct consequence of imperial expansion. Zoos were established on an ever-grander scale as colonial rivalry between European nations demanded ever more conspicuous symbolic reinforcement. Exotic animals provided a set of concrete synechdoches that represented empire to a metropolitan populace for whom territories thousands of miles away remained abstract and alien, and in the rigid hierarchy between human and animal, they reinforced in metaphorical terms the superiority of the metropolitan European.

Beyond these superficial functions of zoological exhibition, however, zoos are ideological machines that participate in structures of power/knowledge. Firstly, animals have endured a history of marginalisation and hierarchisation that exhibits parallels with the history of political economy (Mitchell 1994: 333). It is not merely, as Harriet Ritvo argues, that zoos valued animals according to their usefulness and docility, privileging the industrious 'servants' of mankind over those that not only refused to serve but challenged human dominance (Ritvo, cited in Malamud 1998: 65). It is also that zoos represented this hierarchical and utilitarian view of nature as, precisely, *natural*, thereby obscuring the cultural construction of class inequality that is the concomitant of capitalism. Secondly, collecting animals is the archetypal act of 'marking-off . . . a subjective domain that is not "other" ' (Clifford 1988: 218). One means by which this is achieved is by naming, classification and recontextualisation, reducing biodiversity to a set of taxonomic labels and resemanticising animals as exemplars of a species. The privileging of Western knowledge over local knowledge legitimises the capture and transportation of animals in the name of scientific progress, while also implying a paternalistic view of native populations whose knowledge of and ability to care for animals in their natural habitat is deemed inferior to the Western ability to protect and nurture. The implications of this paternalism are twofold. On the one hand, it provides a justification for empire in that a nation's ability to maintain captive animals so well demonstrates its capacity for good and benevolent government, and thereby earns it the right to govern subaltern peoples in colonial outposts (Malamud 1998: 67). On the other, it carries with it an implication that exotic animals are better cared for 'here' than 'there', a message reinforced by the politics of conservation. Indeed, it becomes unnecessary to travel at all, since the nurturing care of species and their display in dioramas that mimic the creatures' natural habitats allows 'here' to subsume 'there'. The ultimate implication of this is that, '[F]ollowing the logic of imperialism, it is only minimally necessary for Africa to exist, except to supply Western zoos with elephants (and Western industry with cheap oil, and so on for all the other constituent categories encompassing the functions that "outposts" provide imperial society)' (Malamud 1998: 71–2).

The Antwerp zoo episode addresses all these features of the colonial zoo. The statue of the boy and camel symbolically 'bring home' the colony, while establishing the metropolis as the centre of a global transport network that extends to the furthest reaches of empire. In other words, it stresses the role of modern transport technology – of which the railways, as elsewhere in Sebald, are the predominant emblem – in the process of colonial appropriation. The miniature trains that, so the narrator claims, often transport visitors around zoos – which in the case of Antwerp, at least, are organised according to geographical as well as taxonomic principles – are a symbolic enactment of the literal appropriation facilitated by the railways in the nineteenth century. The entire colonial project can be thus realised in miniature within a domesticated, Western, metropolitan setting, rendering global travel unnecessary and Africa itself effectively irrelevant.

The fact that the narrator is drawn to the Nocturama and devotes significant portions of text listing the exotic animals kept there (A 2, 6/6, 10) signals a fascination that is not entirely compatible with a critical agenda. But Sebald's descriptions of animals in captivity certainly do imply a critique of keeping live animals. The racoon engaged in washing a piece of apple time and time again as though this action could liberate it from its unreal, artificial environment

(A 2–3/6–7) echoes the quail in *The Rings of Saturn*, dementedly running back and forth along the edge of its cage in incomprehension at its own captive condition (RS 36/50), while the narrator notes that all the animals in the zoo wore a 'sorrowful expression' (A 6/10). Later in *Austerlitz*, the protagonist obtains a slow-motion copy of the Nazi film about the Theresienstadt ghetto (discussed in Chapter 8, below), and compares the menacing growl that now constitutes the film's sound with the sounds made by lions and tigers driven insane by their captivity in the *Jardin des Plantes* in Paris (A 349–50/353).

The *Jardin des Plantes* is also the site of the most telling critique of zoos in Sebald's work. When Austerlitz and Marie de Verneuil visit it in the 1950s, it is already dilapidated, with most of the miserable enclosures devoid of the African animals they had once proudly contained. This results in the collapse of the colonial gaze and hence of the zoo's function as a technology for reproducing ideology. The permanent visibility of the zoological exhibit has given way to absence and invisibility, which precipitates a crisis in the visitors. All they can do is ask a series of questions: why are the animals hiding? Why aren't they moving? Are they dead (A 367/371)? Furthermore, Marie herself remarks that captive animals and their human audience are destined to face each other across 'une brèche d'incompréhension' (an abyss of incomprehension) (A 368/372).[21] This episode, then, dramatises the breakdown of the structures of looking that zoos conventionally promote, and destabilises the function of zoos in processes of subject-formation.

What emerges from an analysis of museums, collections and zoos in Sebald is that modernity's regimes of spectacle and surveillance are not as total or continuous in their effects as Foucault's analysis would imply. They are frequently open to contestation and critique. As the following chapters will show, this ambivalent engagement with modernity and its disciplinary subjectivity is a pervasive aspect of Sebald's work.

NOTES

1. Boris Groys notes the centrality of collecting for modern subjectivity, and locates the museum at the heart of this problem. 'Modern subjectivity can define itself only in terms of collecting,' he writes. This desire to collect, however, creates problems for what Groys calls the ecology of culture. The question is: what should be rescued from the growing rubbish-heap of history produced by our ever-accelerating cycles of production, consumption and waste? The problem, Groys argues, is managed through the museum: rather than preserving condemned artifacts from disappearance, the museum makes meaningful selections from the increasing pile of cultural rubbish: '[M]useums are places in which the rubbish of cultural history is processed to form cultural identities' (1997: 48–9). Groys' work focuses on the museum primarily as a hermetic and self-regulating system, whereas my interest lies in the biopolitical effects of the various institutions of collecting.

2. It should be noted that Stewart's contentions cannot claim universal applicability. They refer implicitly to collections that developed in the West from the sixteenth century onwards, and have to be understood in this light.

3. This view of the nineteenth-century art museum is shared by Preziosi 2003: 15–43, Prior 2002: 37–46 and Bennett 1995: 167–8.
4. The concern with public health was, of course, one manifestation of Foucault's 'governmentality', as the population became the primary object of state power.
5. All that is now left of the Norfolk and Norwich museum's collection is a vast collection of bladder stones. See http://www.medicalheritage.co.uk/NORFOLK.htm (consulted 23 January 2007).
6. On Fragonard, see Simon 2002.
7. Anne Fuchs (2004a: 102) also draws attention to Browne's liminal epistemic position.
8. On these and other Renaissance collections, see Blom 2003: 13–49; Hooper-Greenhill 1992: 78–132; and Hauser 2001: 32–4.
9. 'Pathologically malformed organs' are present, but relegated to the middle of a sentence and briefly exemplified by shrunken hearts and bloated livers to which Austerlitz grants no further significance (A 371/374).
10. As we will see in the next chapter, the 'normalising gaze' was also lent considerable support by developments in composite, anthropometric and police photography.
11. Such a shift, of course, suits the thematic tenor of *The Rings of Saturn* better than does the idea of nature as an open book of divine revelation. The view of nature as pathological occurs in *After Nature*, where the narrator writes of 'the absence of balance in nature/ which blindly makes one experiment after another/ and like a senseless botcher/ undoes the thing it has only just achieved' (AN 27/24).
12. I discuss the narratological function of lists and inventories in *The Rings of Saturn* in Chapter 7, below.
13. On this point, see Crary 1990: 17–19. Crary rightly notes that Foucault's rejection of spectacle has to be understood historically, as part of the polemics of post-1968 French intellectual life and as a direct riposte to Guy Debord's *The Society of the Spectacle*.
14. I use the masculine pronoun advisedly throughout this chapter. Since Laura Mulvey's classic essay 'Visual Pleasure and Narrative Cinema' (Mulvey 1989), it has been conventional to assume that the bearer of the gaze is masculine more or less by default, particularly when the gaze implies a degree of (desired) mastery. Sebald's texts, with their repeated exploration of scopic mastery, do not call this assumption into question.
15. For a discussion of public schools in Sebald, see Long 2006a: 224–5.
16. We may note here a secret complicity beneath the schismatic breach between Catholicism and biology in the Fitzgerald family: Austerlitz's devout Catholic uncle Evelyn donates money to the Congo mission 'for the salvation of black souls still languishing in unbelief' (A 123/126). Evelyn is as much an imperialist as any of his naturalist relatives.
17. The cockatoos that are still there at the time of Austerlitz's visits are also part of this fantasy of human–animal reciprocity.
18. See Bal 1994 for an account of collecting that stresses the centrality of fetishism, in both its Freudian and Marxian senses, to the subject-formation of the collector.
19. On Sebald and nature, see especially Bond 2004, Riordan 2004 and Fuchs 2004a: 223–9.
20. In one of the text's few light-hearted moments, Austerlitz also relates a series of anecdotes detailing various unlicensed businesses that are established in remote rooms of the Palais de Justice (A 40/44). These represent localised, anti-disciplinary appropriations of space at the very heart of juridical power.
21. Intertext hunters may be interested to know that this is a quotation from Berger 1980.

3

THE PHOTOGRAPH

SEBALD AND PHOTOGRAPHY

The most conspicuous surface feature of Sebald's texts is the fact that they incorporate reproductions of photographic images. While early reviewers of Sebald's texts found the photographs particularly fascinating and innovative, literature has drawn on the resources of the photograph since the inception of the latter medium, from the photographic activities of Emile Zola and Lewis Carroll, through the nineteenth-century fashion for photographically illustrated books, to more genuinely integrated text-image composites in the work of Georges Rodenbach, André Breton, Kurt Tucholsky, Rolf-Dieter Brinkmann, Alexander Kluge and Javier Marías, among others.[1] Since the publication of Sebald's first prose text, *Vertigo*, the German book market has experienced a sudden glut of books that incorporate photographic images: Monika Maron's *Pawels Briefe* (*Pawel's Letters*, 1999), Stephan Wackwitz's *Ein unsichtbares Land* (*An Invisible Country*, 2003), Jana Hensel's *Zonenkinder* (*Children of the 'Zone'* – i.e. East Germany, 2002), the reissue of Peter Henisch's 1975 novel *Die kleine Figur meines Vaters* (*The Diminutive Figure of my Father*) and a series of fictions by Peter Finkelgrün, to name just a few.

The notable thing about all of these recent texts is that they deploy photography as a way of exploring questions of memory. For Sebald, too, the mnemonic capacity of photographs is of central importance. This emerges implicitly in Renate Just's description of his study: apart from a wooden table, a camp bed and a battered German dictionary, all that this room contains is a wallet file bursting with old photographs and maps: 'family photos, glaciers, volcanic eruptions, girls in 1930s clothing, a child on a rocking horse whose head has faded away over time' (1997a: 40).[2] Sebald always collected stray photographs because, as he noted in a conversation with Maya Jaggi, 'there's a lot of memory in them' (2001a: 6). Memory is frequently coupled with the relation between the verbal and the visual. One insight that crops up repeatedly in interviews with the author is that the photograph demands narrativisation, making what Sebald terms an 'appeal' to the viewer to provide the image with a narrative context,[3] and thereby to rescue it from its nomadic existence (Scholz 2000). But there is also a sense that photographs are able to produce an experience of historical shock. In his last interview, Sebald notes that some photographs derive their unsettling power from their ability to eternalise a moment of prior innocence: a photograph of a relative from his mother's Bavarian clan offers no inkling that he was destined to return from the First World War in a mentally disturbed state (Jaggi 2001b). This comment is, of course, even more apposite in connection with Sebald's use of photography in *The Emigrants* and *Austerlitz*, where the emergence or discovery of photographs is often linked to the experience of shock and traumatic recall. But Sebald also notes that his family's photograph albums from the Nazi period are themselves profoundly unsettling when one revisits them after two decades or more and realises that they document the social role played by one's own relatives in the Third Reich (Scholz 2000).

Of the many critics who have addressed photography in Sebald's works, the vast majority have concentrated on the photographs' mnemonic function, frequently interrogating the interaction of image and text in the reconstruction of the past, or the role of photography in structures of traumatic recall.[4] These are important issues, and I will return to them in Part II. But questions of memory do not exhaust the uses to which Sebald puts photography. Indeed, in numerous interviews, he points to the variety of functions that photographs fulfil both within his writings and more generally. He is keen, for example, to stress the authenticating function of images. By his own admission, some of them are intended to create uncertainty in the reader as to the authenticity of the text (Löffler 1997a: 35), one example being the photograph of Max Ferber. The character is a composite of two figures, the one a Jewish refugee from Nazism who was Sebald's landlord in Manchester in the 1960s, the other the painter Frank Auerbach. But the photograph of Ferber is of someone else again. Significantly, though, Sebald immediately stresses that 'about ninety percent' of the photographs in *The Emigrants* are 'authentic' (Angier 1997: 49). This desire to emphasise the referential nature of the photograph crops up elsewhere. When Sebald comments that he uses photography as an aide-mémoire, as a way of note-taking on his travels (Scholz 2000), he alludes to photography's link with memory, but also foregrounds its status as a recording apparatus that is both quicker and more accurate than written note-taking. In the same interview, he declares that:

> the written word does not constitute an authentic document [*wahres Dokument*]. Photography is the authentic document *par excellence*. People find photographs convincing . . . I have no desire to include images of high photographic quality in my texts; they're just documents of found objects and are themselves quite secondary. (Scholz 2000)

There is a significant rhetorical slippage here between an ontological claim ('photography is an authentic document') and a pragmatic claim ('people find photographs convincing'). This is perhaps inevitable: in his highly influential book *The Burden of Representation* John Tagg (1988) argues that photography's referentiality, its indexical function, is a product of discursive systems and conventions rather than an inherent aspect of the medium itself. Thus the notion that the photograph is a mode of technological rather than human witnessing is taken to imply that it also possesses a greater claim to truth: the apparatus is merely a non-human recording agent that cannot lie. The most important point, however, is that Sebald's texts are intimately concerned with the indexical status of the photograph, the idea that it is a trace of past reality that confirms the existence of a certain thing, person, or event.[5] At one level, of course, the photographs contribute to the *effet de réel*, the reality effect that numerous commentators (including Sebald himself) have noted.[6] But the indexical status of the photograph is also central to the disciplinary aspects of modernity's visual culture, and it is to Sebald's thematisation of this issue to which I now turn.

PASSPORTS, TOURISM, ETHNOGRAPHY

Abigail Solomon-Godeau argues that the 'reality effect' of the photograph is not due to its indexicality alone, but to various other factors. Photographs appear to be self-generated, bearing no signs of their making. Although the precondition of the photograph is (in most cases at least) the presence on the scene of the photographer, the latter is manifestly absent from the image. Furthermore, photographs cannot be lifted from their material substrate, unlike an image on canvas or paper. There is also a structural convergence of the eye of the photographer, the eye of the photograph, and the eye of the spectator, which confers on photography the quality of pure presentness (1991: 180). All these things contribute to the mythic transparency of the photographic image. This assumed transparency lies at the heart of the photograph's status as proof or evidence, and allowed photography to be integrated, by the closing decades of the nineteenth century, into a range of scientific, technical, medical, legal and political apparatuses.

It is here that referentiality emerges as a vital aspect of photography's role as an apparatus of power, a role that is bolstered by certain features of photographic optics. Single-point monocular perspective, for example, is far from being a natural mode of perception: human vision is binocular, has no vanishing point, is unbounded, in constant flux, and fades at the edges. But Renaissance perspective is such a powerful representational convention in the West that its conventional status is often forgotten: it appears natural. This naturalisation conceals a set of ideological implications, chief among them being the illusion of visual mastery conferred upon the spectator whose all-seeing eye becomes the commanding point of the pictorial field. The position of visual mastery that this entails has been seen by Jean-Louis Baudry as an ideological construction:

> The world is no longer an 'open and unbounded horizon'. Limited by the framing, lined up, put at the proper distance, the world offers itself up as an object endowed with meaning, an intentional object, implied by and implying the action of the 'subject' which sights it. (cited in Solomon-Godeau 1991: 181)

The differential power relationships implied in this conception of photography emerge clearly in psychiatric, colonial and anthropological, medical, and forensic photography, but they are also operative at numerous other sites where photographs are taken and displayed: on vacation, in the family, at school, in the army, and, of course, in the passport.

Sebald's passport photograph is reproduced in *Vertigo* (V 114/135) in the context of a longer narrative tracing the loss of his passport in Limone and the acquisition of a new one in Milan (Fig. 3.1). I return to this episode in the next chapter, because it says much about the role of archival practices within the disciplinary regimes of modernity. But it also alerts us to the disciplinary aspect of photography: in order to possess a valid passport, one must submit to a rigorous disciplining of the body. This consists in subjecting oneself to the photographic apparatus: sitting in a booth, one must ensure that the background, full-frontal face-on view, framing, and degree of exposure are all correct if the resulting image is to possess legal validity.[7] The fact that it is a machine that takes the portrait demonstrates, incidentally, that the power effects of photography operate independently of any individual human agent. But beyond submission to the exigencies of the photobooth, one also has to control one's own facial gestures: a blank, emotionless expression is required. The passport photograph demonstrates the workings of the 'microphysics of power' at two levels. First, the very concept of the passport is disciplinary, facilitating social regulation by tracing the movement of bodies both within and across national boundaries, and establishing inclusion in or exclusion from the citizen body of a given state. Secondly, the subject is in part constituted by the apparatus, right

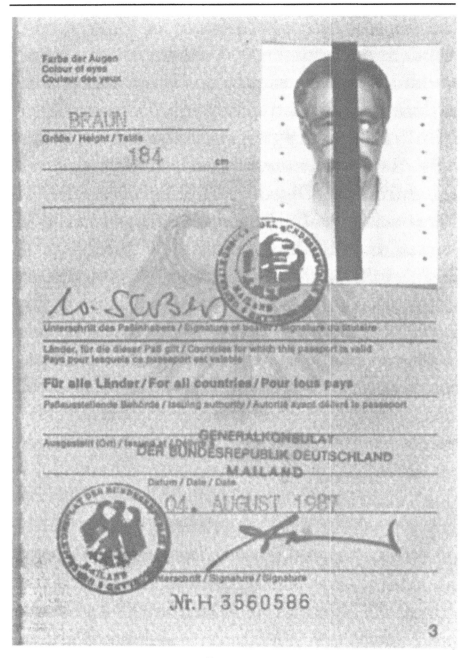

Figure 3.1

down to the most intimate bodily performances. An undisciplined smirk at the wrong moment and the legal validity of the photograph vanishes.[8]

In the case of the passport, the power invested in photography derives largely from the state, as shown in Sebald's text by the fact that the narrator goes to the German consulate in Milan in order to obtain the document. As noted above, though, photography also operates within other regimes of power. Ethnographic and anthropological photography, for example, is now widely seen as deeply implicated in the politics of colonialism and the construction of visual typologies of race. Such typologies fed into emerging theories that located the essence of difference in the racialised body (rather than in language and material culture, which had formed the primary focus of early anthropology and produced a sense of cultural relativism). As we saw in the previous chapter, the conceptual pairing that legitimised this racialist discourse was that of norm and deviation, and a series of photographic innovations of the later nineteenth century were explicitly constructed around the norm-deviation binary.[9] Their ultimate effect was to constitute the white male body as a normative standard, against which degrees of deviance could be measured.

By participating in this discursive construction, colonial photography, as Anne Maxwell points out, allowed the European public – be they colonisers or tourists – to take possession of foreign places and peoples without radically questioning the presupposition of their own superiority. This was partly achieved, she goes on to argue, by the photographic reproduction of racial stereotypes, which 'strengthened European imperialism by providing consumers with an outlet for their exotic fantasies and affording them a heightened sense of their own worth as a distinctive racial and cultural ideal for the rest of the world to follow' (1999: 59).[10] The implication of this was that other cultures were uncivilised, or that they occupied a lower position on the evolutionary scale, two assumptions that necessarily led to the conclusion that these cultures were destined to die out either as a result of the encroachment of modernity and Western civilisation, or as a consequence of their own biological lack of adaptability. The notion of the moribund culture was a self-fulfilling prophecy, as native populations became targets for the European *mission civilisatrice* and were systematically looted under the aegis of the salvage paradigm in ethnography.[11] And such a trend in ethnographic thought found its most destructive distortion in the racial politics of Nazism.

It is this latter fact that draws attention to an unsettling continuity between the tourist photography of Ambros Adelwarth in *The Emigrants* (E 134/199) and the trophy photograph of the gypsy woman in *Vertigo*, which finds its way into the photographic album that the narrator's father presents to his wife as a souvenir of his participation in the German invasion of Poland (V 184/210). During his journey to Constantinople with his lover, Cosmo Solomon, Adelwarth sees a twelve-year-old dervish of surpassing beauty. Later the same

Figure 3.2

day, Cosmo announces his intention to return with a photographer and take a photograph of the boy as a memento (E 134–5/199–200). The resulting image is reproduced (Fig. 3.2). It shows the boy, who looks younger that his supposed twelve years, standing in a yard of cobbles and grass. The part of the yard behind him is in shadow, as is the stuccoed dwelling that forms the upper half of the background. Because the sun is falling over the boy's left shoulder, his face is in partial shadow. This fact, combined with the small format of the reproduced image, prevents the viewer from judging the beauty of which this photograph was intended to be a souvenir. What remains is an image that encodes the power relationship between the tourist and the indigenous populace. The child poses stiffly, arms locked by his sides, and gazes frontally and expressionlessly into the lens. He is situated some distance from the camera, with the result that most of the photograph consists of background. His smallness relative to the image as a whole combines with his position in the very centre of the frame to emphasise the fact that he is *exposed* in more than just the photographic sense: he has nowhere to run or hide, but has to yield to the photographer's gaze, offering himself up for later visual consumption. While the text strives to prevent this kind of reading by casting the image as a harmless token of the familiar and benign Western ritual of tourism, it also foregrounds the desire for possession. Indeed, the way in which the verbal text foregrounds the boy's beauty and his close-fitting garments implies that the photograph functions as a surrogate for sexual possession of the body. Furthermore, the text also emphasises the lack of reciprocity in the encounter, for when Adelwarth addresses a few words of Turkish to the boy, he remains silent.

Such a reading of the dervish photograph relies not only on the immanent formal features of the image, but on its contrastive relationship to an earlier photograph of Adelwarth himself in Arab costume (E 94/137). In the course of the nineteenth century, the head-on stare established itself as a widespread portrait technique in all kinds of repressive photographic practices, and was deemed to signify the 'bluntness and "naturalness" of a culturally unsophisticated class' (Tagg 1988: 36) – or, we might add, race. Honorific portrait photography, on the other hand, borrowed heavily from the compositional conventions of eighteenth-century painting in its drive to democratise the traditional function of portraiture, namely the ceremonial presentation of the self.[12] This involved photographers' and their bourgeois clients' adopting the cultivated asymmetries that typified aristocratic posture. The relationship between rigid frontality and relaxed three-quarter profile constituted a visual codification of social relations, with the result that, as Nancy Armstrong writes, 'the distinction between a portrait of a loved one and that of a criminal became just as obvious as that differentiating either a celebrity from a native or a sentimental illustration from a political cartoon' (1999: 130).

The image of Adelwarth is a studio portrait, which already signals that the image is the result of a collaboration between photographer and sitter (Fig. 3.3). The three-quarter profile, furthermore, is a formal sign of bourgeois self-presentation, as is the emphasis on the face and hands. Such features of the photographic portrait owe their continuing signifying power to the

Figure 3.3

physiognomic discourse with which nineteenth-century portrait photography was deeply enmeshed, and which continues to linger over a century later. The assumption of physiognomy was that the moral characteristics of the person could be gauged from the shape and distribution of facial features, and photography was deemed to provide empirical evidence of the truth of this proposition.[13] The three-quarter profile signifies 'character', while the hands, lying dormant in the lap or (in this case) clutching an instrument of leisure, reveal a 'truth' that Suren Lalvani sees as central to bourgeois ideology, namely that 'the world may be civilized by the domestication of the hand by the head' (1996: 52).[14] Photography thus comes to signify not merely the qualities of the individual, but also that individual's position on the scale of socio-economic privilege. It is a gauge of social power. Beyond this, however, there is the moment of performance in the Adelwarth image. By dressing in Arab costume and holding a hookah, Adelwarth arrogates to himself the right to usurp the identity of the colonised other in a way that is congruent with the appropriation implied in the act of photographing the dervish. Though Sebald has rightly been praised for the pervasive critique of colonialism in his work, we should not be blind to moments where his critical distance collapses, giving way to a more affirmative representation of colonial desire.

In the light of the above considerations, which link formal composition of the image to questions of race, sexuality and power, the image of the gypsy prisoner in *Vertigo* becomes all the more unsettling (Fig. 3.4). The motivation for its inclusion is a childhood reminiscence of the narrator, who recalls a gypsy camp on the periphery of his native village in the summers following the Second World War. His mother would pick him up whenever they walked past the site on the way to the swimming pool (V 183/209). The pool itself had been built, we learn, in 1936 'zur Förderung der Volksgesundheit' ('to promote public health') (V 183/209). Given the year of its construction, it is clear that the *Volk* that was the target of this particular measure was the 'Aryan' people of Germany. Nazi social policy encouraged improvement of one's bodily strength and fitness through various physical activities, of which the mass rhythmic gymnastics familiar from Leni Riefenstahl's propaganda films are emblematic. The pool endures into the post-war years as a reminder of the legacy of Nazism. So, too, does the fact that there was no congress between the gypsies and the villagers (V 184/209), testifying to the persistence of an irrationally phobic attitude on the part of the Germans towards what was by 1945 a persecuted and decimated people, and to an all-too-rational fear, perhaps, on the part of the gypsies themselves.[15] The passage continues:

> Where they came from, how they had managed to survive the war, and why of all places they had chosen that cheerless spot by the Ach bridge for their summer camp, are questions that occur to me only now – for

Figure 3.4

example, when I leaf through the photo album which my father bought as a present for my mother for the first so-called Kriegsweihnacht. In it are pictures of the Polish campaign, all neatly captioned in white ink. Some of these photographs show gypsies who had been rounded up and put in detention. They are looking out, smiling, from behind barbed wire, somewhere in a far corner of Slovakia where my father and his vehicle repairs unit had been stationed for several weeks before the outbreak of the war. (V 184/209–10)

The narrator's strangely inconclusive commentary ends there. His brief puzzling over how the gypsies survived the war could be seen as an example of the oblique representation of the Holocaust that critics have identified as a consistent feature of Sebald's narrative project.[16] But in this context it is clearly also linked to questions of the family's implication in Nazism, questions that are intimately connected to representation and trans-generational transmission.[17] In the absence of explicit reflection on these issues, the photograph itself, and the fact that it formed part of a souvenir album, acquire a semantic density that is unusual even for Sebald's texts.

The photograph shows a gypsy woman cradling a small baby in her arms and smiling at the camera from beyond a crude barbed-wire fence (V 184/210). The background shows the side of a building fashioned from wooden slats or corrugated iron, while the right side of the image contains a looming presence in deep shadow, which can be identified as the right shoulder, arm and head of another incarcerated woman. As the German army swarmed over Europe in 1939 and 1940, it became a widespread practice for Wehrmacht soldiers to take photographs of the inhabitants of occupied territories.[18] For soldiers on the Eastern Front, the evidence furnished by these photographs confirmed racial stereotypes that were already well-established by the end of the First World War in Germany, and had been reinforced by six years of Nazi rule: Eastern European peoples were backward, uncivilised, primitive and worthy of nothing but contempt (Bopp 2003: 109–13, Schmiegelt 2000: 29). This is a radicalised Nazi variant of the ethnographic gaze that assumed the inferiority of a racialised other.[19] The gypsy woman in Sebald's image clearly falls into this category, as the simplicity of her dress and headscarf, and her ostensible lack of teeth, are made to signify a level of cultural backwardness that served to affirm German superiority. The labelling of the image, which consists of the single word 'Zigeuner' ('gypsies'), is a further component of the ethnographic gaze. The woman is seen not as an individual with her own biography and interiority, nor as an inhabitant of a specific place. Even the fact that she and the other captives are women becomes elided: rather than the term Zigeunerinnen, which would signal specifically gypsy women, the compiler of the album leaves gender unmarked by employing the generic masculine plural term Zigeuner. The women are thus reduced to an example of a type, a rhetorical move that bears more than a coincidental similarity to the operations of the collector that we explored in Chapter 2: the example stands metonymically for a larger abstract whole.

There is, however, more to this photograph. To the left of the image can be seen the arm and tunic tails of a man. His arm is bent upwards with the elbow protruding, as if he, too, is in the act of taking a photograph. This possibly inadvertent inclusion of another photographer turns this image into what W. J. T. Mitchell terms a 'metapicture': it is an image that reflects on the nature and production of the image.[20] In particular, it foregrounds the fact that representation is inseparable from questions of power: who has the right and the means to represent whom under what circumstances and for what ends. Like the dervish in The Emigrants, the gypsy woman is forced to submit to the gaze not of one but of several cameras, and to constitute herself as an ethnographic spectacle while being excluded from access to the means of representation. It might be objected that the woman's smile shows a degree of willing participation in the photographic process, and that a resistant reading of the image might allow us to rescue her subjectivity and humanity from the very apparatus that set out to destroy it.[21] Such a reading, however, is precluded by the depiction of another photographer in the frame and by the barbed wire that cuts diagonally across the image, radically separating the taker of the photograph from his subject. This separation constitutes a visible sign of the gypsy woman's fundamental disempowerment; she and the photographer cannot occupy the same discursive terrain, and any sense of reciprocity in the production of the image is therefore illusory. The image thus *depicts* the differential power relationship that is also its own condition of possibility.

If these considerations form the discursive field within which the gypsy image becomes readable, they still do not account for the function of the image within the narrative economy of *Vertigo*. The photograph is reproduced at a point in the text in which the narrator seeks to reconstruct past events by reading the material traces that they left behind. This is, of course, a narrative method that Sebald exploits more fully in his later narratives. Here, the narrator's walk from the Krummenbacher Kapelle to the village of W. takes him past a memorial to four men who had died in one of the last, pointless battles of World War Two (V 181–2/206–8). The photograph of this curious metal cross is much larger in the German edition of the text, taking up almost a whole page. The names are clearly legible, as is the legend on the lowest plaque: 'fürs Vaterland gefallen' ('they gave their lives for the Fatherland') (V 182/207). The last skirmish in which the men died was much talked about in the village, we learn, and the narrator:

> imagined the combatants with soot-blackened faces, crouching behind tree trunks with their rifles at the ready or leaping from rock to rock across the deepest chasms, suspended motionless in mid-air, for at least as long as I could hold my breath or keep my eyes shut. (V 182/208)

The two photographs are not explicitly related to each other in the text, but their close proximity implies a link of some kind. A clue to this link is provided a little later, when the narrator describes the weekly newsreels that were shown in the function room of the inn in which the narrator and his parents lived. Almost every film, he writes, showed images of the bombed-out ruins of cities like Berlin and Hamburg, and yet he never associated these with the war, seeing them rather as the natural state of big cities (V 187/213).

Like the gypsies and the memorial cross, these films point to an epistemological lack. The narrator is confronted with material traces of a past that he does not understand, and for which he therefore seeks to compensate by means of fantasy and imagination. This narratorial position corresponds to what Marianne Hirsch has influentially termed 'postmemory':

> Postmemory is distinguished from memory by generational distance and from history by deep personal connection. Postmemory is a powerful and

very particular form of memory precisely because its connection to its object or source is mediated not through recollection but through an imaginative investment and creation. (1997: 22)

Though he does not use the term, Sebald notes the relevance of postmemory to his own experience as a German born in the penultimate year of the war. In the introduction to his extended essay *Air War and Literature*, a text that is based on a series of lectures delivered in Zürich in 1997, and forms the longest chapter of *On the Natural History of Destruction* he writes:

> Born in a village in the Allgäu Alps in May 1944, I am one of those who remained almost untouched by the catastrophe then unfolding in the German Reich. In my first Zurich lecture I tried to show, through passages of some length taken from my own literary works, that this catastrophe had none the less left its mark on my mind. (NHD vii–viii/5–6)

In the German text, the catastrophe leaves not a 'mark on Sebald's mind', but 'deep traces in his memory', and these correspond to Hirsch's postmemories: the events in question took place before the author's birth, and yet cannot be consigned to mere 'history' because of the profound affective connection to the recent past that no member of the so-called second generation can escape.[22] As we will see in later chapters, postmemory is a central concern of *The Emigrants* and *Austerlitz*. The difference between those texts and this brief episode in 'Il ritorno in patria' is that the latter is concerned not with the victims of history, but with the legacies of the perpetrators. Sebald's exploration of postmemory thus goes beyond Hirsch's own explicit focus on the descendants of Holocaust survivors, and aligns him with the numerous other German writers who have, in recent years, explored the postmemorial position of the descendants of the perpetrator collective: Marcel Beyer, Kurt Drawert, Günter Grass, Ulla Hahn, Uwe Timm, and many others.

The content of the narrator's postmemories is fanciful. They are, of course, the imaginings of a child, and the narrative episodes are focalised as though through a child's consciousness. But they link up with other comments that Sebald made in interviews to diagnose a serious deficit in the public memorial culture of post-war Germany. Speaking of his own inadequate historical education, Sebald comments:

> Until I was 16 or 17, I had heard practically nothing about the history that preceded 1945. Only when we were 17 were we confronted with a documentary film of the opening of the Belsen camp. There it was, and we somehow had to get our minds around it – which of course we didn't. It was in the afternoon, with a football match afterwards. (Jaggi 2001b)

In another interview, he terms the showing of the Bergen-Belsen film a 'moralische Pflichtübung' – a moral duty discharged without conviction

(Löffler 1997b: 131). The gypsy camp, the iron memorial cross, the cities on the weekly newsreel, and the film of Bergen-Belsen are not provided with a historical context that would allow them to be fully assimilated, with the result that we are offered a romanticised narrative of the soldiers in action, and the notion that all cities exist in a state of ruin – fantasies that bespeak a profound ignorance that is upheld by pervasive social silence. As Sebald sees it, public memorial culture in Germany offers the second-generation subject insufficient material and narrative resources for the kind of imaginative investment and creation that are the prerequisites of postmemory.[23]

The gypsy photograph has to be understood in this light. Speaking of his own family albums, Sebald admits that he is not entirely comfortable with them:

> As a rule, you look through these albums as a child, completely naively, without any sense for history or of history or any knowledge of the Third Reich. You didn't know what role your parents played during this period of history, what position they adopted. You just leafed idly through the things. And then you left them lying in a drawer. When you then get them in your hands again, say as a forty-year-old, after a gap of twenty or twenty-five years, the whole thing is something of a negative revelation. Because in the interim you've learned what history is. (Scholz 2000)

An analogous moment of belated historical realisation is experienced by the narrator in 'Il ritorno in Patria', but he does not explicitly articulate its implications. The image produces the strangely truncated commentary quoted above, rather than the more extensive narrativisation that Marianne Hirsch sees as an integral part of the postmemorial act, and that is one of the structural principles of the family narratives of which *The Emigrants* is constituted (as we will see in Chapter 6). The narrator's gaze stops at the surface of the photograph, and the drive to contextualise is arrested. One reason for this is that the ethnographic gaze that is inscribed in the gypsy photograph implicitly aligns the narrator's father with Nazi racial ideology and implicates him in the genocidal war in Eastern Europe. Furthermore, while the photograph itself was originally a gift, intended as a memento of war experience, it is also, as we have seen, the heavily coded bearer of ethnographic assumptions. As such, it contributes to the reinforcement of stereotypes designed to reproduce Nazi racial ideology within the family. Located at the intersection of ethnography, family albums and (post)memorial practices, the gypsy photograph thus contains a sedimented history of perpetration, racial politics and the attempts of those born later to deal with this legacy, traces of which are inscribed in the private spaces of the bourgeois home. Significantly, the narrator shies away from exploring these implications of the photograph. As a non-Jewish German telling the stories of Jewish Holocaust survivors, Sebald has been both condemned for his ethically dubious appropriation of victims' life stories and praised for the ethical seriousness with which he approaches such a highly sensitive issue. What a reading of the gypsy photograph reveals, however, is a reluctance to confront the legacies not of survival, but of perpetration. In this light, Sebald's concern with Jewish fates and families can be seen as a substitute for far more difficult engagement with the past that he and his narrators share.

Discipline and Resistance

The disciplinary uses of photography do not necessarily entail such extreme and polarised structures of power. Sebald's works also contain, for example, ostensibly benign images of school classes, sports teams or professional groups. Such photographs function as a powerful means of constituting the individual as a member of a group at an institutional level. By means of annual repetition, school photographs additionally produce the individual as a member of a specific generation. The anatomo-political power invested in the camera's gaze is particularly clear in the photograph of Austerlitz's school rugby team. Not only are all the boys dressed identically and posed identically (with the sanctioned exception of the Brylcremed captain, who holds a ball marked '1951 2nd XV'), but they all stare frontally into the lens, as does the teacher who stands at one side as the representative of institutional power *within the frame*. As we have seen above, such conventions possess meaning in excess of their aesthetic value: they bespeak photography's power to encourage strict but consensual conformity to normative bodily conduct. Furthermore, the arrangement of those in the back row – tallest in the middle, falling by gradations to the shortest at either end – is a concrete manifestation of the anthropometric distribution beloved of statistical thinking. Adolphe Quetelet, widely credited as the inventor of modern social statistics, noticed that the anthropometric data he collected fell into the pattern of the Gaussian binomial curve. Conflating individual human difference with mathematical error, Quetelet defined the central portion of his bell-shaped curve as the area of normality, with divergent measurements shading off into areas of various forms of deviance (Sekula 1992: 355). The symmetrical arrangement of the rugby players enables precisely this kind of immediate visual apprehension of height distribution among the boys (albeit in terms of median rather than mean values), and thus the measurement of both norm and deviation. It embodies the normalising gaze that Foucault identifies as typical of disciplinary institutions (1979: 177–84).

There are moments in Sebald's work, however, in which the power invested in photography is subverted or called into question. In *Austerlitz*, the protagonist ends up in the Salpêtrière in Paris after a suffering a breakdown on the Métro. He describes the Salpêtrière as a 'gigantic complex of buildings where the borders between hospital and penitentiary have always been blurred' (A 376/378) – a comment that is thoroughly Foucauldean in its understanding of the relationship between power, knowledge and architecture. The Salpêtrière is, of course, famous primarily because of the early psychiatric work of Jean-Marie Charcot, who enlisted photography in order to confirm the visual morphology of hysteria and thereby to produce knowledge about hysterical symptoms.[24] And yet the reader who seeks such images or others culled from the canon of psychiatric photography in Sebald's work looks in vain. Indeed, as Martin Klebes has argued, while Sebald frequently reproduces photographs at points in the verbal text that thematise madness or psychiatric disorders, the images fail to fulfil their putatively evidential function: there is a disorientating incongruence between the claims of the text and the images designed to illustrate them (2006a: 71). Klebes gives three examples. The first is the fairground photograph of Kafka in 'Dr K. Takes the Waters at Riva', in which the photograph appears to contradict Dr K's persistent headache and feelings of profound antipathy towards his companions (V 143–4/166). The second is the picture of a mentally-ill volunteer at the Romford nursery where Austerlitz himself works for a time. The assistants 'all bore the scars of their mental sufferings' but often seemed 'carefree and very cheerful' (A 326/330). It is impossible to tell from the photograph that accompanies this passage whether the person depicted falls into the former or latter category. Thirdly, Klebes mentions the image of the horse in 'Il ritorno in patria', which seems intended to illustrate the proposition that 'horses often have a somewhat crazed look in their eyes' (V 190/216), but whose gaze does not allow any such diagnosis.

Klebes relates the disorientating relationship between text and image in these episodes to the critique of pathography that emerges in Sebald's later critical works as well as elsewhere in his literary texts. This argument can be extended to encompass the wider question of power/knowledge. For by subverting photography's assumed evidential claims, the images to which Klebes draws our attention refuse to confirm the diagnoses offered by the verbal text. The indeterminacy of the text–image relation implies that the equine and human subjects of these images cannot be reduced to diagnostic categories, and exceed the determinations of the power/knowledge matrix.

Group photographs, too, prove to be sites of resistance, where the subjects of the photograph refuse to yield to the strictures of the institutional and photographic apparatus. The photograph of Paul Bereyter's teacher training college depicts a set of stiffly posed, formally clad, becapped seminarists standing on the front steps of an imposing public building, with a row of four masters seated on chairs in front of them (Fig. 3.5, E 46/69). The uniformity of attire and the presence of the masters place the image in the same generic category as the Stower Grange rugby team. There are, however, major differences between the two. Firstly, and most strikingly, few of the seminarists are actually looking at the camera, even though all their masters are. This represents a moment of subversion: the boys refuse to return the gaze of the camera, adopt in many cases a three-quarter profile, and in so doing assert their own embodied subjectivity

Figure 3.5

against the conformity demanded by the situation. The exception is the figure on the far right, who distinguishes himself by his exaggeratedly upright posture and the physical gap between himself and the other boys, throwing the distraction of the other seminarists into greater relief. At the same time, the teacher on the far left is distinguished from his colleagues by means of his beard, the pale colour of his jacket, and his slouching posture. His upper body and right foot are tilted towards the edge of the left-hand frame of the photograph implying a desire to dissociate himself from the other three teachers or even to flee the photographic gaze altogether. A formulation that Sebald's narrators use to describe boarding schools is 'ans Karnevalistische grenzend' – bordering on the carnivalesque. This phrase occurs in both the description of Stower Grange in *Austerlitz* (A 84/88) and in Max Ferber's narrative of his school days in *The Emigrants* (E 189–90/283).[25] In 'Paul Bereyter', the teacher training college is represented as the very antithesis of these carnivalesque institutions. And yet it is the image of the trainee teachers and not the photograph of the Stower Grange rugby players that seems to hint at a level of anti-disciplinary disorder.

A photograph that is genuinely carnivalesque can be found in 'Il ritorno in patria', as the narrator reminisces about the performances of Schiller's *The Robbers* in his native village of W (Fig. 3.6). On Shrove Tuesday, the high-point

Figure 3.6

of carnival in Germany's southern and Rhineland regions, the actors don their costumes one more time, and along with the carnival fools pose for a group portrait with members of the fire brigade (V 191/217). The result is a bizarre image in which the quasi-military postures of the uniformed firemen contrast with the massed ranks of actors, musicians, a few masked harlequin-like figures in the foreground, and even a pantomime cow lounging in the bottom right-hand corner. The asymmetrical composition, the chaotic distribution of bodies, the open frame and the promiscuous melange of attire foreground photography's limitations as a disciplinary medium. As befits an image of carnival, the photograph collapses hierarchical values as the fire brigade – the guarantors of social order – are both outnumbered and marginalised by various kinds of entertainers. Indeed, the firemen seem to be absorbed by the troupe of actors and clowns, and become themselves merely participants in the general masquerade and spectacle.[26]

<h2 style="text-align:center">SPECTACLE</h2>

As we saw in Chapter 2, spectacle is the other aspect of modernity's visual culture, an aspect to which photography made a significant contribution. Furthermore, photography's capacity for limitless reproduction meant that it also became a means of social exchange within an expanded field of commodity circulation. Sebald's narrators thematise the role of photography in both the constitution of the spectacle and in networks of circulation and exchange. In particular, they evince a pervasive fascination for postcards, which, though invented in 1869, became a medium of mass communication only in the late 1890s. In 'Il ritorno in patria', the narrator frequently visits the landlady of the Engelwirt, Rosina Zobel, and leafs through the three large folio volumes that contain her collection of several hundred postcards (V 196/222). The collection, we learn, had been put together by her husband in the years before their marriage, when he had used up most of his sizeable inheritance on global travel (V 197/224), and shows a large number of cities in Germany, Austria, Switzerland, Bohemia, Italy and the Far East. The album is thus not a collection of postcards that have been received by the collector, but a set of souvenirs. Susan Stewart sees the souvenir as replacing memory of the body's relation to the phenomenological world with the memory of an object, a process that emerges under an exchange economy in which 'authentic' experience becomes increasingly mediated and abstracted (1993: 133). In this sense, the album is a technology of recollection that is part of the 'archival consciousness' that we will investigate further in Chapter 5.

There is, however, another aspect to this collection, which concerns photography's capacity to reduce everything to universal equivalence. Sebald's narrative implicitly thematises this feature of the photographic image: going through the album involves nothing more than the narrator's pointing at each picture and Rosina's supplying the name of the city depicted. This generates a list: 'Chur, Bregenz, Innsbruck, Altaussee, Hallstadt, Salzburg, Vienna, Pilsen, Marienbad, Bad Kissingen, Würzburg, Bad Homburg, and Frankfurt am Main' (V 196/222). The list represents, at the surface level of the text, precisely the same paradigmatic, non-hierarchical ordering that characterises the arrangement of the photographic archive itself. Severed from their referents, the photographs lack all geographical and biographical contextualisation. All that remains is equivalence. Theories of modernity often point to the fact that the production of equivalences is a salient feature of advanced exchange economies, and Jonathan Crary explicitly links money and photography as:

> homologous forms of social power [and] equally totalizing systems for binding and unifying all subjects within a single global network of valuation and desire . . . Both are magical forms that establish a new set of abstract relations between individuals and things, and impose those relations as the real. (1990: 13)

While Crary's claims for the 'global' and 'totalising' reach of photography may be exaggerated, the decontextualisation and abstraction that characterise Rosina's postcard albums suggest that they participate in the reconfiguration of subjectivity that Crary sees as a function of modernity's visual field. It is not only that the experience of place is mediated by the image, but that all places lose their geographical specificity and subjective significance once they are mass-produced in postcard format, enter the space of commodity circulation, and are enshrined within the pages of the album. The postcard transforms space into spectacle. In so doing, it exercises a disciplinary effect by establishing a hierarchy of spaces by excluding from representation those places that are not worthy of being seen/photographed, and decreeing in advance how those spaces that are represented are to be seen. It is in this very concrete sense that photography binds subjects into a 'global network of valuation and desire'.

The photographs in Sebald's texts ultimately suggest that there is little that is beyond the reach of spectacle. The postcard of the herring fishermen in *The Rings of Saturn* turns labour into spectacle (RS 54/71), while the postcard of the army encampment in Egypt, which Austerlitz sends to the narrator, demonstrates that war, too, has become an object of spectacular mediation (A 166/170). Both fishing and war, however, are acts that have material effects in the world and are not reducible to their representations. The same cannot be said of the image, reproduced in *Vertigo*, of Kafka, Lise Kaznelson, Albert Ehrenstein and Otto Pick sitting in the cockpit of a painted aeroplane flying over Vienna's famous *Riesenrad* or giant Ferris wheel (Fig. 3.7, V 144/166). While this image, as we have seen, fails to provide confirmation of Kafka's inner

Figure 3.7

turmoil, it is a symptom of the emerging leisure economy, of which novelty photography was both a record and a component. Photography has long gone hand in hand with commodified leisure activities, implying not only that experience is inauthentic unless it is accompanied by photographic proof, but that obtaining the photographic record is the very purpose of undertaking the activity in the first place. The Kafka image is a particularly radical variant of this structure of mediated experience, since it is a photographic record of nothing beyond the act of being photographed. This image has abandoned all pretence of reference to a real experience. It is spectacle as pure mediation.

Sebald's use of photography, then, goes beyond questions of memory. By drawing on photography's role in the constitution of bourgeois subjectivity and its concomitant implication in state, ethnographic and colonial processes of identity formation, Sebald shows that photography as a medium lies at the heart of modernity and its structures of power/knowledge. He also shows, however, that even photography can function as a site of resistance, that the power of the photographic gaze is not all-encompassing, does not produce the subject without remainder, and offers scope for the assertion of individual embodied subjectivity. At the same time, several of Sebald's photographs dramatise the increasing role of spectacle and the mediation of experience, which hints at the erosion of subjective authenticity that numerous commentators have identified as a consequence of modern technologies of representation. In Part II, I will return to these considerations in the discussion of *Vertigo* and *The Emigrants*.

NOTES

1. On nineteenth-century photographically illustrated books, see Stiegler 2001 and Carol Armstrong 2001. A good introduction to the interactions of photography and literature is provided by Koppen 1987. He discusses Rodenbach, Breton, Tucholsky, Brinkmann and Kluge. Marcus Nölp (2001) explicitly situates Sebald within this tradition. Sebald was an admirer of Javier Marías' remarkable fictions, and provided an endorsement for the cover of the English edition of *Dark Back of Time* (see Marías 2003). The collaborative volume *Unrecounted*, which combines short poems by Sebald with hyperrealist etchings of eyes by Jan Peter Tripp, includes an image of Marías (U 8).
2. In another interview with Just, Sebald confesses to an omnivorous interest in heterogeneous photographic material (1997b: 30).
3. This proposition recurs in various interviews. See, for example, Scholz 2000, Jaggi 2001b.
4. See the discussion of photography in the Introduction. This aspect of Sebald research is becoming increasingly congested and predictable, as a seemingly endless series of variations on the theme of 'photography and trauma in *Austerlitz*' suggests. Duttlinger's outstanding and pioneering work (2004) has been followed by Crownshaw 2004, Kouvaros 2005, Pane 2005 and Restuccia 2005. In terms of photography, these critics have an exceedingly narrow frame of reference. Indeed, their work leaves the impression that the only theorist to have said anything interesting and relevant about photography is Roland Barthes. For this reason, it is

refreshing to read Barzilai's anti-Barthesian account of photography and uncanny memory in *The Emigrants* and *Austerlitz* (2006). Two commentators who have sought to resist the memory paradigm are Klebes 2006a, and Horstkotte 2005a.

5. Roland Barthes is the best known critic to have put forward an ontological case for photography's indexicality. It is perhaps no coincidence that Sebald names Barthes (along with Susan Sontag and John Berger) as a photograph critic who has particularly interested him. See Baker 2001.

6. See, for example, Swales 2004: 27 and Furst 2006: 220–1.

7. This kind of standardisation is also typical of police photography, which relies on a series of technical procedures to establish its authority as a referential document. On police portraits, see Sekula 1992: 360. On the protocols for taking photographs for later use as evidence in court, see Tagg 1988: 95–8.

8. It is, of course, significant that the passport photograph in *Vertigo* has a thick black line down the centre, obviously drawn with a chisel-edged marker pen. Commenting on this fact, Martin Klebes points out that the image has been voided, 'its validity as a lawful means of identification struck out'. This cancellation produces an experience of vertigo, which Klebes sees as a textual effect rather than a personal weakness of the narrator (2004: 131). And yet the fact that the passport loses its validity as a legal document because the image is obscured (rather than, for example, the name) also draws our attention to the role of the photograph in constituting identity in the first place.

9. One might mention in this context the anthropometric photography of Henry Huxley and J. H. Lamprey, the *signalement anthropométrique* of Alphonse Bertillon, and the composite portraiture of Sir Francis Galton. On Huxley and Lamprey, see Maxwell 1999: 38–42. On Galton and Bertillon, see Sekula 1992.

10. The best-known text on colonial stereotypes is Alloula 1986. Alloula reproduces dozens of postcards that demonstrate precisely how persistent and systematic were the racial and, of course, gendered stereotypes that circulated in late-nineteenth and early twentieth-century France and Algeria.

11. On salvage ethnography in the German context, see Penny 2002. Elizabeth Edwards discusses the salvage paradigm in relation to photography in *Raw Histories* (2001: 157–80).

12. The most detailed account of the development of the standardised frontal view is provided by Regener 1999. See also Sekula 1992, Lalvani 1996: 43–136, and Nancy Armstrong 1999: 128–30.

13. An interesting variation on physiognomic discourse emerges in *The Rings of Saturn*, where the narrator comments on the unparalleled ugliness and deformity of the Belgians. He reads this as a symptom of the 'Congolese secret' that they carry within them (RS 122–3/149). In other words, they are a walking physiognomic archive of historical guilt.

14. The disciplining of the hands is a recurrent feature of bourgeois studio portraiture. There is a repertoire of hand positions (folded in the lap, placed on the arm of a chair, or raised to the side of the head) that recur in literally millions of studio photographs from all over Europe and North America.

15. Anne Fuchs puts it even more strongly, claiming that the gypsy episode demonstrates the persistence of a totalitarian mechanism of exclusion of the strange or foreign (2004a: 149), which contributes to an archaeology of *Heimat* that sees it as simultaneously historically compromised and a site of fascination and imaginative investment on the narrator's part (152).

16. See especially Williams 2000: 102–3.

17. Mark M. Anderson (2006: 32) notes that Sebald discovered the album from which the gypsy photograph is taken while visiting his parents in Sonthofen in the early

1980s. It also included various images of war, including villages that had been completely destroyed moments before.

18. An exhibition organised in the Museum Berlin-Karlshorst entitled *Foto-Feldpost: Geknipste Kriegserlebnisse 1939–1945* [*Photographic Forces Mail: Snapshots of Wartime Experiences, 1939–1945*] documented this trend. A selection of relevant images can be seen in the exhibition catalogue of the same name (Jahn and Schmiegelt 2000: 106–9).

19. Gypsy photography in Germany already had a long and inglorious history. The notorious *Zigeunerbuch*, a register of gypsies produced by Alfred Dillmann (1905) under the auspices of the Munich police department, contained pages of frontal portraits in the style of criminological identity photographs. Its foreword repeatedly notes that gypsies constitute a 'plague' because of their ability to elude the customary procedures of state control. Photography is thus deployed to assuage anxieties about the limits of discipline. For a photographically illustrated example of gypsy ethnography produced in the Nazi period, see Block 1936.

20. See Mitchell 1994: 35–82. The metapicture is defined in pragmatic rather than formal terms: 'Any picture that is used to reflect on the nature of pictures is a metapicture' (57).

21. See, for example, Ulrich Baer's reading of the photographs of the Łódź ghetto produced by the ghetto accountant, Walter Genewein (2001: 128–49). Baer accuses those who view the images as incarnating a totalising Nazi gaze as having 'a simplistic understanding of the photograph as originating with an all-knowing, morally vacated, and near-demonic subject behind the viewfinder, someone who wields absolute powers of execution and cognition over what is seen' (138). He goes on to argue that Genewein's images include contingent details that cannot be reduced to the Nazi gaze, but which can point to a traumatic reality of which Genewein, later critics, and, indeed survivors themselves have been unaware. Baer's reading of the images is governed by the ethical imperative to acknowledge the humanity of their subjects, which the Nazi gaze sought to deny. This is a perfectly valid project, but to dismiss notions of a totalising Nazi gaze as simplistic is itself simplistic. The telltale word in Baer's analysis is 'someone' – the idea that the ethnographic gaze is somehow dependent on a person rather than on a vast, impersonal discursive apparatus with a long history and considerable biopolitical efficacy.

22. Eva Juhl expresses puzzlement that Sebald should see himself as personally involved in collective repression in spite of the *Gnade der späten Geburt* – the assumption that being born too late to have been involved in Nazism is a guarantee of absolution (1995: 643). The notion that the *Gnade der späten Geburt* could somehow render one immune to such repression, however, is based on the faulty supposition that the relationship between the Nazi past and 'those born later' ceases to be characterised by any sense of emotional investment. Sebald himself demonstrates a much more differentiated understanding of this highly problematic aspect of *Vergangenheitsbewältigung* or coming to terms with the Nazi past. Of the many critics to address this question, see especially Hell 2003 and 2004, and Huyssen 2001.

23. Susanne Vees-Gulani puts forward a similar argument with regard to the aerial bombardment of German cities by the allies (2006: 344). She reads the argument of Sebald's *Air War and Literature* in terms of postmemory, drawing on Andreas Huyssen (2001), who sees *Air War* as betokening, among other things, a desire for vicarious experience of the air raids. I emphasise that the critique of German memorial culture is Sebald's. As his attacks on Germany as lacking history and memory became increasingly strident in his later years, they also began to look increasingly out of kilter with the vigorous memory debates that have intensified markedly since

German Reunification (see, for example, Niven 2002 and the contributions to Fuchs, Cosgrove and Grote 2006). To accept Sebald's diagnosis of German amnesia wholesale, as do Mark McCulloh (2003: 1) and Frances Restuccia (2005: 304) among others, also ignores decades of philosophical, literary and political attempts to address the Nazi past.

24. On Charcot and photography, see Didi-Huberman 2003.
25. It is only in *Austerlitz* that the translation renders this accurately – it appears as 'to the point of anarchy' in *The Emigrants* (E 189/283).
26. Bearing in mind the devastating fire at the sawmill (V 182–3, 204/208, 231) and the later demolition of the fire station (V 185/211), the association of the fire brigade with clowns is perhaps not coincidental!

4

DISCIPLINE

TORTURED BODIES

The narrators of *Vertigo* and *The Rings of Saturn* are obsessed with pre-modern methods of exercising power. In *Vertigo*, the narrator paraphrases the *Italian Diary*, an 1819 work by the Austrian poet and dramatist Franz Grillparzer in which he broods over the uncanny and mysterious nature of the Doge's palace and the invisible principles of justice that it conceals (V 53/65). In the ensuing section about Casanova's famous escape from the palace, these principles are revealed to be arbitrary and prejudicial in the most literal sense: the very fact that somebody is called before the court is tantamount to a pronouncement of guilt (V 56–7/68). Casanova also remarks on the inventiveness of eighteenth-century Venetian penal justice, describing a strangulation machine in which the captive is throttled by a silk band attached to a spool (V 55/66). In Pisanello's fresco of Saint George and the dragon, the narrator notes the presence of a publicly hanged man who paradoxically lends the painting a singular lifelikeness and stresses the earthly nature of punishment (V 75/90). In *The Rings of Saturn*, the narrator records the bodily mutilation and summary executions carried out to maintain discipline in the Belgian Congo (RS 127/155),[1] while his narrative of nineteenth-century China thematises that empire's dependency on meticulous ceremonial (RS 139–40/167–8) and spectacular displays of wealth and opulence (RS 149–50/180) combined with equally spectacular forms of corporal punishment involving removing, cooking and eating the heart of an executed man (RS 142–3/172) or killing the prisoner through dismemberment and cutting him up into slices (RS 147/178). Finally, in his periphrastic and selective account of Thomas Browne's *Musaeum Clausum*, he quotes almost verbatim a paragraph detailing a series of sketches that depict methods of torture (RS 273/323). Browne's text reads:

> Some Pieces delineating singular inhumanities in Tortures. The Scaphismus[2] of the Persians. The living truncation of the Turks. The hanging Sport of the Thracians. The exact method of flaying men alive, beginning between the shoulders, according to the description of Thomas Minadoi, in his Persian War. (1946: 137)

Capital punishment, particularly that involving public torture, is a judicial ritual that forces the body to speak the truth of the crime (Foucault 1979: 35–47) and a political ritual of display that made everyone periodically aware of the unrestrained presence and power of the sovereign (or, in the case of the Congo, the sovereign's representatives) (49). The kind of trial endured by Casanova, in which the accused is effectively guilty *a priori*, was not, Foucault argues, uncommon in Europe before the late eighteenth century (35), while Casanova's imprisonment, involving not only detention but consignment to oblivion, is a feature of the extra-judicial exercise of sovereign power, a privileged instrument of despotism (Foucault 1979: 119).

As we saw in previous chapters, Sebald more or less implicitly integrates present disciplinary practices into an archaeology of power/knowledge, and that is true also of the multifarious disciplinary archives that form the subject of this chapter. The pre-modern actualisations of power that are repeatedly evoked in his texts provide a foil against which his exploration of modernity and its disciplinary regimes takes place.

SEXUALISED BODIES

While he is confined in the leaden chambers of the Doge's Palace, Casanova discovers an archive, consisting of:

> piles of old ledgers with records of trials held in the previous century. They contained charges brought against confessors who had extorted penances for improper ends of their own, described in detail the habits of schoolmasters convicted of pederasty, and were full of the most extraordinary accounts of transgressions, evidently detailed for the delectation solely of the legal profession. Casanova observed that one kind of case that occurred with particular frequency in those old pages concerned the deflowering of virgins in the city's orphanages . . . No doubt the dispensation of justice in those days, as also in later times, was largely concerned with regulating the libidinous instinct, and presumably not a few of the prisoners slowly perishing beneath the leaden roof of the palace will have

been of that irrepressible species whose desires drive them on, time after time, to the very same point. (V 58/69–70)

The interpolation 'as also in later times' constructs a continuity between seventeenth-century Venetian justice and later juridical models for regulating sexual behaviour. This continuity is upheld by the seamless transition between the quotation from Casanova's account of his escape and the narrator's own commentary. As was the case with Thomas Browne, this technique leads here to a superimposition of early modern and modern discourses. For the assumption that the prisoners included a high proportion of those whose own insatiable desires repeatedly led them to perform the same acts is not a concept that would have been familiar to a seventeenth- or eighteenth-century jurist.

The reason for this concerns the changing nature of the subject and its rela-tion to sexual transgression. Foucault notes, for example, that ancient civil or canonical codes defined sodomy as a category of forbidden acts whose perpe-trators were nothing more than the juridical subjects of those acts. The nine-teenth century, on the other hand, sees the emergence of the sexual deviant as a type. The homosexual became:

> a personage, a past, a case history, and a childhood, in addition to being a type of life, a life form, and a morphology, with an indiscreet anatomy and possibly a mysterious physiology . . . The sodomite had been a tem-porary aberration; the homosexual was now a species. (1990: 43)[3]

In other words, homosexuality ceased to be defined in terms of acts, and became instead a psychological, psychiatric and medical category that encap-sulated the essential truth of the individual.

As we noted briefly in the Introduction, Foucault's account of sexuality seeks to refute the assumption that speaking the truth about sex is a way of resisting the power that would repress this truth. On the contrary, he argues, the entire discourse of sexuality is intimately connected to power through the technology of the confession:

> The confession is a ritual of discourse in which the speaking subject is also the subject of the statement. It is also a ritual that unfolds within a power relationship, for one does not confess without the presence (or virtual presence) of a partner who is not simply the interlocutor but the author-ity who requires the confession, prescribes and appreciates it, and inter-venes in order to judge, punish, forgive, console, and reconcile. (1990: 62)

While this basically describes the Christian pastoral, which, Foucault argues, was for centuries the means by which the truth about sex was produced, confession has now become secularised and generalised, taking the form of interrogations, consultations, autobiographical narratives, letters, dossiers and published case histories (63).

We see this intersection of the categorisation of peripheral sexualities and the confessional *mise-en-discours* of sexuality that proliferated during the nineteenth century in the narrative of Roger Casement that concludes Chapter 5 of *The Rings of Saturn*. Casement was executed for treason in 1916, having sought to secure German assistance for an Irish uprising against the British in the early months of the First World War, as Sebald's narrator tells us (RS 130–4/158–62). But what effectively sealed his fate was the discovery and dissemination of his so-called *Black Diaries*. These contained detailed records of his numerous and varied homosexual encounters, and the circulation of the documents to the king, the American president, and the pope was designed to prevent high-profile pleas for clemency from influential quarters (RS 131/159). The narrator argues that the only conclusion that can be drawn from the diaries is that Casement's homosexuality was decisive in sensitising him to the victims of oppression, exploitation and slavery (RS 134/162). While Anne Fuchs argues that Sebald's thematisation of Casement's sexuality is less concerned with subject-formation than with Sebald's desire to cast Casement as a heroic outsider whose anti-imperial struggles were divorced from the political context of his times (2004a: 205), it is clear that the assumption that homosexuality was a fixed component of Casement's identity underpins both the circulation of the diaries to the political leaders of the day *and* Sebald's claim that Casement's solidarity with the oppressed could be traced to his sexual orientation. Whether criminalised or lauded, the text leaves us in no doubt that homosexuality constitutes the fundamental truth of Casement's being.

Significantly, this truth is archivally produced. In the first instance, Casement compulsively commits his confession to paper, detailing not only his encounters but the effects they have on his mood. The facsimile copy of the 1903 diary reproduced in *The Rings of Saturn* includes an entry for 29 March that reads: 'Pepe & Juan again – stayed in cabin. Feeling very seedy. Bleeding badly aft as in Santa Cruz . . . Feeling very seedy indeed.' In the top margin, there are further details of what are presumably sexual conquests: '17 Lauro of Santa Cruz. Manuel Violetta 19 gone to Las Palmas' (RS 132–3/160–1). Sebald's reproduction of this particular entry of the *Black Diaries* implies that they constitute an archival accumulation of carnality and introspection. An examination of this passage within the context of the diaries as a whole undermines such an assumption. Far from being the result of frequent sexual activity, Casement's rectal haemorrhage is actually a symptom of dysentery, as his diary entries for 24 and 25 March 1903 make clear (Síochláin and Sullivan 2003: 206–7). Furthermore, the term 'seedy', though nowadays meaning morally shabby, is used by Casement throughout his diaries to mean ill, tired and out-of-sorts. The way in which this decontextualised excerpt from Casement's journals is integrated into *The Rings of Saturn*, however, encourages a reading based on Casement's sexual behaviour. Sebald's narrator here surreptitiously demonstrates his alignment with a medico-judicial apparatus that forces the diaries to speak the truth, while simultaneously defining homosexuality as an innermost principle of identity and criminalising it. Knowledge of the individual thus facilitates the exercise of power that operates in full view of but ultimately independently of the judicial process.

We witness a similar case of homosexuality being posited as the prime mover in the individual life in the case of Ambros Adelwarth, the narrator's great-uncle in the third narrative in *The Emigrants*. Adelwarth, we are told, was 'of the other persuasion, as anyone could see, even if the family ignored or glossed over the fact. Perhaps some of them never realised' (E 88/128–9). As Maya Barzilai points out in what is so far the only essay to explore the question of male–male relationships in Sebald, the family's failure to acknowledge Adelwarth's sexual orientation is matched by his own difficulties in accessing his memories, and his transformation into an empty shell of a man for whom personal appearance substitutes for any kind of interiority (2004: 205). The causal relationship between sexuality and the dissolution of subjectivity resulting from a lack of acknowledgment by the other is implied, and becomes explicit when Sebald talks of the photograph of his own great-uncle in an interview with Carole Angier. The great-uncle concerned was the model for Adelwarth, and it is probably his photograph that is reproduced in the pages of *The Emigrants*. 'I knew about this uncle and had met him when I was a boy,' Sebald says, 'but I couldn't really see what was going on there. But then as soon as I saw this photo [of him in Arab costume], I understood the whole story . . .' (Angier 1997: 48). The reduction of 'the whole story' to Adelwarth's homosexuality demonstrates Sebald's more or less unconscious assumption that sexuality is the determining factor in the constitution of subjectivity. It also implies that homosexuality is characterised by a fundamental lack that can be compensated for only through an exaggerated outward performance that paradoxically writes homosexuality on the body with a transparency that is both unambiguous and amenable to preservation in the family archive.

BODIES IN SPACE: PASSPORTS, MAPS, FILES

Elsewhere, Sebald's accounts of power are more mundane. In *Vertigo*, for example, the narrator remarks on the extensive ritual of form-filling that has to be undertaken when registering in Italian hotels. In Limone, he checks into a hotel, where the owner's wife spends an excessive amount of time leafing through the narrator's passport and comparing his photograph with the person before her, and stows the passport in a drawer before handing over a room key (V 91/109). This provides a fine illustration of a disciplinary apparatus linked to an archival technology. The passport is in many respects one of modernity's most important inventions, particularly in the German-speaking lands, where it facilitated and regulated the freedom of movement that dramatically increased as old quasi-feudal prohibitions on travel broke down in the face of a developing market for industrial labour (Torpey 2000: 57–92). Both the passport itself and the registration form are part of state administrative bureaucracy whose aim is the control of the country's floating population. It is a form of anatomo-political regulation that fixes the position of bodies in space: without a passport, the traveller cannot leave the country. Indeed, he cannot even change hotel. Given the narrator's itinerancy in *Vertigo*, the system of hotel registration not only represents the action of power on the narrator's body (he cannot go just anywhere, but has to return to an identifiable location periodically), but would also have produced an extensive archive of knowledge about his personal movements that would be available to a variety of state organs, from the police to the Agenzia Nationale del Turismo.

The emphasis on the extensive registration arrangements in *Vertigo* is not, of course, purely thematic; it is also a significant narrative moment, because the passport that has been stored so carefully in its drawer later goes missing. In one of the few episodes in Sebald whose comedy relies not purely on the discrepancy between the banality of the subject matter and the excessive verbal resources used to describe it but on plotting and situation,[4] a series of searches by the receptionist, the owner's son Mauro, and the owner's wife Luciana, and finally the *padrone* himself fails to locate the missing document (V 98–101/117–20). In an intertextual nod to Goethe, we are told that the *padrone* provides a summary of 'these incredible occurrences' ('der vorgefallenen unerhörten Ereignisse', V 100/119). Discussing the particularly German genre of the *Novelle*, Goethe famously remarked in conversation with Eckermann on 29 January 1827: 'Was ist eine Novelle anders als eine sich ereignete, unerhörte Begebenheit' ('What is a *Novelle* but the occurrence of an incredible event', Eckermann 1984: 194–5).[5] The narrator thus stylises the loss of his passport into something 'unerhört' – a word that covers not only the incredible, but also the scandalous, outrageous and overwhelming. Such grandiloquence is, of course, humorous, but it conceals a more serious point, which concerns, yet again, the role of the archive in the production of subjectivity. Once the disappearance of the passport has been acknowledged, the question faced by the narrator is 'how I was to be provided with provisional papers proving my identity, in the absence of my passport, so that I could continue my journey and leave Italy' (V 100/119). What the narrator needs in order to establish his identity is a piece of paper (cf. Wohlleben 2003: 339–40). Without it, he cannot continue on his journey or leave the country, a situation that is later remedied when he acquires a new passport from the German Consulate in Milan. He describes it as an 'Ausweis meiner Freizügigkeit' – not merely proof of his freedom to come and go, as the English translation would have it, but a legal document confirming his right to free passage (V 115/135). He thus finds himself in the paradoxical position of being free to move only insofar as his movements are controlled by the archival apparatus of the state, whose biopolitical effects produce him as a free subject. At the very moment of its failure, then, the power of the archival apparatus is asserted all the more strongly, foregrounding the inextricable entwinement of subjectivity and discipline.

If the passport represents a kind of archiving that acts on the body of the individual in an immediate and clearly-defined way, the map does so much more surreptitiously. Cartography is a significant component of the generalised 'archival desire' that, as we saw in the Introduction, is a salient feature of modernity. Maps play a significant role in Sebald's work, and are often also reproduced photographically, so it is perhaps surprising that little critical attention has been paid to them so far.[6] A passing and puzzling reference to maps of 'the far north' in *The Rings of Saturn* alerts us to what is at stake in Sebald's thematisation of cartography. Having been shown to a dilapidated room in the Ashburys' house, the narrator describes it as follows: 'The paper had been stripped off the walls, which had traces of whitewash with bluish streaks like the skin of a dying body, and reminded me of one of those maps of the far north on which next to nothing is marked' (RS 210/249–50). The original of the last clause reads: 'Die . . . Wände glichen, so sagte ich mir, einer jener *bewundernswerten* Karten des höchsten Nordens, auf denen fast gar nichts verzeichnet ist' (my emphasis). The English translation omits the word 'bewundernswert' ('admirable'), thereby removing all mystery from the sentence. But what is so admirable about these maps? Is the narrator praising the skill of the cartographer or the maps' aesthetic purity? Or is he, on the other hand, alerting us to the fact that maps of the far north represent a world largely untouched by human civilisation and therefore not amenable to political intrumentalisation? The latter seems a more likely explanation of an otherwise strange adjective, for maps are repeatedly linked in Sebald's work to state oppression, colonial exploitation and industrialisation.

The role of maps in the project of colonialism is addressed in the section of *The Rings of Saturn* that deals with Joseph Conrad. In his biographical account of Conrad's boyhood, Sebald has him poring over maps on which almost nothing was marked. They were devoid of railways, roads and cities, and the River Congo was represented by a snake (RS 117/143). This passage is familiar to readers of Conrad's *Heart of Darkness*, whose second-degree narrator, Marlowe, says: 'At that time there were many blank spaces on the earth, and when I saw one that looked particularly inviting on the map (but they all looked like that) I would put my finger on it and say, When I grow up I will go there' (1983: 33).[7] What Sebald's text suppresses and Marlowe's narrative makes clear is the urge to colonise, take possession, fill in the blanks – all of which happens before either Conrad or his fictional narrator Marlowe gets to Africa: Sebald writes in his Conrad narrative that by this time the map had been filled in with detail (RS 117/143), while Marlowe declares, 'True, by this time it was not a blank space any more' (1983: 33).

'To catalogue the world,' writes influential geographer J. B. Harley, 'is to appropriate it' (1992: 245). In a Foucauldean account of cartography, Harley notes that in maps, polity and territory are fused in images which are part of the intellectual apparatus of power. In particular, maps were central to the project of colonialism and empire-building. They derived their power-effects by claiming land on paper before effective occupation; by providing information leading to the political and military containment of subject populations; by legitimising the realities of conquest and empire; and by imposing a regular grid on territory, thereby homogenising it in a way that favoured European control (1988: 282). The grid reduces space to a homogeneous surface defined by punctual co-ordinates. This mode of representation divests space of all symbolic value and local meaning, reconfiguring it as abstract and empty and facilitating, amongst other things, the exploitation of natural resources and the imposition of Western-style geopolitical boundaries with no regard for indigenous political and social structures.[8] What we see in Sebald's Conrad episode is precisely the process whereby the symbolic representation of space in the cartographic archive produces effects of power in the world whose consequences are exemplified by accounts of Western atrocities in the Congo and Casement's anti-colonial interventions.

Beyond this, however, mapping emerges as a means by which colonial ideology is subtly reproduced from one generation to the next. In the fourth narrative of *Vertigo*, the narrator relates his experiences of reading Mathild Seelos' atlas during visits with his grandfather to the Café Alpenrose. Accompanying this passage is a putative reproduction of one of the pages from the atlas (Fig. 4.1). It shows the world's longest rivers and highest peaks, reducing them to a schematic representation of length or height, and giving no sense of their actual geomorphic features or geographical locations, let alone the local cultural and religious significance they may possess (V 220–1/250–1).[9] The map implies that value is determined by purely quantitative data that can be made available only by Western surveying techniques. Like the grid system, it homogenises space and makes it potentially available for exploitation and division. This ideological coding of space is then disseminated by means of such popular forms as the atlas that falls into the hands of the young narrator. His reading replays, at the level of representation, the colonial desire of the Conrad narrative, decipherment of the map's legend substituting for geographical conquest:

> [T]here were wonderfully coloured maps, even of the most distant, scarcely discovered continents, with legends in tiny lettering which,

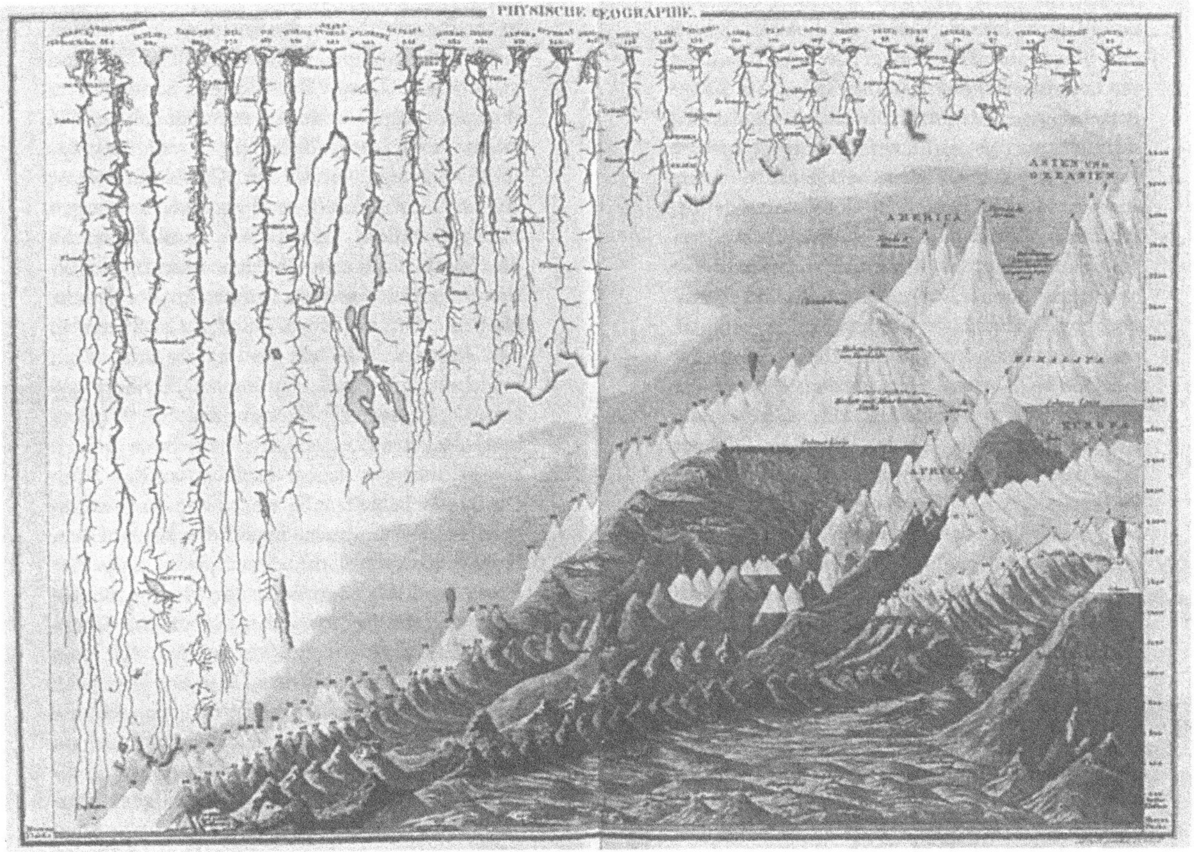

Figure 4.1

> perhaps because I could decipher them only in part just like the early car-
> tographers were able to picture only parts of the world, appeared to me
> to hold in them all conceivable mysteries. (V 222/252)

This is a clear example of colonial desire such as we also saw in the discussion
of the photographs of the dervish and Adelwarth in the previous chapter.

But one need not travel so far from home to see cartographic power in operation. In *Austerlitz*, there is a short passage detailing the slum clearances that
took place in East London in the 1860s and 1870s to make way for a rail ter-
minus. On the engineers' plans, we are told, the railway lines running into the
station look like muscle and nerve fibres in an anatomical atlas, a comment
that is corroborated by the reproduction of a recent map of Bishopsgate and
Liverpool Street Station (A 187/191). For Sebald's readers, the mention of an
anatomical atlas instantly connects the development of the railways to the
public dissection of Aris Kindt in *The Rings of Saturn*. Sebald's celebrated and
much-discussed reading of Rembrandt's *Anatomy Lesson* notes that the
onlooking members of the guild of surgeons stare past the outstretched corpse
at the anatomical atlas (RS 13/23), thereby betraying the rigid Cartesian gaze
(RS 17/27) that views the human body in utilitarian terms as a mechanism
that must either be made useful or disposed of (RS 13/26). In a similar vein,
the way in which railways were constructed through inhabited districts of
Britain's nineteenth-century cities was enabled by a utilitarian conception of
space such as we have already witnessed in the colonial context. Austerlitz
briefly outlines the consequences that the arrival of the railways had on the
Bishopsgate area:

> Soon the site in front of Bishopsgate was nothing but a grey-brown
> morass, a no-man's-land where not a living soul stirred. The little river
> Wellbrook, the ditches and ponds, the crakes and snipe and herons, the
> elms and mulberry trees, Paul Pindar's deer park, the inmates of Bedlam
> and the starving paupers of Angel Alley, Peter Street, Sweet Apple Court
> and Swan Yard had all gone. (A 186/190)

Modernisation is thus predicated on the destruction of nature and certain kinds
of human *Lebensformen* or ways of life that can be seen as expendable according to the economistic logic of industrial capitalism (cf. Eshel 2003: 85). But
such coercive biopolitical intervention is dependent on the knowledge provided
by cartography. In 1841 an Act of Parliament granted the Ordnance Survey,
Great Britain's official mapping agency, unlimited access to land in order to
produce large-scale maps of England whose sole purpose was to facilitate
expansion of the railways.[10] The wholesale resettlement of urban populations
that this expansion entailed was thus an effect of power generated by a vast
archive that catalogued the space of the nation.

If maps emerge as a means by which knowledge and power come together in modernity, this process can be seen in radicalised form in the Theresienstadt ghetto, which employs disciplinary tactics in the service of overt oppression. The map that Sebald reproduces in *Austerlitz* (A 328–9/332–3) is taken from H. G. Adler's *Theresienstadt 1941–1945*, which includes the map in a pull-out section at the end, and also has a key to the various locations represented. The map aims for an effect of total and exhaustive knowledge of bodies in space.

The example of Theresienstadt also alerts us, however, to other ways in which control of the archive serves the immediate interests of power. Towards the end of *Austerlitz*, the protagonist relates how he happens upon a photograph of the *Registraturkammer* or file room in the little fortress of Terezin (A 395/397). The photograph is reproduced on the following pages. While at one level 'the room is an enigma that triggers the kind of cultural memory that points to the ghostly presence of the absent other',[11] it also demonstrates that the distribution of bodies in space inside the walls of the ghetto itself had a symbolic correlate in the distribution of files in a room. Writings on modernity frequently stress the uses of the archive as a mode of controlling populations. Systems of registration in turn-of-the-century Berlin, for example, were extensive, from the issue of birth certificates through records of baptism, vaccinations, school registration and attendance, fitness for military service, occupation and marriage. Upon marriage, a new household was established that, along with all family members, domestic servants and lodgers, had to be registered with the police.[12] This vast documentary apparatus was organised in an integrated index that broke the city down into districts, streets, houses, floors and households (McElligott 2001: 235). The archive thus constituted a technique of power that mobilised statistical knowledge in order to fix the position of individuals within urban space, and to allow more efficient management of the population in terms of social hygiene, welfare and housing policy, as well as police surveillance. These practices, as Austerlitz tells the narrator, were fully evident in Theresienstadt, but as a grotesque and fearful distortion of their pre-Nazi form in which everybody had a precise, bureaucratically regulated place and role. Austerlitz adds:

> [T]his system had to be constantly supervised and statistically accounted for, particularly with respect to the total number of inmates in the ghetto, an uncommonly time-consuming business going far beyond civilian requirements when you remember that new transports were arriving all the time. (A 337/341)

The Theresienstadt *Registraturkammer*, and its relative proximity within *Austerlitz* to the map of the ghetto, make the biopolitical effects of such archives utterly transparent, and emphasise the fact that the Nazi murder of the Jews was predicated, as Zygmunt Bauman and others have noted, on administrative and bureaucratic structures that are fully characteristic of modernity.[13]

Austerlitz's discovery of the *Registraturkammer* photograph leads him to the conclusion that his true workplace is the fortress of Terezin. The disturbance caused by this thought manifests itself on Austerlitz's face, upon which he is addressed by a library employee, Henri Lemoine, who recognises Austerlitz from his visits to the old Bibliothèque Nationale in the Rue Richelieu. Just as Austerlitz becomes aware of past suffering when he senses a cool draught on his forehead in Liverpool Street Station (A 183/187), so Lemoine experiences the flow of time on his forehead and temples (A 400/402), though he puts this down to a 'reflex of the awareness formed in my mind over the years of the various layers which have been superimposed on each other to form the carapace of the city' (A 401/402–3). As so often in Sebald, consciousness is here a function of externality.[14] More importantly, Lemoine's archaeological consciousness allows him to inform Austerlitz that the site of the new Bibliothèque Nationale had been used by the Nazis as a large storage yard for the collection, classification and redistribution of the property of Parisian Jews interned in the transit camp at Drancy (A 401/403). The fact that this was a vast, state-sponsored archival operation becomes clear as Lemoine's description continues:

> Over five hundred art historians, antique dealers, restorers, joiners, clock-makers, furriers and couturiers brought in from Drancy and guarded by a contingent of Indo-Chinese soldiers were employed day after day, in fourteen-hour shifts, to put the goods coming into the depot in proper order and sort them by value and kind. (A 402/404)

While all this material was shipped back to the ruined cities of the German Reich, the major beneficiaries of confiscated Jewish assets – valuables, bonds, shares, and real estate – were and remain the city of Paris and the French state (A 400–2/402–4). The same French state is, of course, responsible for the erection of the new Bibliothèque Nationale. Rather than fulfilling its purpose as an accessible repository of knowledge, we saw in the Introduction that this imposing new building is designed to deter, dehumanise and intimidate. At the same time, it is wholly inefficient, its electronic cataloguing system showing constant signs of seizing up (A 392/394). The catalogue is a kind of archive-within-an-archive, and dramatises in microcosmic form the paralysis that affects the entire ensemble. Furthermore, readers are subjected to rigorous controls if their requests exceed the most basic, having to take a number and wait to be invited into a small booth where they are questioned as to the purpose of their visit (A 390/392).

The juxtaposition of the map of Theresienstadt, the *Registraturkammer*, the Nazi storage yard and the Bibliothèque Nationale implies a critique of archival practices that is operative at several levels. The Theresienstadt episode demonstrates the immediate political instrumentality of both cartography and archiving, exposing the potential totalitarian implications of the techniques of liberal government. The description of the palaver one has to endure in order to gain access to the new Bibliothèque Nationale thematises techniques of discipline. Control of the archive here is not overt or prohibitive, but is rather a question of various spatialising techniques – from the architecture of the whole to the system of waiting, being summoned to a private cubicle and so on – that constitute a set of deterrent measures to which one must perforce submit voluntarily in order to gain access to the holdings of the library. While, as I claimed in the Introduction, this passage is at one level comical, its more serious import is that the difficulty of gaining access to the state's library holdings is metaphorically linked to the historical and legal cover-up surrounding the confiscation of Jewish assets and their appropriation by the French state. The French state is, of course, metonymically represented by its national library. Lemoine's archaeology of the Bibliothèque Nationale site thus suggests that the state is built on a willed historical amnesia and sustains itself through the ongoing exercise of disciplinary power. If there are continuities between the Nazi period and the present, Sebald's text suggests that they consist not in the continuity of the *Registraturkammer* and the museum in Theresienstadt (as Crownshaw argues), but in the continued biopolitical regulation of bodies and space.

THE LIMITS OF DISCIPLINE

Sebald's work is also, however, abundant in moments that dramatise the limits of discipline. The conversation between the narrator of *The Rings of Saturn* and William Hazel, the gardener of Somerleyton House, addresses a different kind of cartographic practice. As a young man, Hazel had become obsessed with the allied aerial bombing war against Germany, and traces the course of the campaign on a relief map (RS 38–9/52–3). Superficially, this practice is reminiscent of the vast operations room maps on which the progress of military campaigns was charted in real time. The homogenising conventions of Western cartography have an enabling effect not only on the colonial and industrial projects, but on the prosecution of modern warfare. This effect is produced by sanitising battle and palliating 'the sense of guilt which arises from its conduct: the silent lines of a paper landscape foster the notion of socially empty space' (Harley 1988: 284). The one significant difference is that Hazel's maps foreground the social aspect of space by incorporating iconic images of gables, battlements and turrets that vary in number according to the size of the settlement (RS 39/53). The result is to create an imagined geography of Germany as a mysterious medieval place, and to kindle Hazel's interest in the actual experience of the bombings from the point of view of the victims. In the 1950s Hazel learns sufficient German to be able to conduct research into the victims' experience of the bombings, but claims to be astonished at the lack of published testimony – an assertion that clearly presages the argument of *Air War and Literature*. More important in the current context is that Hazel's narrative adumbrates an alternative politics of cartography in which interests of state and the military are subordinate if not to solidarity, then to intercultural curiosity. This, of course, generates a certain will to knowledge of its own, but this is itself thwarted by the lack of confessional literature that Hazel seeks. Hazel's narrative both invokes and resists the power/knowledge matrix in its cartographic guise.

There are other episodes in Sebald that demonstrate the failure of the map. In Chapter 5 of *The Rings of Saturn*, we learn that Conrad's uncle's sleigh-driver – a boy of just eleven – has internalised the map of the terrain so accurately that it is as though the knowledge were innate (RS 115/140). What remains ambiguous here is whether the word 'map' refers to a purely cognitive structure, or whether it refers to an actual map of paper or parchment that has been so thoroughly integrated into the psyche that it has become a fundamental component of his subjectivity. There is no such ambiguity in 'All'estero', whose narrator admits to being a regular purchaser of street maps. On his arrival in Milan, he asks 'How many street plans have I not bought in my time?', adding that he always tries to build up a reliable sense of space. The English translation talks of 'find[ing] reliable bearings', while the German reads: 'Immerzu versuche ich, wenigstens vom Raum mir eine zuverlässige Vorstellung zu verschaffen' (V 106/126–7). This wording is significant, implying that a mental representation (*Vorstellung*) of space can be gained only from a two-dimensional paper representation (*Darstellung*): spatial consciousness is externalised. The map he chooses reassures him because it includes a plan of a labyrinth on one side, and a claim that this general map of Milan (*Pianta Generale Milano*) will offer 'una guida sicura per l'organizzazione del vostro lavoro' ('a reliable guide to organising your work or business') (V 108/128). The utilitarian function of the map is plainly announced: its function is to aid the efficient organisation of labour. Beyond this, the narrator assumes that the street plan will help the process of cognitive mapping, and thereby serve to consolidate his sense of self.

And yet the irony is that Sebald's map proves completely useless. It is not only that the narrator is almost immediately mugged, thereby making a mockery of the idea of 'una guida sicura'; it is also that despite his ability to trace the precise route he followed and to list the streets and squares he traversed – Via Moscova, Giardini Pubblici, Via Palestro, Via Marina, Via Senato, Via della Spiga, Via Gesù, Via Monte Napoloeone, Via Alessandro Manzoni, Piazza della Scala – he eventually loses all sense of spatial orientation. Undoing his shoelaces in the cathedral, he suddenly has no idea where he is, and also suffers a loss of memory: 'Despite a great effort to account for the last few days and how I had come to be in this place, I was unable even to determine whether I was in the land of the living or already in another place' (V 115/136). Climbing to the highest gallery of the cathedral and taking in the panoramic views does not help: 'Where the word "Milan" ought to have appeared in my mind, there was nothing but a painful, inane reflex' (V 116–7/137). The ability to name streets does not constitute a reliable sense of urban topography, and the resulting loss of spatio-temporal co-ordinates produces a momentary dissolution of the narrator's subjectivity; his embodied materiality proves resistant to the cognitive prosthesis that the map represents.[15]

The ambivalence towards the archive in the above passages is repeated elsewhere in Sebald's texts. In 'All'estero', the second story of *Vertigo*, the tale of the narrator's travels is, as it were, shadowed by another narrative that emerges only in fragments, but implies that the narrator could be somehow caught up in a criminal plot. While drinking a coffee in the buffet of Venice station, the narrator believes himself to be observed by two men (V 68–9/82), who later turn up in the amphitheatre in Verona (V 72/87). These are followed by a series of other unsettling omens, such as the name of a pizzeria owner (Carlo Cadavero) and a newspaper article about the Organizzazione Ludwig, which the narrator reads in the pizzeria and which concerns the group responsible for carrying out a string of murders and terrorist attacks in northern Italy in the late 1970s (V 77–8/93–4). When the narrator of 'All'estero' later makes the acquaintance of Salvatore, the latter provides the background to the story (V 131/154), but its dénouement exposes the inadequacy of the archive. For Salvatore claims to find no definitive knowledge in the psychiatric reports on the two young men. As one of the human sciences whose genealogy Foucault traces in *Discipline and Punish*, psychiatry is central to structures of power/knowledge. 'The "epistemological profile" of psychiatry is weak,' Foucault states, 'and psychiatric practice is linked to a series of institutions, immediate economic exigencies, political urgencies and social regulations' (1980: 109). Thus the knowledge gained from psychiatry has to be understood in terms of its economic or normalising functions. In the criminological context, it is clearly one way of specifying the type of criminal one is dealing with, theoretically then allowing one to decide upon the correct regime of punishment and rehabilitation.[16] The inability of psychiatry to provide such knowledge in the case of the Organizzazione Ludwig bespeaks a failure of the disciplinary institution and its archival apparatus. Both psycho-socially and narratively, this failure is deeply unsettling, preventing identification of a plausible motive or exculpatory psychopathology and thus also preventing narrative closure.[17]

Thus while Sebald extensively thematises disciplinary subjectivity in modernity, the map of Milan and the psychiatric reports in *Vertigo* show that discipline is neither total in its scope nor fully predictable in its operation. These moments of archival failure go hand in hand with a series of archival projects that are deliberately anti-disciplinary. In *The Rings of Saturn*, the paper landscape in Janine Dakyns' office constitutes an archive that is completely devoid of systematicity or a publicly accessible ordering principle, effectively excluding it from structures of power/knowledge (RS 8/17–19). The narrator provides a list of Edward FitzGerald's various archival projects, including a lexicon of commonplaces, a glossary of seafaring vocabulary, and a colossal commentary on the letters of Mme de Sévigné (RS 199–200/237), all of which is destined to remain unpublished. The Ashburys' library contains no books, signalling a complete abandonment of any kind of organised knowledge whatsoever (RS 211/252). In an illustration of various lepidoptera from a book on entomology, the principles of taxonomy are subordinate to the aesthetic considerations that govern the way in which the moths and butterflies are arranged symmetrically on the page (RS 274/325), a feature shared by the butterfly cabinets at Andromeda Lodge (A 118/122). In *Austerlitz*, Gerald Fitzpatrick develops his own classification of birds based on their aerial competence, betokening a simultaneous desire for taxonomy and an escape from conventional principles of classification (A 160/164). And Austerlitz learns to count in Aunt Otýlie's glove shop, whose quasi-archival ordering, like Janine Dakyns' office, is incomprehensible to anyone but Aunt Otýlie herself (A 225–6/229–30).

The disciplinary archive is thus susceptible to failure from within, to the recalcitrance of embodied human materiality, and to local subversion by archival and taxonomic practices that elude the power/knowledge nexus. This possibility for resistance is one of the key concerns of Part II, in which I continue the investigation of the image, the archive and modernity in close readings of Sebald's four major prose narratives.

NOTES

1. While these atrocities took place in the late nineteenth century and are therefore contemporaneous with the full flowering of Foucauldean biopower, I describe these modes of punishment as 'pre-modern' because they are not regulated by a desire to reform the offender's soul or reclaim him as a productive economic agent, which are two fundamental characteristics of modern penal practice. Rather, the mutilations and executions take place within a penal economy of pure expenditure whose only function is the spectacular display of Western power.
2. From the Greek 'skaphe', meaning 'boat', this torture involved inducing diarrhoea in the victim, smearing him with honey, and placing him in a boat with his extremities protruding over the sides. The combination of honey and excrement attracted insects, which slowly consumed the victim's flesh. Death occurred as a result of starvation, dehydration and toxic shock.
3. The English translation of 'jene Unstillbaren' (literally: 'those insatiable ones') as 'that irrepressible species' underlines the point more strongly than the German text.
4. Sebald's comedy is one significant aspect of his work that remains largely unexplored. Thomas Kastura (1996: 209) and Greg Bond (2004: 39–40) have noted the 'involuntary' comedy that sometimes surfaces. Bond quotes what is probably the funniest episode in Sebald's work, namely the meal of fish and chips served in Lowestoft's Victoria Hotel (RS 43/58), but attributes the discrepancy between banal subject and linguistic extravagance to a stylistic faux pas generated by the

need to maintain the melancholy pose at all coasts. I see this discrepancy as a comedic device that ironises the narrator's strenuous efforts to remain permanently melancholic. The fact that Sebald was himself not averse to a little sly humour emerges clearly from an interview with Michaël Zeeman for Dutch television (Turner 2006).

5. This allusion, like many in Sebald, is invisible in English, alerting us to the fact that approaching Sebald purely through translation allows only a partial understanding of his work in all its richness and complexity.

6. I will return to cartography in Chapter 7.

7. As Anne Fuchs and Susanne Schedel note, the account of Conrad's journey to the Congo is also modelled extensively on Marlowe's narrative (Fuchs 2004a: 199, Schedel 2004: 115).

8. See Aleida Assmann 1999: 321, Harley 1988: 282. See also Black 1997: 148.

9. In a concession to location, the mountains are admittedly grouped by continent.

10. See http://www.ordnancesurvey.co.uk/oswebsite/aboutus/history/index.html (consulted 5 December 2006).

11. Fuchs 2006b: 182. Fuchs conjectures that this image might be a hyper-realist painting like those of Sebald's friend, Jan Peter Tripp. In fact, it is part of *Deathly Still*, a photographic work by Dirk Reinartz that portrays the banal functional architecture of Nazi camps. See Mack 1999: 52. For a discussion of Reinartz's work in terms of landscape and trauma, see Baer 2001: 61–85.

12. See E. Hirschberg, *Bilder aus der Berliner Statistik* (Berlin, 1904), quoted in McElligott 2001: 233–4.

13. In an article on postmemory and the archive in *Austerlitz*, Richard Crownshaw argues that both the ghetto itself and the ghetto museum presuppose the death of that which they archive: the ghetto organised and catalogued lives only to destroy them, while the heaped possessions of the dead in museums risk perpetuating the means by which the perpetrators would have memorialised their Jewish victims. The Terezin museum, he argues, is not vastly different from the *Registraturkammer*: both are predicated on death, and can represent Jews only in terms of an abstract, universalised identity (2004: 225–7). Archival violence, Crownshaw concludes, is 'continuous from ghetto to museum' (227). The neatness of this argument, however, should not blind us to its problematic aspects. Although Nazi racial politics clearly depended on universalised and essentialist notions of racial identity, the actual technologies of power employed by the Nazis relied on individuation, not only in Theresienstadt, but generally by means of the so-called *Volkskartei*. This was a systematic ethnographic archive of the German people that recorded racial details and the degree of 'biological health' of every individual along with their address, thereby facilitating efficient implementation of the campaigns of sterilisation, euthanasia and mass extermination (see Fritzsche 2005: 26–8). What Crownshaw fails to address are the biopolitical effects of archiving, which leads him to commit the solecism of equating memorial practices and the bureaucractic apparatus of genocide and to offer a reading of the archive that is essentialist and ahistorical. Curiously, he also manages to argue that the Prague Theatre archive captures Austerlitz's mother in life, not death. Why theatrical archives should be exempted from the Derridean logic of archival violence that dominates the rest of Crownshaw's argument remains unclear.

14. The chapters on *Vertigo*, *The Emigrants* and *Austerlitz* below all address this aspect of Sebald's work.

15. John Zilcosky notes that the dominant trope of travel writing involves losing one's way only to reorientate oneself and thereby discover a more robust sense of selfhood (2004: 103). He argues that Sebald's texts thematise the inability to lose one's

way, and the repeated uncanny return of the homely and familiar. This is a persuasive thesis, but it does not account for passages like the one discussed here, in which there is an unambiguous moment of disorientation.

16. On the intersection of psychiatry, the law and crime writing, see Kern 2004: 226–65.

17. I return to the relationship between discipline and narrative in Chapter 7, below.

PART II

5

WONDER: *VERTIGO*

Vertigo, Sebald's first major prose text, is also his most heterogeneous, its two lengthy quasi-autobiographical segments, 'All'estero' and 'Il ritorno in patria', alternating with short biographical sketches based on the diaries and letters of Stendhal and Kafka. The other of Sebald's works to consist of four independent narratives, *The Emigrants*, explicitly signals in its very title the characterologi-cal and thematic links between the four narratives, and the stories are also con-nected by narratological similarities involving structures of repression and the belated return of buried memories as a result of mediation by the narrator. The title *Vertigo*, on the other hand, is significantly less determinate, particularly in the German original – *Schwindel.Gefühle* – which denotes a sensation of dizzi-ness while implying also the possibility of being duped, conned or deceived (though quite who the victim of this 'swindle' is meant to be is a question that the text leaves open).

The multiple indeterminacies of the title and the thematic heterogeneity of *Vertigo* go hand in hand with weak narrative cohesion. Even within the indi-vidual stories, the usual mechanisms of narrative – the posing and solving of enigmas that Roland Barthes (1970) terms the 'hermeneutic code' – are present only in greatly attenuated form, even in 'All'estero', which always promises to develop into a full-blown detective story but never does. Yet both within and between the stories there is a dense pattern of repeated motifs that lends the text as a whole a high degree of coherence. Many of these, such as the recurrence of the year 1913 and the frequent allusions to and quotations from Kafka, have been much discussed by critics,[1] and I will further explore their function later in this chapter. One of the motifs that has so far gone unnoticed, however, is that fact that the narrator of *Vertigo* is forever reading newspapers. He twice studies the Venetian *Gazettino* (V 53, 77/65, 93), has French, English and Italian newspapers brought to him (V 95–6/114) in his hotel in Limone, reads the local press while staying in Verona (V 116/137), gets depressed reading the *Tiroler Nachrichten* (V 174/198), pretends to peruse the paper while actually listening to the conversations going on around him in the Engelwirt (V 204/232), and returns to England with several newspapers, even though they remain unopened (V 253/288). Sebald's other narrators are also readers of newspapers: in *The Emigrants*, the narrator comes across a report in a Lausanne paper about Johannes Naegeli, the mountain guide who had been a close friend of Henry Selwyn before his accidental death in 1914, and whose remains had resurfaced on the Aar glacier in 1986 (E 22–3/36–7). He later laments the weirdly skewed sense of history that emerges from the calendars of birthdays and deaths contained in the *Saale-Zeitung* that he reads on his visit to Bad Kissingen (E 220–1/330–1). In *The Rings of Saturn*, the story of George William Le Strange is based on an article from the *Eastern Daily Press*, a facsimile of which is incorporated in the text (RS 62–3/80–1), while a photograph from the *Independent* accompanies the paraphrase of an article about Croatian atrocities against the Serbs during the Second World War (RS 96–9/119–22). In *Austerlitz*, the narrator's decision to visit the fortress at Breendonk is precipitated by his reading a newspaper article about it (A 24/29). He also comes across a story about a man who commits suicide by means of a home-made guillotine. When he later paraphrases it for Austerlitz, he receives a sombre response to the anecdote, which he had himself found absurdly comic (A 138–9/142–3). In these texts, the newspapers serve a clearly identifiable narrative purpose: they function as sources of information, evidence, the occasion for explicit meditations on the philosophy of history, or character development. In *Vertigo*, on the other hand, the content of the newspapers is seldom divulged. Reading newspapers is significant as a repeatedly performed generic activity, rather than for the specific information that may be gleaned.

Newspapers were one of the communications technologies that aided the binding together of diverse and geographically dispersed audiences, facilitating the development of national and historical consciousness as newspapers allowed individuals to see themselves in relation to wider patterns of ongoing history. Each newspaper-reader, argues Benedict Anderson:

> is well aware that the ceremony he performs is being replicated simultaneously by thousands (or millions) of others of whose existence he is confident, yet of whose identity he has not the slightest notion. Furthermore, this ceremony is incessantly repeated at daily or half-daily intervals

throughout the calendar. What more vivid figure for the secular, historically clocked, imagined community can be envisioned? (1991: 35)

These integrative aspects of the press, however, went hand in hand with more
disruptive effects. Newspapers, like archives, are structured additively: articles
are discrete, decontextualised, detached and possess no necessary connections
to each other beyond those imposed by the exigencies of layout. Newspaper
culture, as Richard Terdiman remarks, produces a 'disorganization of consciousness', and provides a 'structured experience of confusion that naturalizes
new forms of cultural and perceptual contents'. The ensuing cognitive abstraction, he argues:

> defeats the associative structure of natural memory and induces in its
> place a different form of the habitus or technology of recollection that we
> could call 'archival consciousness'. Its principle would be the increasingly
> randomised isolation of the individual *item* of information, to the detri-
> ment of its relation to any whole, and the consignment of such informa-
> tion to . . . 'extra-individual' mnemonic mechanisms. (1993: 37)

Newspapers, then, thematise two of the central problems addressed within the
pages of *Vertigo* itself. First, there is the question of memory, its relation to the
archival practices that characterise modernity, and the kind of subjectivity that
is produced by 'archival consciousness'. Second is the hermeneutic problem of
relating individual events and pieces of information to the wider whole.

Numerous commentators on *Vertigo* have noted that the first narrative,
'Beyle; or Love is a Madness Most Discrete', describes the loss of authentic individual memory. Upon finding an engraving entitled *Prospetto d'Ivrea* among his
papers, Henri Beyle (alias Stendhal) realises that the memory he retained of Ivrea
was based not on his lived experience of the vista, but on the engraving: memory
emerges as the reproduction of a pre-existent image that is external to the self
(V 8/11–12). Anne Fuchs reads this episode psychoanalytically, as a Freudian
screen memory whose function is to veil Stendhal's traumatic experiences of war
(2004a: 83–6). Stendhal's visit to the battlefield of Marengo, she argues, then
confronts him with the reality of war that has been displaced by the screen
memory (84). Such a depth-psychological reading of the text, however, attributes to the experience of the Marengo battlefield a degree of authenticity that
the text does not support. For the purported 'reality' of the Battle of Marengo
is itself a function of external mnemotechnical supplements: firstly the unfolding progress of the Napoleon's North Italian campaign as relayed in military bul-
letins (V 14/18), then the countless narrative variants told by third parties, then
the skeletons of 16,000 men and 4,000 horses that Stendhal sees strewn across
the battlefield (V 17/21–2). These human and equine remains invalidate
Stendhal's imagined visions of what the battle was like, but they do so not by

providing knowledge of what it was *really* like, but by functioning as indexical proof that the conflict had actually taken place ('daß die Schlacht sich wahrhaftig ereignet hatte'). The bones confront Stendhal with the facticity of the battle, but still convey nothing of its nature. Far from revealing a reality that the screen memory concealed, then, the episode at Marengo shows once again that mnemotechnical prostheses offer no access to authentic experience.

The role of such prostheses is thematised once more in the narrative of Sebald's relationship with Méthilde Dembowski Viscontini. When Méthilde, a married mother of two, goes to Volterra to visit her sons at boarding school, Stendhal follows her in disguise. But Méthilde easily sees through his incognito and abruptly breaks off the affair (V 19–20/24–6). Shortly before she does so, however, Stendhal succeeds in obtaining a plastercast of her left hand 'as a memento of Méthilde' (V 20/26). As an artificial body part, this is a prosthesis in a very literal sense, but it also fulfils a mnemotechnical function. Indeed, Sebald's narrative stresses that 'the hand now meant almost as much to [Stendhal] as Méthilde herself could ever have done. In particular,' the narrator adds, 'the slight crookedness of the ring finger occasioned in him emotions of a vehemence he had not hitherto experienced' (V 21/26–7). Not the woman herself, then, nor even the memories of her, but the plastercast, is the object of affective investment and the cause of violent emotion. Authentic experience, it appears, has been displaced by an external mnemonic mechanism.

It is not uncommon for photography theorists to claim that this loss of authentic memory is a largely twentieth-century phenomenon, coming into being only with the widespread availability of the technical media. In her influential book *On Photography*, for example, Susan Sontag comes to the conclusion that photographs are 'not so much an instrument of memory as an invention of it or a replacement' (1979: 165), while Roland Barthes claims that 'not only is the Photograph never, in essence, a memory, but it actually blocks memory, quickly becomes a counter-memory'. To corroborate this claim, Barthes relates an anecdote in which his friends recount their childhood recollections, while Barthes finds that he has none, his memory having been evacuated as a consequence of looking at old photographs (1984: 91). What *Vertigo* demonstrates, however, is that earlier technologies of reproduction have an equally unsettling effect on notions of authentic memory. Indeed, one of the images reproduced shows a pre-photographic mechanical means for producing and reproducing images. The section that recounts Stendhal's infatuation with Angela Pietragrua is accompanied by a detail taken from a portrait of Angela. It is a pencil or charcoal sketch, and is overlaid with a hand-drawn grid (V 12/16). It is thus an example of a drawing technique that involves placing the object to be drawn (be it a three-dimensional thing or an existing two-dimensional representation) behind a grid. This has the effect of dividing the object into a set of regular modules. By viewing the scene thus divided through a fixed eyepiece, the artist can transfer each module to another surface overlaid with a corresponding grid, and thereby reconstruct the whole.[2] The technique dates from at least the sixteenth century, as Albrecht Dürer's famous instructional woodcut of 1538 makes clear (see Williamson 1986: 19). However, the widespread application of the grid as an illusionistic device emerges only in the late eighteenth and nineteenth centuries, with an increase in the publication of drawing manuals and commercial availability of mechanical 'drawing aids' (Korsmeyer 1989: 142–3). It is a process that relies on a highly abstract apprehension of space, a dismantling of the object into equivalent segments, and the reconstruction of the totality through the replication of each atomised square. Furthermore, successful results demand perfect integration of the eye and the mechanical aid: even the slightest slip (occasioned, for example, by breathing) results in a skewed reproduction (Korsmeyer 1989: 142). Any 'natural' or 'organic' relationship between hand and eye is here subordinated to the demands of a rudimentary apparatus. As Claudia Öhlschläger has shown, the original portrait of Angela Pietragrua shows no signs of a grid, which is thus an addition by Sebald himself (2006a: 64–6).[3] Its purpose is to establish thematic connections with the *Prospetto d'Ivrea* and the plastercast of Méthilde's hand. The grid-based drawing method, like the engraving and the plastercast, suggests that the abdication of lived experience to the external supplement existed well before photography. Once again it becomes clear that Sebald sees modernity as an *époque de longue durée* that stretches back, as we noted in the Introduction, at least as far as the revolutionary period of European history.

This argument is congruent with that put forward by Doren Wohlleben. She writes that individual memory is shown to be dependent on the formation of stable, externalised models for the storage of experiences, and the realisation of this fundamental difference between experience and memory goes hand in hand with a loss of self (2003: 339).

If 'Beyle' deals with archival consciousness in the nineteenth century, the final story of *Vertigo*, 'Il ritorno in patria', continues this theme into the post-war era. It explicitly thematises the belated arrival of modernisation in the Bavarian village of W. In an interview with Marco Poltronieri, Sebald draws attention to the impact of modernisation on rural Bavarian life. 'Imagine a place like Wertach', he says:

> cut off from all traffic arteries. In my childhood there were no cars, but today the farmers all drive BMWs and have shed-loads of money. That's what's so difficult to cope with: having to get from the nineteenth century into the twenty-first in just a few decades. (Poltronieri 1997: 134)

During his return to the village of W. in 'Il ritorno in patria', however, the narrator comments on the lack of cars as he looks out from the windows of the bus at the stretch of road lying ahead (V 177/201). This leads Susanne Finke to interpret W. as a location that is immune to modernity. The various characters in the story, she argues, are immutable stereotypes who remain untouched by industrialisation and modernisation:

> Sebald's characters are integrated into a typically provincial *Lebensform*. Their lives are determined by the rhythms of nature, they all know each other, carry out small-town occupations (watchmaker, blacksmith, barber, and country doctor), and consciously shield themselves from all that is foreign and new. (1997: 214)

But there are numerous details that suggest that W. has in fact been slowly accommodating itself to the rhythms of an encroaching modernity since the years immediately before and after the Second World War. The narrator himself draws attention to the shop-window display consisting of a huge pyramid of Sanella margarine cubes, which he sees as heralding the beginning of a new age (V 244/277). Given the uniformity and quantity of the margarine blocks, it is clearly a new age dominated by a consumerist ethos and serial production of commodities. A more potent symbol of the transition to modernity is the painting by Hengge – whom the narrator dismisses as a crypto-Nazi monumentalist – on the façade of Ulrich Seefelder's car and machinery workshop (Fig. 5.1). While the narrator mentions only the motor race depicted on one side of the building, the other side is adorned with an image of agricultural workers and a horse-drawn trap (V 205–6/233–4). Furthermore, as a businessman engaged not only in selling and repairing agricultural machinery, but in hiring cars (the sign above his door reads *Miet-Auto für Nah- und Fernfahrten* ('Hire-car for local and long-distance trips')), Seefelder caters to both the agrarian economy that continues to be the dominant generator of the region's wealth, and the emerging leisure economy that is a concomitant of mechanisation. His workshop thus embodies the very process of modernisation that is allegorised in Hengge's mural. The consequences of this process are witnessed as the narrator travels by train through the German countryside to Hook of Holland in 1987: there is not a single human form to be seen, even though there are plenty of cars racing along the wet country roads, and even agriculture itself has fallen prey to extreme rational planning: every scrap of available land has been segmented and made productive (V 254/288).[4]

In her analysis of *Vertigo*, Finke writes, 'In the provinces, the clocks run differently' (1997: 212). But the point is surely that once clocks become the means by which time is measured and regulated, the notion of different temporalities becomes slowly eroded. Indeed, a whole raft of literary and philosophical projects in the early twentieth century, such as the Bergsonian *durée* and the various stream-of-consciousness techniques developed by Dujardin, Schnitzler, Joyce, Woolf and others, can be seen as responses to the externalisation, rationalisation and reification of time that had already come to dominate industrial societies. Strict management of time in the factory system, the invention of the telegraph (which allowed instantaneous communication across vast distances and thereby

Figure 5.1

annulled temporal difference), and the standardisation of time zones and railway schedules led to the emergence of what has been called the 'homogeneous empty time of capitalism'.[5] This external temporality, however, is then reintegrated into subjectivity by means of the pocketwatch, worn on the body as a kind of prosthetic. Historian Karl Lamprecht estimates that in the last decades of the nineteenth century, some twelve million watches were imported into Germany to meet demand from a population of fifty-two million (cited in Kern 1983: 110). The increased use of the pocketwatch, as Georg Simmel noted in 'Metropolis and Mental Life', was responsible for both accelerating the pace of modern life and instilling a greater sense of punctuality, calculability and precision in both business transactions and human relations more generally (1950).

Vertigo thematises the invasion of the rural provinces by clock time at several points. Shortly after catching sight of the corpse of the recently-deceased Dr Rambousek, the narrator goes with his grandfather to the village horologist to collect a pocketwatch that his grandfather had had repaired. The shop is filled with the cacophonous simultaneous ticking of myriad clocks, 'as if one clock on its own could not destroy enough time' (V 233/265–6). This represents a conception of time that is linear and irreversible, each segment of time being demarcated and destroyed by the mechanical movement of the clock. Within the immediate narrative context, this view of time is intimately linked to the experience of death and an existential awareness of mortality. But the very variety of clocks that the narrator enumerates here also demonstrates the degree to which mechanical time-pieces are fully integrated into the domestic lives of the rural populace: grandfather clocks, wall-mounted regulators, clocks for living rooms and kitchens, alarm clocks for the bedroom, and pocket- and wristwatches for wearing on the person.

Just as memory is consigned to external mnemotechnical supplements in *Vertigo*, so the body's capacity to measure time is extended and externalised by means of clocks and watches. It is the huntsman Schlag who best exemplifies this process. He spends the evenings in the Engelwirt doing little beyond gazing at his precious pocketwatch as though he cannot afford to miss an important appointment (V 237/270). When he dies as a result of an accidental fall, the watch emits a few bars of the well-known song 'Üb' immer Treu und Redlichkeit' (V 248–9/282). Those present react as though profoundly shaken by the experience, the German word 'Bestürzung' signalling a significantly greater degree of shock and alarm than the bland translation 'bewilderment'. This shock is occasioned by the fact that a mechanically produced sound emanates from a dead body; Schlag literalises the metaphor of having 'internalised' the temporal regimen of modernity.[6]

The implications of these considerations for an understanding of narrative can be seen in the way photography functions in the text. As briefly noted in Chapter 3, many of the photographs in *Vertigo* are acquired as souvenirs. This applies not only to the postcard album compiled by Rosina Zobel's husband, but to many of the photographs that are implicitly attributable to the narrator of the text. As we saw in Chapter 3, Sebald used photography as an aide-mémoire, a means of 'proving' that what he reports really happened. His narrator, too, evinces a singular concern to obtain a photographic record of events and locations. Hence the lengths he goes to in an ultimately successful effort to persuade a German tourist to photograph the Pizzeria Verona and send it to him (V 127/148–9). Hence also his disappointment at not being able to photograph the twins on the bus to Riva, who are not only identical to each other, but identical to the young Kafka (V 89–90/105–6). Among the numerous souvenir photographs reproduced in the text are images of the Danube (V 41, 42/50, 51), a dilapidated building in Klosterneuburg (V 44/53), various kinds of tickets (V 69, 85/83, 101), postcards of the Giardino Giusti in Verona (V 70/85) and the Cimitero di Staglieno in Genoa (V 123/145), a restaurant bill (V 79/94), a map cover (107, 108/127, 128), the Pizzeria Verona (V 126/148), and the Hengge paintings (V 206, 207/234, 235).

The souvenir, as Walter Benjamin noted, is 'a secularised relic' and 'the complement of the *Erlebnis*. In it is deposited the increasing self-alienation of the person who inventories his past as dead possessions . . . The relic comes from the corpse, the souvenir from the atrophied *Erfahrung* that euphemistically calls itself *Erlebnis*' (1973: 177). *Erfahrung* and *Erlebnis* are both translated as 'experience', but Benjamin famously differentiated them: *Erfahrung*, continuous with past and future and containing elements of both the past and the future in itself, is, according to Benjamin, progressively eroded in modernity, and experience breaks down into isolated and singular moments or events (*Erlebnis*). As the complement of the *Erlebnis*, then, the souvenir is fragmentary, incomplete and severed from any putative experiential totality. Susan Stewart (1993: 133) notes that the souvenir derives its value from its material relation to its 'natural' location, a proposition that is intimately linked to the indexical status of the photograph: both the souvenir and the photograph operate metonymically. They are traces of one's 'having been there', and thus function as evidence, a kind of proof. Sebald's critics have rightly realised that the images in his texts exceed the purely illustrative function, but as Lilian Furst points out, our reading of Sebald is inflected by ingrained conventions of viewing that encourage us to accept the photograph as a true image (2006: 220–1). To ignore this aspect of Sebald's work is to overlook one of his central rhetorical strategies: the souvenir photographs prove that the narrators of his texts have been to such-and-such a place and seen such-and-such a sight. But the ultimate significance of this is not to confirm a naïve empiricism; it is, rather, to show the reliance of narratorial subjectivity on what Terdiman terms 'extra-individual mnemonic mechanisms' (Terdiman 1993: 37).

This brings us to the question of narrative. Susan Stewart argues that the event of which the souvenir is a metonym is accessible only through narrative (1993: 133), and that narrative is therefore a supplementary discourse 'that both attaches [the souvenir] to its origins and creates a myth with regard to those origins' (136). This implies that such narratives can operate only retroactively. While the narrative purports to explain the origin of the souvenir, it is in fact the souvenir that functions as the origin of the narrative. Memory, as it emerges in the pages of *Vertigo*, is thus figured as a *post-hoc* construction that, like Stendhal's imagined vision of Ivrea, reconstitutes a fantasy of interiority on the basis of external supplements. The problem, however, is that in a era that sees the progressive erosion of *Erfahrung* and the waning of the storytelling faculty that Benjamin (1999) saw as a concomitant of this process, these retroactive narratives are no longer able to suture *Erlebnis* and *Erfahrung*. The fragmentary and incohesive state of narrative in *Vertigo* suggests that it has itself succumbed to archival consciousness.

WONDER

As the foregoing analysis has shown, archival consciousness is repeatedly foregrounded in *Vertigo*. From the various mnemotechnical prostheses of which Stendhal avails himself and the various souvenir photographs collected by the narrator, to the diaries and clocks that structure the temporality of the represented world, the text thematises the substitution of external mnemonic technologies for any sense of 'natural' memory. Bearing in mind also the functioning of disciplinary and photographic archives in *Vertigo* discussed in earlier chapters, it would seem that the possibility of autonomous subjectivity is severely curtailed in a world where identity is fixed by means of a series of photographic and state apparatuses, where memory itself can no longer claim to be the site of authentic selfhood, and where *Erlebnis* has usurped *Erfahrung* as the dominant mode of experience.

The reduction of experience to a series of isolated moments possessing no necessary temporal or causal links produces a narrative whose cohesion is greatly attenuated, leading to the hermeneutic problem of relating parts to a putative whole. This brings us back to newspapers. While in Verona on the trail of Kafka, the narrator visits the civic library – yet another archive – and peruses newspapers from August and September 1913. The classified advertisements are of particular fascination to the narrator. An advert for one Dr Ringger, specialising in diseases of the skin and the urinary tract, inspires a fantasy narrative of well-dressed men stepping furtively into Ringger's surgery, while a similar one for pain-free dental surgery gives rise to a vision of a young woman whose body is contorted in pain as the treatment is carried out. On seeing an announcement for Ferro-China table water, the narrator imagines a pyramid, made up of the ten million bottles of Ferro-China sold annually, silently shattering at the soundless roar of the lion that is the company's trademark (V 118–20/139–42). This final advertisement is motivically linked to the pyramid of Sanella margarine in 'Il ritorno in patria'. But whereas the Sanella pyramid signalled the arrival of consumerism in a tiny rural outpost of post-war Germany, the Ferro-China advertisement does far more than merely serve the commercial interests of the water company. It generates a narrative that, in its gigantism and transgression of physical laws, is nothing short of magical. Indeed, the narrator claims that newspapers are a source of (albeit fleeting) revelation (V 119/141). The stories have neither beginning nor end, and should, the narrator notes, be followed up some time. But of course he does not follow them up; they remain 'soundless and weightless, these images and words of times gone by, flaring up briefly and instantly going out, each of them its own empty enigma' (V 120–1/142). So although they are structured additively, devoid of narrative closure, and characterised by a 'structured experience of confusion' (Terdiman 1993: 37), the Verona newspapers of 1913 are more than mere symptoms of an archival consciousness; they become objects of wonder.

In his analysis of early modern European narratives of encounters with the New World, Stephen Greenblatt (1991) notes that wonder is a polysemous term.[7] He registers the moral ambiguity of the category: wonder is 'thrilling, potentially dangerous, momentarily immobilizing, charged at once with desires, ignorance, and fear' (20), and contains within itself the potential for pleasure and pain, longing and horror. What is most relevant in Greenblatt's account is the notion that wonder is 'the decisive emotional and intellectual experience in the presence of radical difference' (14). Whereas for the Renaissance traveller, radical difference was embodied by the indigenous peoples of the Americas, however, Sebald's traveller pursues familiar itineraries. It is not merely that he retraces routes that have been followed before him by the writers in whose footsteps he treads (Casanova, Grillparzer, Stendhal, Kafka), nor even that the places he visits have already given rise to a rich literary tradition, as the wide-ranging intertextual studies of Marcel Atze (1997b) and Gabriella Rovagnati (2005b) have shown. It is also that the acquaintance with existing textual representations of these places seems to preclude the experience of otherness; everything is known in advance, to the extent that the narrator, disappointed with all he sees, muses that he would have been better off staying at home with his maps and timetables (V 53–4/65). Furthermore, Aleida Assmann argues that a fundamental characteristic of modernity is a waning sense of the symbolic significance of place (1999: 303).[8] This seems to be borne out by the representation of travel in *Vertigo*, for in an age of fast, reliable trains and cheap hotels, travel itself involves the repetitive passage through 'non-places' that Marc Augé identifies as characteristic of what he terms 'hypermodernity'. Non-places are places of transit such as airports, motels, petrol stations and supermarkets, in which identity is suspended, and human beings are reduced to conformity and pervasive similitude (1995: 103–4). In other words, they are everywhere the same, predictable, the very antithesis of radical difference.

Like the Surrealists, however, Sebald seeks to reinvest the urban spaces of modern life with a sense of magic, and numerous episodes in *Vertigo* thematise the hidden presence of the marvellous on the city streets. The opening of 'All'estero', for example, relates the strange phenomenon of the narrator's walks through Vienna which, when he consults a map, turn out to have been restricted to a 'sickle- or crescent-shaped area, the outermost points of which were the Venediger Au by the Praterstern and the great hospital precincts of the Alstergrund' (V 33–4/41–2). John Zilcosky identifies links here between similar urban wanderings in Kafka's *The Trial*, Thomas Mann's *Death in Venice* and Freud's essay on the 'Uncanny', but sees it as evidence for the 'uncanny paradigm, in which the subject is always, against his will, returning to familiar places' (2004: 106). Zilcosky's reading is, ultimately, psychological: in his desire to get lost, the narrator hopes to cure himself of the unspecified psychological difficulties announced at the start of 'All'estero', and to lay the literary ghosts (Dante, Casanova, Grillparzer, Kafka) that continue to haunt him. But what his wanderings actually bring home to him are the limits of his mind and his writing (105). These limitations, however, do not seem amenable to a depth-psychological reading of this kind. In fact, the episode is characterised by a process of estrangement followed by an experience of wonder. The sudden shift to the third person is telling: if one were to ink in the narrator's wanderings on a map, 'it would have seemed as though *a man* had kept trying new tracks and connections over and over, only to be thwarted each time by the limitations of *his* reason, imagination, or will-power' (V 34/41–2). There is a moment of self-alienation here, as the narrator's behaviour appears to belong to someone else.

It is understood less in terms of uncanny repetition (there is no identifiable psychological content that is here being repeated), than in terms of an external compulsion that is 'incomprehensible', 'invisible', 'arbitrary', and can be recuperated only as an experience of wonder.

What this means for an understanding of Sebald's response to modernity emerges most clearly in the episode surrounding Casanova's escape from the prison chambers beneath the roof of the Doge's Palace in Venice. The narrator reproduces a facsimile of his appointment diary which, like the clocks discussed above, is one of the technologies by which capitalism accommodates the time of the individual to the time of industrial labour (V 60/72). David Harvey notes that it was monastic orders that first promoted explorations of the calendar and time measurement in order to impose religious discipline, but found their innovations appropriated by the nascent bourgeoisie as a means of organising and disciplining populations to the secular labour discipline of emerging capital production (1990: 228). The late twentieth-century diary bears traces of both forms of temporal discipline. But although Sundays are shaded a darker colour to mark them off from the rest of the week, and 5 October is marked as the annual Harvest Festival – a residual sign of the cyclical time of the liturgical calendar – the more important division of time is into weekdays and weekends, serving to institutionalise the distinction between work and leisure within a system that sees leisure as means of reproducing the worker's labour-power.[9]

But in *Vertigo*, the diary comes to signify something altogether different from a regime of temporal discipline. The image of the diary page in the text is preceded by the narrative of Casanova's escape from the Doge's Palace. In order to calculate the most auspicious date for the attempted break-out, Casanova consults Ariosto's *Orlando Furioso*, but does so on the basis of a complex and largely arbitrary numerical procedure that involves writing down the question that concerns him, deriving a set of numbers from the words, arranging these numbers in an inverted pyramid, subtracting nine from each pair of figures, and arriving at the first line of the seventh stanza of the ninth canto of Ariosto's poem (V 59/71). Since this line reads '*Tra il fin d'ottobre e il capo di novembre*' ('between the end of October and the beginning of November'), the timing of the escape is fixed to the hour. Casanova's attempt to fathom the unknown by means of such a bizarre and arbitrary system itself represents a moment of wonder. What is more striking, however, is the fact that when the narrator leafs through his 1980 pocket diary, he realises to his 'amazement' ('Verwunderung') and 'considerable alarm' ('Schrecken') that he had been sitting in a café near the Doges Palace on 31 October, an anniversary of Casanova's escape (V 59–60/71–3). Thus a photograph of the diary – the very object that symbolises the externalised temporal schemes by means of which daily life is organised in modernity – comes to serve as evidence for the experience of wonder in all its ambiguity, as amazement combines with horror (Fig. 5.2).

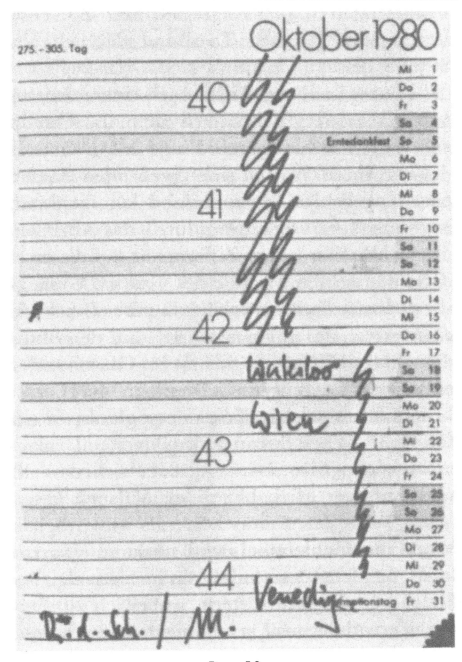

Figure 5.2

There are numerous examples of such ambiguous experience in *Vertigo*. While drinking his cappuccino in the chaotic but perfectly regulated café of Venice station, the narrator becomes convinced that he is being observed by two men who, he now suspects, have actually crossed his path several times during his stay (V 68–9/82–3), and he fantasises that he is involved in some murky business as he enters the Piazza Bra Arena, Verona's Roman amphitheatre (V 71/85). As the last group of tourists leave, the narrator becomes aware of two figures loitering in the shadows who are 'without a doubt' the men he had seen that morning in Venice, and as he leaves the amphitheatre he imagines an arrow flying through the air and entering his heart via his left shoulder-blade (V 72/87). These episodes are followed shortly afterwards by the narrator's coming across an article about the Organizzazione Ludwig, a group that has confessed to a series of crimes in northern Italy (V 77–8/93), and the near-simultaneous discovery that the pizzeria in which he is dining is owned by one Carlo Cadavero (V 79/94). These episodes occur in the context of what the narrator surmises at one point might become a detective story concerning a series of unsolved crimes in upper Italy (V 94–5/113). But the detective story never actually materialises. Although Salvatore's narrative reveals the identity of the Organizzazione Ludwig, the failure of the psychiatric reports to explain the miscreants' behaviour (discussed in Chapter 4) means that even this elementary structure of enigma and resolution remains incomplete. And the relevance of the two men or Carlo Cadavero is never explained. As a result, the moments of paranoia and alarm that the narrator experiences in Venice and Verona are not integrated into a narrative structure that would guarantee their meaning; they exist as unassimilated moments of wonder in its negative guise: thrilling, but frightening and potentially dangerous.

The spaces traversed by the narrator also become the sites of more positive experiences of the marvellous. In Venice, the narrator experiences hallucinations of people he has not seen for a long time, including some who are already dead, such as Mathild Seelos and the village scribe Fürgut (V 35/43), inhabitants of the village of W. to which the narrator travels in 'Il ritorno in patria'. The illusory nature of these apparitions is attributed to the narrator's increasingly fragile mental state. Elsewhere, however, the narrator offers no such psychological explanation for a series of magical encounters. Even the sighting of Dante, for example, becomes ambiguous: the narrator 'believes' that he sees Dante (V 35/43–4). Though dismissed as a 'turn', it is the first of several visions whose ontological status is not called into question: the narrator 'recognises' both Ludwig II of Bavaria on the streets of Venice (V 53/64) and the Winter Queen in a train compartment in Heidelberg, reading a book that turns out not to exist (V 254/289).[10] These encounters dramatise the invasion of the material world by the fantastic.

Wonder is in part generated by the sense that public messages are in fact addressed directly to the narrator himself: the newspaper preview of a play about Casanova that the narrator finds in the *Alto Adige* (V 96–7/114–15), and the advertisement for Hertz car rentals bearing the slogan 'LA PROSSIMA COINCIDENZA' (V 109/128–9). It is generated by the numerous coincidences that run through the text,[11] and by the use of metaphor in a variety of different contexts. Notable is the recurrence of nautical metaphors to describe the experience of (predominantly urban) space. In order to convey the experience of waking in Vienna, the narrator employs an extended metaphor in which the surge of traffic noise from the Ringstraße is described in terms of surf generated by currents of traffic, while the narrator's leaving his hotel is figured as descending the gangway of a large ferry (V 37–8/46). The same metaphor is later developed more fully: modern city traffic has become the new ocean:

> Ceaselessly, in great surges, the waves roll in over the length and breadth of our cities, rising higher and higher, breaking in a kind of frenzy when the roar reaches its peak and then discharging across the stones and the asphalt even as the next onrush is being released from where it was held by the traffic lights. (V 63/76)

The St Martin's retirement home in which the narrator's friend or partner Clara's grandmother lives is also portrayed as a ship that has loosed its moorings and is already far out to sea, and whose corridors are peopled not by inmates or residents, but by passengers (V 45/55). In one of the narrator's dreams, the Venetian island asylum of La Grazia turns into a ship of fools (V 65–6/79), the Pizzeria Verona is designed to foster the illusion that one is surrounded by water (V 77/92), the narrator's acquaintance Salvatore notes the salutary effects of reading as an antidote to a hectic day at work, and compares the experience of immersing oneself in a book to rowing out to an island (V 128/150), and the stone walls of the Krummenbach chapel are transformed into the wooden hull of a boat. 'The moist smell of lime became sea air,' the narrator writes, 'I could feel the spray on my forehead and the boards swaying beneath my feet, and I imagined myself sailing in this ship out of the flooded mountains' (V 179/203–4). These metaphors not only transfigure the mundane topography of familiar settings, but constitute a central device by means of which similarities are constructed between disparate events and locations.

The fact that the perception or construction of such similarities is central to the poetics of *Vertigo* emerges in one of the many self-reflexive moments in Sebald's work. The narrator sits in a hotel restaurant in Limone, with his various papers and notes spread out around him, drawing connections between events that are distant from one another in time and space, but which seem to belong to the same order of meaning (V 94/112). This constitutes an attempt to discover or construct a narrative and epistemological model that will allow the disparate events of the text to coalesce into a more meaningful whole. The desire to link events that belong to the same order of meaning is a fundamentally metaphorical process, and implies that paradigmatic equivalence is the structuring principle on which *Vertigo* is based. In this sense, Sebald begins to explore the possibility of an archival text that will in some way compensate for the centrifugal tendencies inherent in the diversity of his subject matter. This is *Vertigo*'s answer to its own hermeneutic problem.

For Theodor Adorno, the proper subject of the bourgeois novel was the portrayal of the disenchanted world (*entzauberte Welt*) of modernity (1974: 41). Although Sebald refused to give his works a generic label beyond the blandly denotative term 'prose', his texts betray an almost obsessive need to anchor their narrative worlds in named physical spaces and to fill these spaces with objects that are described at length or accumulated in long inventories and lists. In this sense, they clearly participate in the discourse of bourgeois realism. And yet numerous critics have pointed out that Sebald's realism exists in tension with other dimensions of his work. Martin Swales, for example, notes that Sebald's texts evince a high degree of literariness, which manifests itself not only in his conspicuously elevated style, but in the frequent intertextual allusions to earlier forms and writers (2004: 23). Swales notes, too, that Sebald's materiality is always 'made eloquent by the implied "metaphysical lining"' of reality (28). In a similar vein, Eric Santner writes of Sebald's 'spectral materialism', by which he means 'the capacity to register the persistence of suffering that has in some sense been absorbed into the substance of lived space, into the "setting" of human history' (2006: 57). What these critics allude to (and they are not alone) is that the physical world in Sebald always signifies something – be it metaphysical, psychological or historical – that lies beyond itself. In *Vertigo*, the dense web of motivic repetitions constitutes the material world of the text as a site not of metaphysics, nor even of sedimented history, but of wonder.

In an essay on Robert Walser, Sebald comments on the kind of correspondences at work in *Vertigo*. Noting the similarities between the life of Walser and the life of his own grandfather, he initially speculates on the nature of such similarities:

> What is the meaning of these similarities, intersections, and correspondences? Are they simply a matter of illusionary memory images (*Verxierbilder der Erinnerung*), self-deceptions or sensory deceptions, or are they the schemata of an order that is beyond our ken, but that is programmed into the chaos of human relationships and extends over both the quick and the dead? (LL 137–8)

In a later passage in the same text, he comes down firmly on the side of the latter explanation:

> I have slowly come to realise that everything is connected with everything else across times and places . . . dates of birth with dates of death, happiness with unhappiness, the history of nature with that of our industry, and the history of home with that of exile. (LL 162–3)

Many of Sebald's critics quote this passage. There has been a tendency, however, to see the correspondences that dominate not only *Vertigo*, but the later prose works too, as meaning the same in each text. As we will see, this is far from being the case. The motivic and metaphoric repetitions and the numerous coincidences in *Vertigo* represent the moment when an archival epistemology combines with the fantastic and flips over into magic, constituting urban space in terms of wonder and thereby transfiguring the fragmentation and disorganisation that characterises the archival consciousness of modernity.

NOTES

1. On the repeating Kafka allusions, see particularly Atze 1997b: 156–8, Sill 1997a, Klebes 2004, Kilbourn 2006 and Prager 2006. On the significance of 1913, see Schedel 2004: 154–65 and Santner 2006: 49, 119.
2. The same method is thematised in *The Emigrants*, in the episode where Paul Bereyter expounds the technique to his young charges (E 31/46–7).
3. Following Rosalind Krauss, Öhlschläger sees the grid as a fundamentally anti-mimetic device that is part of a wider anti-mimetic strategy that characterises not only 'Beyle', but Sebald's poetics more generally (2006: 64–7).
4. Sebald's original stresses the consequences for the landscape of capitalism and its utilitarian demands for ever-greater productivity. The term 'nutzbar machen' (to make useful or productive) is applied here to the land, but it is also the term used by Sebald in his gloss of Cartesianism in *The Rings of Saturn* (RS 13/26), thereby linking the exploitation of the land to the exploitation of human labour power. This resonance is totally lost in the English translation of *Vertigo*, which reads: 'the landscape which had been so thoroughly parcelled up and segmented'. Fast cars and the efficient parcelling up of land are also the things that Austerlitz notices on his trip from Prague to Hook of Holland, and that differentiate the German landscape from the Czech countryside (A 312/316).
5. Kern 1983: 11–15; Schivelbusch 2004: 42–5.
6. This episode is reminiscent of the description of Paul Bereyter, who speaks as though he were a clockwork contraption on the brink of permanent malfunction (E 35/52).
7. In Renaissance aesthetic theory wonder is associated with the overcoming of great difficulties and with a strange blend of chance and human intention (Castelvetro); or with the spectacle of the unexpected and the extraordinary (Robortelli); or with passions, reversals, and discoveries (Vettori); or with the reconciliation of unity and variety (Tasso); or with novel and surprising twists of narrative (Denores, Talentoni); or with the effects of awe and wonder associated with religious feelings and hence with sublimity and high gravity (Patrizi). (Greenblatt 1991: 80)

   Apart from the last definition, these can all, at various points, be identified in *Vertigo*.
8. Assmann goes on to argue that one cultural function of the Gothic novel and the ghost story was to reinvest place with mystical value (1999: 322). This aspect of

Sebald's engagement with place has been discussed in overtly spectral terms by Eric Santner (2006: 57–8), and in terms of the landscape tradition and the sedimentation of historical traces by Anne Fuchs (2004a: 227–31). See also Christopher C. Gregory-Guider (2005: 428): 'Each place in Sebald thus opens onto a ghostly version of its past existence, allowing a kind of traffic between the present and the past, the living and the dead.'

9. This is the classic Marxist understanding of capitalist leisure, and is clearly articulated in Bertolt Brecht, *Der Dreigroschenprozeß*:

> [T]he sharp distinction between work and leisure peculiar to the capitalist mode of production divides all mental activities into those that serve the purposes of labour and those that serve the purposes of leisure, turning the latter into a system for the reproduction of labour-power. (1992: 475)

A similar view informs Adorno and Horkheimer's discussion of the culture industry in *Dialectic of Enlightenment*.

10. As well as being the location of this magical encounter, railway journeys in continental Europe are frequently represented in *Vertigo* as soothing and pleasant (V 49, 80–1, 84–5, 103–4/59–60, 95–6, 101, 123–6). It is only once the narrator arrives in England that trains become an alienating mode of transport, a theme that is picked up in more detail in *The Rings of Saturn* and in Chapter 7, below.

11. These coincidences are well documented in the critical literature. In addition to Atze 1997b, see particularly Fuchs 2004b: 87–93 and Loquai 2005b: 245–6.

6

FAMILY ALBUMS: *THE EMIGRANTS*

The Emigrants consists, as its subtitle baldly states, of 'four long stories', which reconstruct the biographies of the exiles and émigrés whose names form the stories' titles. 'Dr Henry Selwyn' is a Lithuanian Jew who emigrated to England in 1899, who has had a distinguished academic and medical career and married Hedi, a woman whose inherited wealth had allowed them to live in a grand style in the 1920s and 1930s. The narrator encounters the couple when he rents a flat in Prior's Gate, their capacious Norfolk home. 'Paul Bereyter' is the narrator's much-admired schoolteacher. As a so-called *Dreiviertelarier* or three-quarter Aryan, Bereyter is initially forced out of his job as a schoolmaster in the 1930s, and spends some time as a private tutor in France before returning to Germany and serving in the Wehrmacht for six years. After the war he takes up his former post in 'S.', before moving, more or less permanently, to Yverdon. He commits suicide on his final visit to S. in 1984. 'Ambros Adelwarth' tells the story of the narrator's great-uncle, who emigrates to the United States and spends most of his life serving the Solomons, one of New York's wealthiest Jewish banking families. Adelwarth accompanies the Solomons' youngest son, Cosmo, on numerous trips through Europe and the Middle East. After Cosmo's premature death, Adelwarth eventually admits himself to a mental hospital where he hastens his own death by subjecting himself voluntarily to a lengthy course of electroconvulsive therapy. 'Max Ferber' is the last and longest of the stories. The narrator shares an intense friendship with Ferber during his period of study in Manchester in the mid-1960s. Ferber is Jewish, and leaves Germany to escape persecution in 1939, settling in England where he establishes himself as a successful painter. After a gap of almost two decades, the narrator re-establishes contact with Ferber, who gives him his mother's posthumous papers that consist of a description of Jewish middle-class life in the Bad Kissingen region before the Nazi period.

All the stories in *The Emigrants*, then, deal with experiences of dislocation that, as Anne Whitehead (2004: 118) and Stuart Taberner (2004: 185) note, are a function of modernity. Modernity's dislocations are not merely geographical; the four main characters undergo experiences of cultural displacement, economic migration, political exile and, in two cases, racial persecution at the hands of the Nazis, whose impact on the individual psyche becomes apparent only belatedly. Furthermore, Selwyn, Bereyter, Adelwarth and Ferber are representatives of families – and ultimately of entire societies – that have been destroyed or scattered by the political upheavals of the twentieth century.

As the text makes clear, these upheavals take place within the context of a wider dialectic of human and environmental history in which nature is constantly being destroyed by mankind, but simultaneously attempting to reclaim the products of civilisation and turn them back into the dust from which they originated – witness, for example, the buildings that are slowly being engulfed by sand (E 87, 118/127, 174), or Dr Abramsky's entropic vision of his asylum slowly succumbing to an army of mice, woodworm and deathwatch beetles, and collapsing into a pile of dust (E 112–13/165–6).[1] And yet the exile, loss and entropic decline that constitute the thematic core of Sebald's text are counterbalanced by the narrative discourse itself, which involves weaving together the disparate strands of fragmented biographies within the same tale. To this end, Sebald mobilises techniques of narrative embedding that dramatise acts of remembrance and recuperation. The function of the discourse is to integrate two or even three narrative levels: the story of the narrator's investigations frames both the biography of the main protagonist, and the life of another character whose story either mediates that of the central figure (Aunt Fini, Lucy Landau, Dr Abramsky) or is mediated by it (Ferber's mother). As with all framed narratives, a central concern of *The Emigrants* is transmission.[2] Unlike many framed narratives, however, transmission here is primarily *archival*, archives being understood not in terms of state administration, public institutions of storage and cultural display, or regulation, but in terms of individual and familial archives: diaries, letters, family albums and slide collections, and autobiographical writings. All of these things are central to the narrative enterprise, and all – with the possible but by no means necessary exception of diaries – are situated on the threshold between the public and the private, moments where the self records and displays itself for itself and a limited number of others within a set of shared conventions. The question I wish to pursue in this chapter concerns the extent to which such personal and family archives participate in the determinations of power/knowledge, and what effects this might produce within Sebald's text.

FAMILY PHOTOGRAPHY

The Emigrants reproduces numerous photographs that are clearly taken from family albums, their subjects being either tourist sights depicted on postcards, or the traditional occasions on which family photographs are taken: outings, communal meals and celebrations, studio portraits, the completion of a work contract, school class groups and prize-giving ceremonies.[3]

Accounts of family photography almost invariably stress its imbrication in structures of social power, class affiliation and identity formation. The role of the family in modernity is addressed by Foucault in his essay 'Governmentality'. Foucault argues that in early treatises on the art of government, which emerged in the sixteenth century as more or less explicit critiques of a Machiavellian model of sovereignty, government is characterised in terms of continuity between self-government, the management of the family, and the science of ruling the state (2002b: 206). In other words, the family initially functioned as a model for the state. But, Foucault notes, its status within the theory of government shifted as the problem of population became central. Statistics demonstrated that populations have their own regularities of births, deaths and disease, their cycles of scarcity, and so on. And since the population is not reducible to the family, the latter becomes a segment rather than a model. At the same time, however, the family is a uniquely important segment in the sense that it is a conduit through which information about the population (in terms of sexual behaviour, demographics, consumption) is relayed. The family thus becomes 'the privileged instrument for the government of the population and not the chimerical model of good government' (216). For Foucault, the family as institution is intimately bound up with the acquisition of new knowledge about the body and its modes of functioning, and hence with the power/knowledge complex.

This was not the only reason for the enhanced importance that the family began to take on as the eighteenth century progressed. Under an agrarian economy, all family members, including young children, worked to support themselves, and the boundaries between the household and the family were fluid, with lodgers, apprentices and resident servants all considered to be family members. With the rise of large-scale industry, urbanisation and changes in housing, there was an increasing focus on the nuclear family, differentiated from the household and consisting of blood relations: parents and children, with possibly older relatives and unmarried adults living with them. This unit better suited an industrial economy's demands for wage labour (Hamilton and Hargreaves 2001: 11).

Thus the rise of the nuclear family was determined by the dual imperative of capitalist production and efficient administration. At the same time, however, the family became subject to increasing sentimentalisation, with the ideology of the 'love marriage' coming to displace, in both representation and (eventually) reality, marriages based on shared property interests, and children becoming the objects of intense affective investment. It was under these conditions, in which the family was understood primarily in terms of the bloodline and emotional ties, that photography came to play a central role. In Chapter 3 we investigated photography's function within the human sciences, particularly ethnology and psychiatry. Suren Lalvani extends the discussion of photography's disciplinary aspects to include domestic portrait photography which, he argues, played a variety of insidious roles in the perpetuation of bourgeois hegemony by inscribing individual bodies within a discursive field that reduced them to a representational type. The very homogeneity of these images, their profound conventionality, is what allows their 'density of meaning' to emerge: they represent normative fantasies of the bourgeois family, and are hence ineluctably implicated in familial ideology (1996: 56). Lalvani sees photography as fundamentally disciplinary. In the studio, the body was forced to signify in terms that were underwritten by the discourses of physiognomy, phrenology and gender, a process that remained operative even after the invention of Kodak roll film had turned the middle-class domestic amateur into the primary producer of family photographs (Smith 1999: 118). The photograph then continued its ideological work within the bourgeois home, establishing 'the normative "scene" of the family with its appropriately gendered subjects, its self-evident hierarchy, and passive children on display' but also evoking 'a discipline of love' (Lalvani 1996: 63–5). Lalvani extends this analysis to the family album which, he contends, asserts the family's social status and records sentimental ties. It also represents a space of non-productive domesticity that is staged to be recorded by the camera and preserved in the album. The album's function thus confirms continuity in the face of the fragmentation of quotidian existence and reveals 'the power of domestic fictions to conceal the contradictions of lived experience' (65). For Lalvani, photography's panoptic effects (the production of self-regulating bourgeois individuals) goes hand in hand with its capacity to position those individuals within a specific ideological formation.[4]

While similar insights can be found in the writings of other critics and theorists such as Sontag and Bourdieu,[5] I cite Lalvani at length because he provides one of the most interesting accounts of family photography, adopting an explicitly Foucauldean methodology but extending it to encompass the production of ideology as well as subjectivity. It is here that both the force of his analysis and its weakness lie. For Lalvani operates with notions of discipline and ideology that are so monolithic and seamless that they allow for no resistance whatsoever. The family member, whether the subject or the viewer of the photograph, is produced without remainder by the disciplinary structure of the photographic apparatus (studio, image, frame or album, bourgeois interior), leaving no space for alternative readings or subversions of any kind. Lalvani's view of photography, like Foucault's diagnosis of carceral society, stresses the productive functions of power (Lalvani 1996: 29), while being relentlessly negative in its judgment of precisely this productivity. And like Bourdieu, Lalvani is implicitly but unequivocally hostile to the bourgeois family as institution.

A similar sentiment appears to emerge in Marianne Hirsch's book *Family Frames*, but on closer inspection, her initial account of family photography opens up the possibility of a more nuanced approach to the subject. Photography, she writes, 'quickly became the family's primary instrument of self-knowledge and representation – the means by which family memory would be continued and perpetuated, by which the family's story would henceforth be told' (1997: 6–7). Photography as the family's means of self-representation is precisely what Lalvani investigates. But beyond the constitution of ideology in the visual field (which is also one of Hirsch's concerns), the above quotation also addresses the relationship of photography to memory and narrative, questions that become central to our understanding of Sebald's use of domestic photographs in *The Emigrants*.

THE ARCHIVE: FROM THE PSYCHE TO THE ALBUM

As we saw in the Introduction, one of the defining features of modernity is a crisis of memory, one symptom of which is the sense that memory ceases to be a pure matter of consciousness, and comes to reside instead in the materiality of our social or psychic life. Memory is henceforth inseparable from a series of external mnemotechnical supplements, as Jacques Derrida notes in his discussion of Freud's essay on the mystic writing pad. Derrida argues that the metaphor of the mystic writing pad:

> integrates the necessity, inside the *psyche* itself, of a certain outside . . . And with this *domestic outside*, that is to say with the hypothesis of an *internal* substrate, surface, or space without which there is neither consignation, registration, impression nor suppression, censorship, repression, it prepares the idea of a psychic archive distinct from spontaneous memory . . . the institution, in sum, of a *prosthesis of the inside*. (1995: 19)

Such a conception of a prosthesis of the inside is clearly derived from Freud's *Moses and Monotheism*, where the metaphor of photography is deployed in order to clarify the phenomenon of latency:

> The strongest compulsive influence arises from impressions which impinge upon a child at a time when we would have to regard his psychical apparatus as not yet completely receptive. The fact itself cannot be doubted; but it is so puzzling that we may make it more comprehensible

by comparing it with a photographic exposure which can be developed after an interval of time and transformed into a picture. (1964: 126)

Photographic metaphors are also prominent in Benjamin's account of how we know the past, as in the following quotation from the posthumously published *Berlin Chronicle*:

> Anyone can see that the duration for which we are exposed to impressions has no bearing on their fate in memory. Nothing prevents our keeping rooms where we spent twenty-four hours more or less clearly in our memory and forgetting entirely where we passed months. Thus it is certainly not owing to an all too short exposure time if no image appears on the plate of remembrance. More frequent, perhaps, are the cases when the twilight of habit denies the plate the necessary light for years, until one day, from alien sources, it flashes up from burning magnesium powder, and now a snapshot transfixes the room's image onto the plate. (1978: 56–7)

The psychic processes by which the past is remembered can thus be seen as duplicating the process of photography, which entails a necessary delay between light hitting the plate and the emergence of the recognisable image. Conversely, the process of photography corresponds to the sudden recall of buried memories after a period of latency.

At numerous points in *The Emigrants*, this photographic analogy is implicitly invoked, the notion of an internal archive emerging in connection with a form of memory that is visual rather than narrative. Henry Selwyn tells the narrator, 'For years the images of that exodus had been gone from his memory, but recently, he said, they had been returning once again and making their presence felt' (E 18–19/31). This is followed by several sentences beginning 'I can still see . . .' ('Ich sehe . . .'), as Selwyn recalls with astonishing vividness events that happened over seventy years before. Mme Landau is amazed 'at how clear the images that she had supposed buried beneath grief at the loss of Paul still were to her', and again employs the 'ich sehe . . .' formulation in the act of recall (E 45/67).[6] Likewise, Bereyter's eye operation and temporary sightlessness result in his acquiring a kind of eidetic memory: 'he could see things then with the greatest clarity, as one sees them in dreams, things he had not thought he still had within him' (E 51/76). Uncle Kasimir's emigration to the United States is characterised by a combination of a general forgetfulness and an exceptionally vivid vision of the Lloyd's terminal in Bremerhaven (E 81/119). The experience of departure is represented in similar terms by Max Ferber, whose memory of his flight from Germany in May 1939 is likewise purely visual. He cannot remember what his parents said to him, or whether they embraced him or not (E 187/279), but can 'envisualize [Oberwiesen] with fearful precision', right down to the most ostensibly trivial detail (E 187–8/280).

Both Sigrid Korff (1998: 185) and Greg Bond (2004: 44) have noted Sebald's debt to the work of William Niederland, whose case studies of Holocaust survivors foreground the co-presence of hypomnesic memories, which are vague and unclear, with hypermnesic memories, which are not only extremely vivid and laden with affect, but cannot be located within a clear temporal framework (Niederland 1980: 69, 81, 124, 230). And yet the comparison with Niederland tells us little about how these visual memories function within Sebald's text. Their significance becomes apparent when Ferber remarks: 'The fragmentary scenes that haunt my memories are obsessive in character' (E 181/270). The German reads: 'Die bruchstückhaften Erinnerungsbilder, von denen ich heimgesucht werde, haben den Charakter von Zwangsvorstellungen.' This quotation explicitly links Ferber's discourse to that of Freud. The notion of 'Zwangsvorstellungen' – compulsive images or convictions – occurs in many of Freud's writings, and 'heimsuchen' is used, in the German text of *Beyond the Pleasure Principle* (*Jenseits des Lustprinzips*), to refer to the involuntary invasion of repressed traumatic memories. The role of the visual within the constellation of repression, latency and return is also addressed repeatedly in Freud's work. Painfully exact, compulsively repeated visual recall that 'possesses' the individual against his or her will is, as Freud noted in Chapter 3 of *Beyond the Pleasure Principle* (1955: 18–23), the dominant symptom of traumatic neurosis. Unlike normal dreams, which are always encrypted and are concerned to a large degree with wish-fulfilment, traumatic dreams and visions are defined by an ineluctable literalness that cannot be interpreted in terms of the pleasure principle.

Classic psychoanalytic accounts of trauma emphasise the therapeutic effects of narrativisation, which recontextualises compulsively repeated 'traumatic' memories, characterised by visual literalness, via a process of working through that facilitates their integration into the subject's psychic life.[7] This process is attempted by all of Sebald's protagonists, who, towards the end of their lives, seek to tell their stories – in a secular version of the confession – to a third party: the narrator himself in the case of Selwyn and Ferber, Lucy Landau in Bereyter's case, and Aunt Fini in Adelwarth's. And yet narrativisation never fully succeeds as therapy. After unburdening himself to the narrator (E 18–21/30–5), Selwyn fades out of the narrator's life and soon afterwards commits suicide. Bereyter, too, commits suicide after filling his notebooks with excerpts from the work of writers who had themselves died by their own hands (E 58–9/86–8). Ferber realises that the pattern of his entire life has been secretly determined by his parents' deportation and murder (E 191/285), and that his adopted home of Manchester, far from being an escape or refuge from his own German-Jewish past, confronts him with it at every turn (E 192/287). He finds the memory work imposed upon him by his mother's memoirs to be unbearable, and passes them on to the narrator before disappearing from the narrative – a symbolic death, if not a real one. The most interesting figure, however, is Adelwarth, who begins to tell the story of his own past only once his employment with the Solomons, and therewith his life, comes to an end. The reminiscences he drags up are, says Aunt Fini, astonishingly vivid, leading her to the conclusion that he possessed 'an infallible memory, but that, at the same time, he scarcely allowed himself access to it' ('zwar ein untrügliches Gedächtnis . . . aber kaum mehr eine mit diesem Gedächtnis ihn verbindende Erinnerungsfähigkeit') (E 100/146). Sebald is drawing on a distinction in German between *Gedächtnis* and *Erinnerung*, both generally meaning 'memory', but the former implying a mode of storage, the latter the functional reconstruction and transformation of the contents of the past in the light of present imperatives.[8] The translation is slightly misleading here, in that the notion of 'not allowing oneself access' to one's memories implies a degree of conscious agency, whereas the lack of 'Erinnerungsfähigkeit' implies the absence of a particular mnemonic faculty or facility that operates independently of the individual's conscious intentions. Adelwarth thus suffers from a disturbance of memory that prevents him from enlisting his past in the service of present identity-formation. He is devoid of any meaningful interiority: 'Looking back' comments Aunt Fini, 'you might say that Ambros Adelwarth the private man had ceased to exist, that nothing was left but his shell of decorum' (E 99/144).

As we saw in the Introduction, one of Foucault's main contentions in Volume 1 of *The History of Sexuality* is that confession is a central technology by which the modern individual is produced as a subject. Self-examination, in conjunction with a set of interpretative protocols enshrined within medical, legal and moral discourses lead, it is claimed, to the pronouncement of the truth about the self and to the acquisition of forms of knowledge that facilitate ever closer control of bodies and populations. And yet confession in *The Emigrants* fails to fulfil this role.[9] Despite the Freudian rhetoric employed by Ferber, there is no attempt at psychoanalytic interpretation by either the narrator or any of the other characters who play the role of partner within the confessional structure. As a consequence, confession leads not to the pronouncement of the truth – let alone to a diagnosis or cure of mental pathology – but rather to a hollowing-out or evacuation of subjectivity whose issue can only be death. As Fini remarks of Adelwarth, confession is both an attempt at liberation and an act of self-annihilation (E 100/146). Sebald's text implies that there are levels of subjective suffering that are not reducible to power/knowledge.

If narrativisation of the internal archive fails in its therapeutic effects and thus also fails as a technology of the self, and if the psychic archive (the Derridean 'prosthesis of the inside') is congruent with the photographic archive, it might appear that the photographs, too, stress the ongoing unassimilability of trauma. Stuart Taberner (2004: 184) and Maya Barzilai (2006) stress the similarity between photographs and traumatic symptoms, arguing that the images possess an irreducible alterity that keeps open the wounds of traumatic history and resists closure. Such views, however, run the risk of setting up binary oppositions between memory and narrative on the one hand, and trauma and photography on the other. In his critical work, Sebald expresses scepticism about the mnemonic value of photography in strikingly similar terms. In an essay on Adalbert Stifter and Peter Handke he writes:

> The decisive difference between the writer's method and the technique of photography, with its simultaneous greed for and timidity in the face of experience, consists in the fact that describing promotes remembering, while photographing promotes forgetting. (BU 178)

Such an approach precludes an investigation of the interaction between photography and narrative, and the role such interaction might play in the construction of memory. It is distinctly unhelpful when interrogating a text that repeatedly foregrounds acts of reading the photographic archive. To emphasise photography's status as a vehicle of unassimilable trauma in *The Emigrants* ignores its function within the narrative economy of Sebald's text. While *The Emigrants* stresses that photographs can be regarded first and foremost not as memory, but as a kind of belated symptom of familial and collective history, the narrator's engagement with the photographs represents an attempt at narrative recuperation that succeeds where the protagonists fail. In this sense, *The Emigrants* bears out Marianne Hirsch's suggestion that 'it is *only* in subsequent generations that trauma can be witnessed and worked through, by those who were not there to live it but who received its effects, belatedly, through the narratives, actions, and symptoms of the previous generation' (2001: 222). Hirsch's contention is not unproblematic, because it shifts epistemological authority from first to second generation, thereby devaluing the first generation's experience, while also hollowing out the subjectivity of the second generation and replacing it with the effects of the previous generation's trauma. In *The Emigrants*, however, the narrator's highly self-reflexive narrative practice provides, if not a solution, then certainly a mode of representation that thematises an acute awareness of the dangers inherent in adopting this kind of 'postmemorial' position.

As we saw in Chapter 3, the notion of postmemory was coined by Hirsch to characterise a mode of remembering that traverses generations. It has become one of the most influential and useful concepts for interrogating the relationship between photography, narrative and memory. Postmemory, distinguished from memory by generational distance and from history by deep personal connection, 'characterizes the experience of those who grow up dominated by narratives that preceded their birth, whose own belated stories are evacuated by the stories of the previous generation shaped by traumatic events that can be neither understood nor recreated' (Hirsch 1997: 22).[10] Any attempt at reconstruction, furthermore, must be mediated not by memory, but by imagination and creation.

The phenomenon of postmemory is repeatedly foregrounded in *The Emigrants*. In all four stories, the narrator seeks to reconstruct a series of events that took place before his birth. The narrator's relationship with his subjects is characterised by the kind of affective proximity and investment that history as a discipline strives to avoid, suppress or marginalise,[11] so these events are accessible through neither purely 'historical' research nor personal recollection. Moreover, the four life stories pieced together in the course of Sebald's text tend progressively to swamp the narrator's story. The framing narratives in *The Emigrants* tell the story of the narrator's own travels and inquiries, and thematise the transmission of knowledge – in various forms – from one person to another. All the stories, however, evince a similar chiastic structure: in each case the framing narrative becomes increasingly subordinate to the various embedded narratives. The resulting inversion of the hierarchy of narrative levels brings with it a shift of textual interest away from the narrator and on to the four biographical subjects of the narration, illustrating what Hirsch calls the 'evacuation' of the narrator's story by those of the preceding generation, stories dominated by the traumatic effects of history and politics on the individual.

However, Hirsch's claim that postmemory is mediated by an 'imaginative investment and creation' needs modification, because imagination and creation alone could lead to contructions of pure fantasy possessing no connection to the real.[12] On this reading, postmemory would be no different from Korsakov's Syndrom in which, as Aunt Fini explains to the narrator, 'causes lost memories to be replaced by fantastic inventions' (E 102/149). For postmemory to function as a useful analytic tool and to carry the ethical burden that Hirsch places upon it, it must be distinguished from unregulated fantasy. The mental constructions of postmemory must exist in some kind of dialogue with the empirical, must be open to confirmation or contestation by the real. One way in which this can take place is through the archive, whose material traces of the past can check, correct, relativise or prompt both primary memory (based on recall) and postmemory (based on retrospective construction). Among archival artifacts, photography's perceived indexical relationship to reality privileges it as a vehicle for such postmemorial reconstruction.[13]

The importance of narrative can be witnessed in the completely different types of text provided by the narrator and his aunt Fini when confronted with photographs depicting events that preceded the narrator's birth. The narrator can attach names to some of the faces on a photograph depicting a family group, but is ignorant of the identity of others:

> Lina is sitting on the far left, next to Kasimir. On the far right is Aunt
> Theres. I do not know who the other people on the sofa are, except for

Figure 6.1

the little girl wearing glasses. That's Flossie, who later became a secretary in Tucson, Arizona, and learnt to belly dance when she was in her fifties. (E 71–2/103–4)

The captioning here produces only a partial specification of the photograph's referents; the minimal 'belly-dancing' narrative is desultory and contributes little to our understanding of the temporal context or cultural significance of the picture. A commentary offered by Aunt Fini when confronted with a photograph from her pre-emigration days, on the other hand, goes beyond the merely constative, and is much richer in context and narrative purpose (Fig. 6.1). While viewing a snapshot of a school outing, she says:

I had graduated from the Institute at Wettenhausen the previous year, and from autumn 1926 I had worked as an unpaid teaching assistant at the primary school in W. This is a photograph taken at that time. We were on an outing to Falkenstein. The pupils all stood in the back of the lorry, while I sat in the driver's cab with a teacher named Fuchsluger, who was one of the very first National Socialists, and Benedikt Tannheimer, who was the landlord of the Adler and the owner of the lorry. The child right at the back, with a cross marked over her head, is your mother, Rosa. I remember, said Aunt Fini, that a month or so later, two days before I embarked, I went to Klosterwald with her, and saw her to her boarding school. At that time, I think, Rosa had a great deal of anxiety to contend with, given that her leaving home coincided so unhappily with her siblings' departure for another life overseas, for at Christmas she wrote a letter to us in New York in which she said that she felt fearful when she lay awake in the dormitory at night. (E 75–6/109–10)

The difference between the narrator's and Fini's acts of 'captioning' is a question of knowledge and of the ability to understand the photograph as part of a narrative that links the captured moment to those that precede and follow it. The narrator's postmemories, which form much of the text we read, are the result of a complex set of interactions involving photography, memory and storytelling.

The question that remains is this: what motivates the *type* of story that gets told in the service of postmemory? We have noted the importance of family albums to the narrator's enterprise. Such albums, as we have seen, typically impose upon the viewer a particular mode of looking. While the distribution of photographs within the pages of *The Emigrants* seems to rob domestic photography of its ideological or disciplinary function, the narrative strives to re-enlist the photographs in the service of a reconstruction of family narratives. Central to this project is what Marianne Hirsch has termed the 'familial gaze'. By this she means the set of visual relations that constitute both the subjects and the viewer of the photographs as members of the family group. Family photography is governed by the exchange of looks between the subject and the camera, but these looks are themselves determined by the ideology of the family. Furthermore, the way in which family photographs are usually read reinscribes the familial gaze in the act of reception.[14] Although the sole story to which this theory can be directly applied is Ambros Adelwarth (the only one of the four emigrants to whom the narrator is related), Hirsch's concept actually turns out to be more elastic than her initial definition implies. Indeed, she expands the concept of the gaze beyond the narrow confines of kinship ties, using the term 'affiliative gaze' to describe the ways in which other intimate social groups – particularly friendships – are constructed in the visual field.

Because of Sebald's close acquaintance with and affective proximity to all four of his biographical subjects, it is this affiliative gaze that dominates his reading of the various family photographs of which he is the recipient. This in turn both conditions and is conditioned by his ability to adopt, as his own postmemories, the memories of the people whose lives he narrates. We have seen that the photographs themselves generate the acts of remembrance and storytelling that then surround them and provide them with a context. The precise nature of these narratives is determined by the way Sebald views the photographs, which is itself governed by the affiliative gaze.

This can be seen with particular clarity in the story of Paul Bereyter. In describing Bereyter's album, the narrator writes:

> The earliest photographs told the story of a happy childhood in the Bereyter family home in Blumenstrasse, right next to Lerchenmüller's nursery garden, and frequently showed Paul with his cat or with a rooster that was evidently completely domesticated. The years in a country boarding school followed, scarcely less happy than the years of childhood that had gone before, and then Paul's entry into teacher training college at Lauingen, which he referred to as the teacher processing factory in his gloss. Mme Landau observed that Paul had submitted to this training, which followed the most narrow-minded of guidelines and was dictated by a morbid Catholicism, only because he wanted to teach children at whatever cost – even if it meant enduring training of that kind. Only because he was so absolute and unconditional an idealist had he been able to survive his time at Lauingen without his soul being harmed in any way. (E 46–7/69–70)

In this extract, there are three acts of interpretation taking place as three agents add their linguistic supplement to the photographs under discussion. Firstly, the statement that the early photographs 'told of' Paul's happy childhood masks the fact that it is actually the narrator who is responsible for the narrative construction placed upon a specific set of images. Secondly, Paul's caption 'teacher processing factory' conveys his judgment of the institution, and his verdict is finally supported and glossed by Lucy Landau, who offers a psychological explanation for Paul's perseverance in the training institute depicted in the photograph.

Interestingly, the childhood photographs are absent. Sebald's narrator suppresses the photographs of the young Bereyter in a way that allows him to foreground his own fantasy narrative of Paul's childhood without fear that other interpreters, who are not caught up in the viewing relations of the affiliative gaze, should produce different symbolic readings of the photographs. Hirsch argues that the referentiality of a photograph persists, even if it is only described in a text and not reproduced (1997: 202). Description itself is always also interpretation, of course, but because the described photograph is absent, the interpretation is not open to contestation. As readers, we are robbed of any criteria that would allow contradiction of the Edenic reading of Paul's childhood put forward by the narrator.

The negative affect dominating the representation of the teacher training college, on the other hand, is lent authority by the fact that Paul's own caption is reproduced along with a group photograph that depicts the uniformed seminarists and their masters posing formally on the front steps of an imposing edifice. Indeed, the typographical layout of the text means that in the German text, the word 'Lehrerabrichtungsanstalt' actually *contains* the image to which it refers (E 46/69).[15] Lucy Landau's comments, based on genuine recollection of her conversations with Paul, further strengthen the condemnation of the teacher training college and constitute Paul as the quietly rebellious outsider figure that Sebald's narrative reveals him to have been.[16] The narrator's 'postmemory' is thus a hybrid construction consisting of and mediated through the narratives of others, the narratives implied by the continuity and captioning of the family album, and the fantasy interpretations that the narrator places upon photographic images.

The role of language in determining photographic meaning is here particularly evident. As we saw in Chapter 3, the photograph of the teacher training college actually hints at a high degree of anti-disciplinary disorder and a pervasive desire among the students to assert their embodied subjectivity in the face of the institution's disciplinarity. And yet the captions provided seek to anchor and limit the meanings that can be ascribed to this particular image, bringing it within the compass of the affiliative gaze and resolutely refusing the kind of reading of the image that I offered in Chapter 3.

The interpretation of the seminary photograph throws yet more light on the processes of postmemory. The main contention of Hirsch's *Family Frames* is that reading family photography can be a subversive act, a means of resisting the 'familial gaze'. This can serve two functions: it can allow tensions, rifts and rivalries to emerge from the surface of images whose function is to perpetuate the myth of the cohesive nuclear unit, thereby contributing to a form of *Ideologiekritik* that takes the family as its object. It can also enable the individual subject to emancipate him- or herself from the narrow behavioural norms dictated by the ideology of kinship ties and social roles (1997: Chaps 2, 4 and 6). It may, however, be pragmatically important *not* to read photographs in this way, but to interpret them as a sign or proof of unity and continuity. This is particularly the case when traumatic experiences of loss and exile have severed family ties through geographical distance or violent death. In this connection, Susan Sontag's comment that family photography is a symbolic surrogate for or memorial of the geographically dispersed, extended family that effectively exists only within the leaves of the album (1979: 8–9) becomes apt in a way that Sontag herself had not intended. For Sontag, this phenomenon was just one more symptom of a modernity towards which she seems highly ambivalent. For Bereyter, Landau, Fini and the narrator, on the other hand, the affiliative gaze facilitates the construction and transmission of a set of coherent, consistent life-stories. It also allows the narrator, as both viewer and narrator, to understand his own experience of emigration in terms of the narratives of others, creating a sense of consistency that goes some way towards compensating for the rupture, displacement and bereavement inflicted on the individual by the vicissitudes of political history.

The relationship between photography and narrative in *The Emigrants* is one of mutual dependency: photographs function as the impulse that generates the narrative, and are simultaneously enveloped and fixed in their meaning by the narratives to which they give rise. The alternative readings of Bereyter's teacher training college photograph and the images of Adelwarth and the dervish that I offered in Chapter 3 show that this fixity is fragile. For the meaning of photographs depends on the specific discursive framework into which they are inserted, which allows them to function simultaneously as bearers of the ethnographic gaze or as tokens of anti-disciplinary resistance *and* as vehicles of familial ideology. The narrative economy of *The Emigrants*, however, repeatedly strives to foreground the latter aspect, as the images' meaning is circumscribed by the familial or affiliative gaze.

Reading the family album emerges as one way in which something permanent can be salvaged from the passing of time and the vicissitudes of history. In this sense, *The Emigrants* offers an account of family photography that exceeds the negative evaluations of the medium that one finds in the work of Lalvani, Bourdieu and others. Far from subjecting himself passively and unwittingly to the viewing conventions of family albums, the narrator elects to align himself with this mode of visual consumption. This gesture stresses not the reproduction of an oppressive institution and rigid subject-positions that Lalvani sees as inherent in family photography, but, rather, the importance of preserving affective bonds and genealogical continuity at a time when these have been severed or broken by economic catastrophe and the politics of racial extermination. *The Emigrants* ultimately offers a powerful rehabilitation of local and familial archiving practices that are made possible by modern technologies of representation, and have been regarded with deep suspicion by a particularly paranoid brand of post-Foucauldean theory.

THE EMIGRANTS AS PHOTOGRAPHIC ARCHIVE

As well as the photographs that are passed down to the narrator in the course of his researches, *The Emigrants* also contains photographs whose primary address is to the reader rather than to other characters within the represented world. Here, relations between word and image take two forms. Some of the images are clearly referential, and illustrate the verbal text. The relationship between other images and the surrounding words, however, is characterised by a radical indeterminacy.

At the pole of maximum referentiality are those photographs that are attributable to the narrator and that document both his past life and his investigations into the lives of others. The empty gardens in 'Henry Selwyn' (E 6, 7, 11/12, 13, 19), the drawings of the classroom in S. and of the railway sidings that the narrator prepares during childhood lessons with Paul Bereyter (E 33, 62/50, 91), the snapshots of buildings in Deauville (E 117, 118, 119/173, 174, 175), or the numerous images, in 'Max Ferber', of Manchester (E 158, 159, 167, 231, 232, 233, 235/232, 235, 247, 346, 347, 348, 353) and Bad Kissingen (E 221, 222, 223, 224, 225, 226, 228, 229/332, 333, 334, 335, 336, 339, 341, 343). The referents are clear, and the photographs invite a primarily indexical reading: they appear to function as an authenticating discourse, providing irrefutable evidence for the narrator's claims to have seen and done certain things, and producing the 'autobiography effect' to which many of Sebald's critics have drawn attention.

Many of the photographs, however, possess no such stable referentiality. Take, for example, the first photograph of the text. The link between word and image here is indeterminate. The photograph depicts what is probably a yew tree standing in a graveyard, but whether it is the 'grassy graveyard [with] Scots pines and yews' (E 3/8) near the narrator's home cannot be deduced with any certainty, because the photograph does not contain enough information: the Scots pines and the church described in the text are absent from the photograph.

The connection between the image of railway lines that precedes 'Paul Bereyter' (E 27/41) and the caption that follows soon afterwards is analogous in its effects. The narrator attempts to imagine Bereyter's last moments as he lies on the track awaiting the train that is to kill him: 'The gleaming bands of steel, the crossbars of the sleepers, the spruce trees on the hillside above the village of Altstädten, the arc of the mountains he knew so well, were a blur before his short-sighted eyes, smudged out in the gathering dusk' (E 29/44). The first part of this quotation could refer to the photograph, but the focus of the image is the very inverse of the effects of myopia: the foreground is blurred, while objects in the middle and far distance are in sharp focus. Furthermore, the three mountains Trettach, Kratzer and Himmelsschrofen are not visible at all. Even more disorientating for the reader are some of the photographs in 'Max Ferber'. A description of a train-journey from Norwich to Manchester is accompanied by an image of an utterly flat landscape on which no detail can be made out at all (E 179/266). After narrating his trip to the salina at Bad Kissingen, Sebald incorporates a photograph of a twig into his text which might have been broken off one of the huge stacks of twigs in the salt-works, but which cannot be seen to illustrate the text in any specifiable way (E 230/344). In both these examples, the referents of the photographs remain unclear, and their purpose within the narrative can only be a matter of speculation and conjecture.

On the one hand, then, *The Emigrants* contains images which appear to do nothing but index the real, in all its meaninglessness. On the other hand, there is a set of photographs whose reference to the real cannot be specified with any certainty, and whose relationship to the text is so vague as to open up the potential for a totally unregulated and arbitrary symbolic reading. In both cases, but for opposite reasons, the images ostensibly elude the grasp of the interpreter.

This conclusion, however, only holds if we assume that the photographs in question have to be read in terms of their reference to a reality that is prior and external to the text. But the photographs can be read in another way, namely as images that refer to other images within the same text. So, for example, the cemetery with the yew tree can be linked in terms of subject to the three photographs that Sebald takes in the Jewish Cemetery in Bad Kissingen (E 223–5/333–5), and to mirror compositionally the reproduction of Courbet's *The Oak of Vercingetorix* (E 180/268). The extracts from Paul Bereyter's notebooks (E 58–9/86–7) pre-empt the later pictures of Adelwarth's diaries (E 132, 135/194–5, 200–1), and the narrator's drawing of the classroom in S. (E 33/50) corresponds to the photograph of the same classroom later in the same story (E 47/70). The postcard of the Hotel Eden in Montreux (E 78/113) mirrors compositionally the photograph of the Banff Springs Hotel (E 98/142), both of which have mountains looming behind them. In addition, these images are linked to other pictures of hotels in Deauville (E 118–9/174–5) and Manchester (E 233/348). There are also numerous photographs of houses and dwellings: Selwyn's hermitage (E 11/19), the pagoda-like mansion of the Japanese ambassador for whom Adelwarth worked (E 80/116), the Solomons' Long Island property (E 87/128), the terrace in Manchester's Palatine Road that was once inhabited by Wittgenstein and later by Max Ferber (E 167/247), and the Lanzberg's magnificent Bad Kissingen villa (E 209/313).

As well as being traces of an external reality, then, the photographs in *The Emigrants* are related to other photographs both within and across the four stories. This complex set of pictorial interrelations means that the relationship between the images and the text goes beyond that of photograph and caption. Taken in their entirety, the photographs can be seen as addressing the overall thematic issues that permeate the verbal narrative. The symbolic readings of the photographs, then, result not only from the relationship of photography and language, but from the cross-referencing of photographs to each other. Cemeteries, for example, are an obvious symbol of both death and memorial, and we have seen that the text explores the means by which the stories of the dead may be recuperated and memorialised. Indeed, the text itself fulfils, on one level, a memorial function. The drawings and notebooks reproduced thematise the problems of writing and representation, and our inability to fix a multi-faceted reality on paper. These problems are addressed extensively in 'Max Ferber'. The painter's strange, palimpsestic technique is a response to the ultimate unrepresentability of three-dimensional reality on a two-dimensional canvas, and his aesthetic success consists precisely in the fact that all his attempts end in failure (E 161–2, 174–5/239–40, 260). The narrator's writing enterprise is characterised by precisely the same scrupulous attitude and techniques of erasure:

> I had covered hundreds of pages with my scribble, in pencil and ballpoint. By far the greater part had been crossed out, discarded, or obliterated by additions. Even what I ultimately salvagted as a 'final' version seemed to me a thing of shreds and patches, utterly botched. (E 230–1/345)

The hotels and houses, on the other hand, offer powerful visual images of home and rootednesss – *Heimat* – and the loss thereof. Particularly, temporary dwellings, many of them devoid of visible inhabitants like most other spaces in Sebald, are repeatedly depicted in a way that foregrounds the deracination and fundamental homelessness experienced by Sebald's emigrants.[17]

The technique of mobilising motifs that refer not to external reality but to other motifs within the text has been termed 'the principle of reflexive reference' by Joseph Frank (1963). The concept of 'reflexive reference' occurs in the context of Frank's well-known essay 'Spatial Form in Modern Literature', where he analyses novels by Flaubert, Joyce and Djuna Barnes in order to demonstrate that these authors intended their texts to be apprehended 'spatially, in a moment in time' (9). Spatial form is a highly problematic notion, partly because the word 'spatial' conflates textual form and the phenomenology of perception. In addition, narrative is ineluctably temporal, both in its subject matter and its reading, and so to talk of spatial form entails a wilful refusal to examine the distribution of individual motifs along the narrative syntagma. Nevertheless, the meaning of narratives is not purely dependent on linearity. Indeed, extensive motivic repetitions often exceed the capacity of linear narrative organisation to account for them, and they therefore have to be subjected to another mode of reading.[18] It is in this case that the concept of reflexive reference is useful. Those photographs whose function cannot be understood in terms of narrative linearity can be recuperated as images that refer to other images within the text in order to construct a metaphor for the thematics of the verbal narrative.

Photographs characterised by referential indeterminacy on the one hand and representation of contingent and random reality on the other can initially appear to be arbitrary either in the sense that they merely 'authenticate' the verbal narrative, or in the sense that they are unmotivated by the text that surrounds them. On this reading, their effect would be to underpin the sense of dispersion that characterises the conception of history, environmental change and family life in *The Emigrants*. Such a reading, however, is possible only if we attempt to interpret the photographs in terms of the linear unfolding of the narrative. Reading the photographs in terms of reflexive reference allows them to emerge as part of a network of images that actually fulfil the opposite function: they create patterns of constancy that are repeated within and between the lives of the individual emigrants, including that of the narrator himself.

It is at this point that we can turn once again to the relationship between the photographs and the verbal narrative. One of the features of Sebald's text to which numerous critics have drawn attention is the dense tissue of motivic repetitions. More important than leitmotivs, however, are the numerous events whose configurations are repeated across time in the lives of diverse characters. As the narrator drives away from the home of Aunt Fini, her waving figure becomes the double of Adelwarth at the scene of his final parting from Fini herself (E 103–4/152). Theres' departure for the United States after her last visit to Germany in 'Ambros Adelwarth' (E 69/100–1) mirrors Max Ferber's flight from the same Munich airport (E 187–8/279–80) and the narrator's night-flight to Manchester with which 'Max Ferber' begins (E 149–50/219–21). The caravan of camels painted on the wall of the Wadi Halfa, the café frequented by Ferber and the narrator in Manchester (E 164/243), echoes, right down to the angle from which the fresco is painted, the description of the film that led to Cosmo Solomon's eventual mental breakdown (E 97/141). This list could be extended. The point to note is that reflexive reference operates not only within the photographic discourse, but between motifs and episodes of the verbal narrative as well. Reflexive reference represents a formal analogue of the reflections on correspondences discussed in the previous chapter, turning the entire text into an archival space that allows similarity to be perceived across spatial and temporal distance.

Both the affiliative gaze and the technique of reflexive reference are motivated by the desire to find something stable and constant in the face of historical pessimism. A metaphor that is often used in contemporary criticism is that of 'suturing', the attempt to create some form of durable bond in the face of a perceived historical or post-traumatic fragmentation. The metaphor of suturing allows us to understand Sebald's mobilisation of both the affiliative gaze and reflexive reference. His reading of family albums allows him to suture himself into the stories of others and construct a sense of narrative and biographical continuity as a compensation for exile and loss. Reflexive reference, on the other hand, allows patterns of repetition to emerge that go beyond mere coincidence and hint at a hidden order behind the ostensible chaos of history and entropy of matter. The combination of narrative and photography in *The Emigrants* can thus be seen as an attempt, at the level of form, to counteract the dispersal, dissipation and rupture inherent in the history of modernity.

NOTES

1. The concept of entropy is itself a product of modernity. It is the Second Law of Thermodynamics that recognises that 'usable energy ultimately and irreversibly exhausts itself in the process of transformation and dissipates, leading inevitably to the degeneration and death of a closed system' (Doane 2002: 114). In his critical

essays, Sebald discusses the entropic vision of nature in the work of Adalbert Stifter and Thomas Bernhard (BU 27, 109). Sebald's negative conception of civilisation as one of perpetual destruction has been discussed by Kastura 1996, Williams 2000 and Juhl 1995, and need not be rehearsed here. Eric Santner sees this aspect of Sebald's work in relation to Benjamin's notion of natural history: '[N]atural history is born out of the dual possibilities that life can persist beyond the death of the symbolic forms that gave it meaning, and that symbolic forms can persist beyond the death of the form of life that gave them human vitality' (2006: 17). Santner also notes the prevalence of dust, and goes so far as to suggest that it is 'Sebald's emblem for materiality as such' (100).

2. On framing and narrative transmission, see, for example, Barthes 1970, Brooks 1984 (Chaps 8 and 9), Chambers 1984, Reid 1992.

3. See E 39, 46, 47, 48, 49, 53, 55, 56, 71, 74, 75, 78, 81, 89, 92, 94, 96, 98, 101, 134, 171, 186, 209, 217, 218/59, 69, 70, 71, 73, 78, 82, 83, 104, 108, 109, 113, 118, 130, 134, 137, 140, 142, 147, 199, 255, 278, 313, 325, 326.

4. Lalvani's use of the term 'ideology' seems to oscillate between a Marxian notion of false consciousness and a post-Althusserian view of ideology as a system of representations by which we imagine the world as it is.

5. See, for example, Sontag 1979: 8–9 and Bourdieu et al. 1965: 38–60. For a critique of Bourdieu, see Starl 1995: 142–7. Shawn Smith argues that family albums contributed to reproducing the ideology not only of class but also of race, and were implicated in the popular promulgation of eugenic discourse (1999: 113–35).

6. The translator is freer here, abandoning the literal 'I can still see . . .' in favour of 'Clearest of all, though, were the memories of their outing'. This obscures one of the verbal echoes between stories that combine with motivic and narrative repetitions to constitute a core formal technique of The Emigrants, as we will see.

7. The literature on trauma is vast. In addition to Freud 1955 and 1958b, see especially Caruth 1995 and 1996, and Laub 1992a and 1992b.

8. These definitions correspond largely to Aleida Assmann's distinction between 'storage techniques' and the 'processes of recall' (1999: 28–9).

9. For a more extensive discussion of these issues, see my article 'Disziplin und Geständnis' (Long 2006a: 231–7).

10. Similar definitions are provided in Hirsch 2001: 221 and 1999: 8.

11. Martin Swales, commenting on my earlier essay 'Narrative, History and Photography in W. G. Sebald's Die Ausgewanderten' (Long 2003), denies any emotional connection between the narrator and his biographical subjects (Swales 2003: 86). It is, however, clear that a degree of affective investment on the narrator's part is the very driving force behind all of Sebald's narratives from The Emigrants onwards. As Santner has argued, this is not to be conflated with empathy in the usual sense. He suggests that such subjective involvement with another depends on an involuntary participation in the other's spirit world, on entering the 'enigmatic space of his or her hauntedness' (2006: 58). This comment, typical of the inflationary use of spectral rhetoric in recent psychoanalytic theory, seems to locate such affiliations in the unconscious. Anne Fuchs, on the other hand, claims that Sebald's poetics is dominated by an ethically motivated advocacy on behalf of the victims of history (2004a: 39). Both Fuchs (31) and Santner (58) approvingly quote the opening of 'Paul Bereyter', in which the narrator dismisses empathy as both unethical and lacking in cognitive value. It seems to me that the act of writing is the moment at which the ethical emerges, but without fully displacing the profound sense of affiliation that motivates the narratives in the first place. For the ethical, as Kaja Silverman stresses, 'becomes operative not at the moment when unconscious

desires and phobias assume possession of our look, but in a subsequent moment' (1996: 173). It operates retroactively.

12. This issue is further explored in my essay 'Monika Maron's *Pawels Briefe*: Photography, Narrative, and the Claims of Postmemory' (Long 2006b). There, I offer a critique of postmemory that focuses particularly on the dubiousness of Hirsch's ethical claims. In my view, postmemory's value as a critical concept lies in its describing a structure of (transgenerational) transmission that is not accounted for by other memory paradigms, and it is in this sense that I use the term here.

13. Referring to an earlier article (Long 2003), Anne Fuchs questions photography's ability to provide this 'dialogue with the empirical', given what she terms the massive philosophical critique of mimetic conceptions of reference (2004a: 35). My point, however, is based not on the mimetic capacity of photography, but on its indexical character, which, as we have seen throughout this study, is repeatedly foregrounded in Sebald's work.

14. This is, of course, akin to Lalvani's description of the production of familial ideology in the visual field. As we will see, however, it has several advantages over Lalvani's scheme because it can be extended to encompass social groups other than kinship and because it is less totalising, allowing for a degree of subversion or resistance.

15. 'Lehrerabrichtungsanstalt' is translated as 'teacher processing factory', which modifies the metaphor. For *abrichten* means to train an animal to perform certain tasks. Sebald's original text thus foregrounds the disciplinary rather than the industrial nature of the institution.

16. Sebald's narrative of Paul Bereyter's life casts him as a non-conformist in perpetual, silent conflict with authority, however it should manifest itself. The first thing he does on his arrival at the village school is to scrape off the whitewash with which the previous teacher had painted the classroom windows (E 34/51); he detests the representatives of Catholicism (E 36–6/53–5); and devotes hardly any time to the prescribed school curriculum (E 37/56). During the early Nazi period, he is the victim of Nazi persecution because of his status as a *Dreiviertelarier*, and is never truly at home in post-war Germany.

17. For a reading that emphasises transcendental homelessness in relation to Judaism and the loss of an idealised Jerusalem, see Korff 1998.

18. See Kermode 1981. We will return to these issues in the next chapter.

7

THE AMBULATORY NARRATIVE: *THE RINGS OF SATURN*

Towards the end of Sebald's third major prose text, *The Rings of Saturn*, the narrator arrives at the abandoned Cold War weapons research facility at Orfordness. He includes a map of the area that is produced by the Ordnance Survey, the official mapping agency of Great Britain (RS 232/277). The narrator's interest in the map primarily concerns the fact that it bears absolutely no traces of the military installation, which was, as Sebald's narrative states, shrouded in official secrecy, giving rise to all sorts of conspiracy theories which the opening of the relevant archives failed to lay to rest (RS 231–3/276).[1] Indeed, the very logic of conspiracy theories means that the opening of the files led merely to further conspiracy theories about the suppression or removal of archival material before access was granted,[2] and the fact that the Orfordness base is still absent from OS maps gives little cause to abandon such conjecture.

This absence immediately alerts us to the overt connection between archives and state power that we have seen elsewhere in this study. But beyond this, it also alerts us to the political aspects of cartographic rhetoric. As J. B. Harley has argued, maps are intentional structures that embody social values and power relationships, even though Western cartography seeks to disguise this by conceiving of itself as a scientific exercise involving the development and application of technical procedures in the service of a positivist epistemology (1992). The history of the Ordnance Survey amply illustrates the political instrumentality of map-making. Its precursor was a military survey of the Scottish Highlands undertaken in 1746 as part of a strategy to quell the threat of Scottish rebellion. The Ordnance Survey itself, named after the Board of Ordnance, the forerunner of the Ministry of Defence, was established in 1791 in order to map the south-eastern counties of England at a time when fears of an invasion by Napoleonic forces were at their height. It undertook extensive surveys of Ireland in the 1820s and 1830s, and as we saw in Chapter 4, it was charged by Parliament with the task of mapping the whole of Britain in order to expedite the expansion of the rail network. Cartography was thus central to protecting the integrity of the nation state against sedition and invasion, controlling populations, facilitating colonial administration, and encouraging the processes of modernisation and industrialisation. On this reading, maps illustrate the inextricable entwinement of power and knowledge that Foucault identifies as the defining form of power in modernity: cartographers were given legal rights to survey the terrain, and to record geophysical formations, the location of urban settlements, communication routes, and so on, in a way that enabled power to be exercised all the more efficiently.

The Ordnance Survey was one of several national topographical surveys carried out in eighteenth-century Europe, the other best-known example being the systematic cadastral mapping of post-revolutionary France (Harvey 1990: 259). In its totalising ambition and its desire to record and catalogue the space of the nation for purposes of political control, the maps it generated participated in the 'archival desire' and the practical rationalisation of space that characterise modernity.

Against this background of state instrumentalisation of cartography, certain features of the Orfordness map that might ordinarily go unnoticed (largely because they have become naturalised conventions of Western cartography) begin to acquire heightened significance. First, the terrain is overlaid by a grid running east–west and north–south, and dividing geographical space up into a series of equal-sized squares. Secondly, its primary modern-day use is as a hiking map, and it therefore details not only roads and geological features, but also public footpaths and bridleways. Thirdly, it is a leisure map, and thus indicates tourist attractions and areas owned by the National Trust, the United Kingdom's main administrator of heritage sites.

Starting with the first of these, the imposition of the grid is the most radical and rational means by which the map brings about the homogenisation of space that we noted in Chapter 4. The second feature of this map to which I wish to draw attention is its extensive delineation of footpaths that are designated as public rights of way. While this might at first glance appear democratic, it is of course an assertion of property rights, according to which the hoi polloi are permitted access only to strictly demarcated routes across land that is largely in private ownership. Such a strategy of representation can be seen as a

Foucauldean disciplinary technology: the map functions as an instrument of power that produces effects on the body while concealing its own workings, in this case behind the powerful cartographic ideology of scientific disinterestedness. Finally, by providing details of historic buildings and monuments, churches, museums, campsites, and so on, the map makes space available to the tourist. The map is functionally organised to direct walkers to specific places as an aid to the tourist economy, thereby producing a hierarchy of space in which some things are worth seeing and others are not. These second and third aspects of the map reflect, as Jeremy Black notes, the dual nature of tourism, in which space is something to be both enjoyed and overcome (1997: 92). While providing scenic routes and places of interest, the map is also repeatedly crossed with roads and paths that allow the most efficient journey to be plotted between two points.[3]

All of these features of the Ordnance Survey map – its encoding of capitalist property relations, its disciplining of the walker, its facilitation of efficient route-planning, and the fact that it simultaneously homogenises space and reconstitutes it in hierarchical terms that are dictated by the tourist economy – mark it out as an emblematic artifact of modernity, a modernity that counts among its salient features the commodification of landscape and 'heritage' (exemplified by Somerleyton Hall), and the imperative of efficiency, the need to achieve goals with the maximum speed and minimum expenditure of resources.[4] The map and its relationship to modernity are central to *The Rings of Saturn*, for they provide the context within which the narrator's journey and his narrative enterprise need to be understood.

WALKING

In her book *Wanderlust*, Rebecca Solnit notes the absence of the walking or labouring body from contemporary theories of corporeality: 'A medical and sexual phenomenon, [the body in recent theory] is a site of sensations, processes, and desires rather than a source of action or production' (2000: 28). Indeed, the idea that the body could be the source of anything would be anathema to much contemporary thought that builds on Foucault's work and sees the body as constituted purely through the play of discourse systems. Post-Foucauldean accounts of the body have, as N. Katherine Hayles argues, produced a dematerialisation of the body (1998: 193). She goes on to show how Foucault's insistence on the disembodied gaze of the observer in his description of the panopticon allows the body to disappear into technology, concealing the limitations of corporeality. The bodies of those disciplined 'fade into the technology as well, becoming a universalized body worked upon by surveillance techniques and practices' (194). Hayles uses the term 'the body' to designate this normative, universalised, discursively-produced entity, which she then contrasts with 'embodiment':

In contrast to the body, embodiment is contextual, enmeshed with the specifics of place, time, physiology, and culture . . . Embodiment never coincides directly with 'the body,' however that normalized concept is understood . . . Whereas the body can disappear into information with scarcely a murmur of protest, embodiment cannot, for it is tied to the circumstances and the person. As soon as embodiment is acknowledged, the abstractions of the Panopticon disintegrate into the particularities of specific people embedded in specific contexts. Along with these particularities come concomitant strategies for resistances and subversions, excesses and deviations. (196–7)

Embodiment thus exists in tension with the body, opening up the possibility of resistance to the Foucauldean disciplinary structures outlined in earlier chapters of this study.

As befits a text that has walking as its central theme, *The Rings of Saturn* repeatedly foregrounds the narrator's corporeality. In the light of this it is remarkable that so few critics have addressed the representation of the body in Sebald's work. Anja Maier notes that Sebald's work is extensively concerned with the suffering body. The slight shift of perspective brought about by physical pain is, she argues, both the driving force and the structural principle of Sebald's narratives. Rather then providing a refuge or a fixed position in the world, the body is the cause of a profound irritation that sets free a displaced or vertiginous mode of perception. This mode of perception is essential for the production of the work of art, because it facilitates the metonymic substitutions that generate Sebald's texts (2006: 111–13).[5] Maier identifies Sebald's tendency to romanticise torture by seeing it as akin to writing. In particular, she points out that Sebald repeatedly speaks of pain in terms of shrinkage to a tiny point, but that this point then produces an extension that is the text itself – in other words, the *pleasurable* recounting of all the catastrophes that produced the symptom (117). Eric Santner notes the importance of the cringed body as emblematic of the 'creaturely', by which he understands the condition of the subject under the state of exception or emergency, when the normal functioning of the law is suspended in favour of the sovereign's executive decisions (2006: 29–30). But the walking body of the narrator himself has received little critical attention.

This walking body and its performances constitute, however, the locus of resistance to modernity in *The Rings of Saturn*. The contrast between the body and embodiment is thematised at several points in the text. The only time the narrator mentions that he is using a map, for example, he does so only to emphasise its representational inadequacy and to note his own willingness to strike out randomly across fields when the paths are overgrown or ploughed up and hence no longer discernible (RS 249–50/296). This foregrounds the disparity between the map's inscription of the itinerary of the ideal walker, and the improvisational performance of the embodied narrator, whose movements are governed by contextual knowledge of his immediate environment, even if he uses a two-dimensional schematic representation to help orientate himself.[6] What Hayles would call the narrator's 'instantiated materiality' deviates from the abstract cartographic representation, and it is this that enables him to subvert the map's disciplinary intention. Similar patterns are at work elsewhere in the text. As the narrator approaches Covehithe, he walks along a path bounded on one side by cliffs, and on the other by an electric fence behind which some pigs are dozing (RS 65–6/85). The fact that it is an electric fence stresses, of course, that the boundary employs a specifically modern technology. Indeed, it is analogous to the traffic signals that work upon the body of the urban pedestrian and, as Benjamin pointed out in one of his many proto-Foucauldean moments, subject the human sensorium to a highly complex training (1973: 132). These two boundaries, one natural, one man-made, establish the parameters within which the walker can move, and circumscribe the body's mobility. And yet the embodied narrator, fascinated by the pigs, steps over the electric fence in an act of wilful trespass, once again transgressing the behavioural norms implied not by the map this time, but by actual barriers in the physical environment. Analogous to this is his climbing the perimeter wall of Somerleyton Hall and forging his way through the undergrowth so as to avoid having to circumambulate half of the estate to gain entrance to the park (RS 32/44).

The visit to Orfordness is the episode in which the contrast between the embodied practice of the narrator and the normative expectations encoded in cartographic representations is most marked. Rather than gravitate towards the numerous tourist attractions or places of local interest with which Ordnance Survey maps are generously sprinkled, he visits the unmapped, abandoned terrain of the military base that is accessible only by boat. This is an embodied practice that exceeds both the disciplinary strictures of the map and modernity's imperative of efficiency, for since the end of the Cold War, the space has become quite literally redundant and the narrator's visit therefore has no productive purpose. The important thing to note, however, is that the omission or erasure of the Orfordness installation from the map means that it always *had* been constituted as redundant space. If the base is indeed where the narrator's arrow shows it to be, then the area it occupies exists on the map as nothing but a bank of shingle. There is no evidence of human action on the environment, and the homogenisation effected by the grid-based cartographic system reduces it to a site of non-meaning, devoid of all functional relevance and, in cultural terms, no different from other 'blank' areas of the map. The narrator, on the other hand, shows that Orfordness is far from being empty, homogeneous space. While roaming over the island, he invests it with myriad cultural meanings.

Metaphor after metaphor is produced in order to articulate the specific embodied experience of place: it resembles a Far-Eastern penal colony and feels extraterritorial (RS 233/278) or like an undiscovered country (RS 234/279).[7] The camouflaged concrete bunkers of the research facility look like the burial mounds of prehistoric rulers (RS 236/281) while other buildings resemble temples or pagodas (RS 236/282). Finally, the narrator abandons the idea that Orfordness is an isle of the dead, and imagines himself 'amidst the ruins of our own civilization after its extinction in some future catastrophe' (RS 237/282).[8] As we have seen, Sebald seeks to re-inject a degree of magic into the urban environment in *Vertigo*. His repeated attempts to find adequate metaphors for Orfordness' uncanniness, to invest it with symbolic power, can be read in the same light, and constitute a further means by which embodied experience exceeds modernity's representations.

The Rings of Saturn, then, stages the interplay between the disciplined body as defined by cartographic discourse and physical demarcations in the landscape on the one hand, and the embodied practice of the narrator on the other. As such, it can be seen as a response to the Cartesian view of the body that is subjected to trenchant critique in the narrator's discussion of Rembrandt's *Anatomy Lesson*. This discussion derives its force from the discrepancy between the body and embodiment. For the guild of surgeons, as Hayles would put it, Aris Kindt's corpse 'disappears into information': 'it is debatable whether anyone ever really saw that body, since the art of anatomy, then in its infancy, was not least a way of making the reprobate body invisible' (RS 13/23). The corpse is displaced by the anatomical atlas, which reduces corporeality to a diagrammatic representation that is by its very nature normative. Such a view of the body was congruent with Cartesian rationalism, and as Anne Fuchs notes, the narrator attacks this philosophy for legitimising the 'disastrously anthropocentric world-view of the modern era' and the 'devaluation of the very notion of biological life'. The privileging of the cognitive faculties and the concomitant objectification of the body lead to a utilitarian biopolitics, according to which the body must be made productive and in the event of a fault either repaired or destroyed.[9] In other words, modernity seeks to reduce contingencies of embodiment to a normative notion of the body as nothing more than a productive mechanism. Sebald's reading of the *Anatomy Lesson* shows that Rembrandt deploys the anatomical atlas against itself: by copying the lower left arm directly from the atlas, Rembrandt has painted it upside-down. The resulting 'crass misrepresentation' (RS 16/27) becomes, in the narrator's view, a sign of the violence perpetrated on Aris Kindt and a gesture of empathic identification on the part of the painter. This stress on the suffering of the individual victim reinscribes embodiment at the very moment of its disappearance into the body.[10]

The foregrounding of embodiment at other points in *The Rings of Saturn* can likewise be read not only as a subversion but as an inversion of

Cartesianism. Whereas Descartes' central premise was that the mind can be certain only of its ability to be present to itself, Sebald's text repeatedly emphasises that the body exists in space and time and, through interaction with the environment, defines the parameters of mental activity: thought, dream, memory, imagination.

But the narrator's attempts to resist modernity are not limited to these instances of embodied subjectivity. For if one of the imperatives encoded in the map is modernity's drive for efficiency, then walking *per se* emerges as an activity that challenges that imperative. This is illustrated most clearly (and comically) when the narrator imagines the inhabitants of Middleton coming out of their houses and telling him quite forcefully to be on his way (RS 175/209). Modernity, he suggests, is deeply suspicious of walkers, especially if they fail to conform to socially sanctioned stereotypes: 'After all, every foot traveller incurs the suspicion of the locals, especially nowadays, and particularly if he does not fit the image of the local rambler' (RS 175/209). We can infer from this that the embodied materiality of the narrator himself is at odds with normative representations of 'the hiker' or 'the rambler'. The notion of the *Freizeitwanderer*, or one who walks for pleasure in his spare time, is one means by which modernity rationalises a pursuit that – according to its own logic at least – would otherwise be irrational, for walking as a leisure activity can be seen to fulfil the same purpose as other leisure activities, namely the reproduction of the worker's labour-power. It is not merely that Sebald's narrator does not look like the typical hiker; it is also that he wanders with no ostensible purpose or goal, following the dictates of the land, inadvertently doubling back on himself, inexplicably tracing out the same route time and again, and striking out only to end up back where he started.[11] Destinations emerge as a contingent by-product of walking, not its *telos*.

A brief enumeration of the stations on the narrator's journey will clarify what is at stake both thematically and narratologically in Sebald's text. The narrator boards a train at Norwich and visits Somerleyton Hall before continuing on foot to Lowestoft. The following evening he reaches Southwold where he spends two days, then crosses the Blyth, visits Dunwich, and then gets thoroughly lost on Dunwich Heath. Upon finally leaving the heath, he goes to Middleton and thence returns to Southwold. After a further rest day, he continues on to Woodbridge, Orford and Orfordness, returns again to Woodbridge, then travels inland to the sparsely-populated area south of Harleston. Here, he visits Thomas Abrams' farm, then travels to Harleston itself before betaking himself into an area known as The Saints. After nearly getting lost once more, he finds his way to the village of Ilketshall St Margaret, before making his way via Bungay and the marshlands of the Waverney Valley to Ditchingham. From here he strikes out on the road towards Norwich, stopping at a pub from where he phones for a lift home.

Claudia Albes, to whom I am indebted for this summary of the narrator's itinerary, terms the form of Sebald's ambulatory narrative both 'circular' and 'labyrinthine' (2002: 288, 290). It is difficult to see how it could be both, and I am not convinced that it is either. Although the narrator begins in Norwich and is last seen on the Norwich road out of Ditchingham, the circularity of the text is potential, not actual; the circle remains unclosed and the text refuses the formal satisfaction that completed circularity would bring. Indeed, if *The Rings of Saturn* were structured in this way, it would be a kind of lost-and-found narrative which, as John Zilcosky has shown, is the dominant paradigm of travel writing and functions analogously to the Freudian fort-da game to confirm the travelling and writing subject's sense of self. As Zilcosky has also shown, such a structure is systematically subverted by Sebald's narratives (2004). And rather than a labyrinth, *The Rings of Saturn*, like the journey it recounts, is filled with diversions, recursions and a refusal of teleology. Not only is walking itself an inefficient mode of locomotion in the age of planes, trains and automobiles; the route that Sebald's narrator takes is itself uneconomic, for his meanderings have no goal that would count as such according to the logic of modernity, and no schedule for attaining it.[12]

THE POETICS OF DIGRESSION

The wandering that forms the explicit subject-matter of the 'main' narrative strand goes hand in hand with a poetics of digression. The post-structural narratology of Roland Barthes (1970), Peter Brooks (1984), and others has taught us that the felicitous text moves back and forth between end-directedness and the exploration of what Barthes called the 'dilatory space' of narrative, which retards and impedes the progression of the story. Teleology and dilatoriness are thus typically held in equilibrium, each desire being fulfilled at the expense of the frustration of its opposite and other. Such an equilibrium is fundamentally subverted, however, by a text like *The Rings of Saturn*, which consists almost entirely of digressions. The 'English Pilgrimage' promised by the title almost immediately fades from view, as the view from the narrator's hospital bed, the features of the natural and built environment, a television programme half perceived on the cusp of sleep, newspaper cuttings, paintings and other objects lead the narrator into a series of autobiographical and historical narratives, excavations of biographical itineraries, passages of art criticism, zoological speculations and extensive descriptions, all of which produce a repeated decentring of the tale of the thirty-mile walk from Somerleyton to Ditchingham that constitutes the so-called 'pilgrimage' itself. The pattern of digression in the third chapter of *The Rings of Saturn* can stand as exemplary for the technique of the text as a whole.

At the beginning of the chapter, the narrator has left Lowestoft and walks south over the dunes, commenting on the anglers whose tents remain constant in number despite the comings and goings of individuals. After offering an existential interpretation of fishing as an activity that allows the anglers to dwell in a place 'where they have the world behind them, and before them nothing but emptiness' (RS 52/69), he progresses to an account of the decline of the local fishing industry, notes in passing the effects of pollution on the morphology of sea fish, and then devotes some time to a film about herring fishing that he recalls from childhood. The description of the film merges into more general reflections on the herring, culminating in a discussion of the bizarre nineteenth-century plan to use the phosphorescing corpses of the fish as a source of artificial illumination. Returning to his coastal walk, the narrator continues on his way as the morning haze is burned off, but then immediately launches into the story of George Wyndham Le Strange, the military man who bequeathed his entire estate to his housekeeper. Resuming his journey, the narrator finds himself among high ferns on a cliff near Covehithe. It is here that he climbs over an electric fence to commune with a prostrate pig, and recalls the biblical narrative of the Nazarene swine. The notable thing here is that in this act of trespass, the narrator deviates from both the physical path of his journey and from the narration thereof, as though reliteralising the etymology of 'digression', which derives from the Latin *di-gradi*, a 'stepping aside'. As he thinks of this Bible story, the narrator notices swallows soaring back and forth over the sea, which leads him to a childhood reminiscence and thence to an association with Borges' story *Tlön, Uqbar, Orbis Tertius*, before he returns to the narrative present of the journey and the copulating couple on the sand. This sight causes the narrator some distress, prompting him to recall the Borges story once more, a story that ends with a reference to Thomas Browne. Here, as throughout *The Rings of Saturn*, the quantitative preponderance of micronarratives and associative meditations swamps the story of the journey itself.[13]

But digression does not stop there, for the *The Rings of Saturn* is shot through with similes that call up alternative worlds. Ross Chambers suggests that a feature of such narrative is its awareness of the permeability of contexts: 'The context in which one happens to be working is not only not the only context; but another context is actually interfering with the first' (1998: 12). This is precisely what happens every time Sebald introduces an 'as if' construction or another metaphorical formulation: while visiting Somerleyton Hall, the narrator is unsure if he is in a stately home in Suffolk, on the North Sea Coast, or in the heart of Africa (RS 36/49). Looking down to the beach from the cliffs south of Lowestoft, it is *as though* the anglers on the shore were the last remnants of a nomadic people who had found their way here to the ends of the earth (RS 51/68); the bleached remains of fallen trees *look like* the skeletons of an extinct race of prehistoric creatures (RS 64/83); it is *as though* the world were held together by the paths traced by swallows in flight (RS 67/87); the copulating couple *resemble* a two-headed, many-limbed sea-monster that has been washed up onto the beach and is now in its death-throes (RS 68/88); the narrator *feels like* a member of a nomadic tribe resting on its passage through the desert (RS 85/105), and later like the last survivor of a caravan that has been buried in a sandstorm (RS 229/273). Similar metaphors occur, too, in the Orfordness episode, as we have seen.

Gregory-Guider identifies a pervasive tendency of 'everywhere [to contain] numerous elsewheres' in Sebald's work (2005: 427), and in his interpretation of this phenomenon he oscillates uneasily between psychology, metaphysics and history. It is worth noting, however, that the textual transformation of one space into another is enabled by metaphor, and as such it forms part of a wider pattern of substitutions, as the above list illustrates. The phenomenal world in *The Rings of Saturn* is repeatedly invaded by intimations of a pre-modern or even mythic temporality that allows for the presence of sea-monsters, prehistoric beasts and post-apocalyptic survival. This awareness of the permeability of contexts means that the narrator exists in a permanent state of distraction that leads, in the narrative discourse, to what Brian McHale terms 'ontological flicker', as the physical world in which the text appears to be grounded frequently opens onto alternative spatio-temporal dimensions.[14] This in turn demands from the implied reader a kind of split attention. In both cases, it is not only physical space but also the mind that can rapidly become 'elsewhere', and such absent-mindedness, as Jonathan Crary suggests, runs counter to the carefully calibrated attentiveness required of the normative subject in modernity:

> Because so many forms of disciplinary attentiveness, especially since the early twentieth century, have entailed cognitively 'processing' a stream of heterogeneous stimuli (whether radio, film, television, or cyberspace), the kind of swerves into inattentiveness increasingly have produced alternate experiences of dislocation, or temporalities that are not only dissimilar to but also incompatible with capitalist patterns of flow and obsolescence. (1999: 77)

There is a further element to Sebald's digressiveness, namely his obsession with lists and inventories of all kinds. The most striking example is perhaps the lengthy enumeration of the churches of Jerusalem in *The Emigrants*,[15] but it is no less present in *The Rings of Saturn*. We might think, for example, of the objects transported to Somerleyton by train in its nineteenth-century heyday:

> impedimenta of every description, the new piano, curtains and portières, the Italian tiles and fittings for the bathrooms, the boiler and pipes for the hothouses, supplies from the market gardens, cases of hock and Bordeaux, lawn mowers and great boxes of whalebone corsets and crinolines from London.

This mutates, in typically Sebaldian fashion, into a melancholy enumeration of all the people who no longer frequent the station: 'No stationmaster in gleaming peaked cap, no servants, no coachman, no house guests, no shooting parties, neither gentlemen in indestructible tweeds nor ladies in stylish travelling clothes' (RS 31/44). This kind of inventorisation recurs throughout *The Rings of Saturn*: the furnishings of Somerleyton Hall (RS 33–4/46), the hotels and tourist facilities of nineteenth-century Lowestoft (RS 45/61), the contents of the photographic history of the First World War (RS 94/116), Swinburne's description of Kubla Khan's palace (RS 160–1/193), the topography of the Temple of Jerusalem (RS 248/294), the stations of Chateaubriand's diplomatic career (RS 257/305), the periphrastic summary of Thomas Browne's *Musaeum Clausum* (RS 271–3/322), and the varieties of silk produced by the manufacturers of Norwich (RS 283/335). Many of these examples participate in what Eric Santner terms Sebald's 'spectral materialism', namely the capacity to register the persistence of past affect that has been absorbed into the substance of lived space.[16] But narratologically speaking, inventorisation brings the text to a standstill much more radically than the so-called descriptive pause of classical narratology, since a description of a person or spatial setting will generally entail some kind of ekphrastic syntax akin to the scanning of a framed image, whereas Sebald's lists are purely paradigmatic in nature, and represent a degree zero of story time while facilitating the potentially infinite extension of discourse time.

Sebald's narrator's walking, then, is deliberately inefficient and, one might say, anti-disciplinary. This tendency to explore byways rather than make beelines goes hand in hand with a narrative technique that is multiply digressive: it repeatedly shifts focus, as each digression is soon abandoned in favour of another digression or a brief return to the story of the journey itself; it frequently changes the context within which phenomena are understood, evoking a parallel, mythic temporality that transfigures the quotidian object-world and produces a split attention, a kind of distraction, in both the narrator and the reader; and it frequently gets sidetracked into lengthy enumerations of physical objects.

Like the thematisation of walking, the digressive principle of *The Rings of Saturn* is best understood as a response to modernity. For if modernity is characterised by the drive towards increased efficiency in economic and bureaucratic life, the same imperatives come to govern the practices of writing and reading. One of modernity's great achievements, namely the advent of mass literacy, inaugurated the proverbial Great Divide, after which suspense-driven, teleological narratives became associated with 'low' genres such as romance and detective fiction, against which literary modernism defined itself.[17] The formal innovations of modernism – in terms of convoluted time structures, various kinds of distorted narrative perspective, motivic density or stylistic difficulty – can be seen as deliberately impeding easy consumption of the narrative, or offering an excess of textual material beyond what is necessary to the presentation of plot, milieu, or character. The reading practices demanded by such writing – rereading, for example, or non-linear reading strategies in general – go against the logic of the market, in which the rapid consumption of books both stimulates and is stimulated by the constant flow of new products onto the literary market. And yet *all* writers are tied to this marketplace. As a consequence, authors – even modernists – tend, in Frank Kermode's words, to ' "foreground" sequence and message' – at the expense, of course, of 'back-grounding' large parts of their novels that consequently go virtually unread, 'resisting all but abnormally attentive scrutiny, reading so minute, intense, and slow that it seems to run counter to one's "natural" sense of what a novel is' (1981: 84). Kermode goes on to claim that most readers 'underread' and are encouraged in this practice by authors because the commercial success of their books depends upon it.

The resistant moment in digressive narrative resides in the fact that it is deliberately uneconomic, resolutely refusing the imperative to achieve goals with the maximum efficiency (or, indeed, to achieve goals at all!), and to pander to the culture of impatience. It fails to foreground sequence and message, and shatters the equilibrium between directedness and dilatoriness, as the expansion of the dilatory space of the narrative overwhelms the teleological impulse. The story is not only spun out but is also *clogged up* by the proliferation of inventories and lists, micronarratives and reminiscences, which not only defer the arrival at the end of the main story, but make it impossible to say with any certainty what the main story *is*. The danger, as Kermode implies, is that narratives that do this run the risk of being 'underread' – and numerous readers of Sebald have testified on an anecdotal basis to the fact that his works tempt one to skim long passages of text. They testify, too, to the fact that despite being absorbing when one is reading them, Sebald's books cannot easily be held within the memory or effectively summarised. Iris Denneler has written of the '*erzeugte* Langeweile', the calculated boredom produced by the non-narrative inventories in Sebald's prose (2001: 151), while Geoff Dyer (2001) notes that Sebald's texts are always teetering 'on the brink of being boring' because of their sense of 'suspended narration'. For Dyer, this goes hand in hand with a certain readerly anxiety, because:

> any clue as to what was going to make the book work always seemed likely to be hidden in the least interesting passages, the passages one was most tempted to skim. The reader was thereby forced to attend (in every sense) with a patience-straining diligence that proceeded in tandem with the narrator's weary tramping through the Suffolk lowlands.

This patience-straining diligence is precisely the kind of reading practice that Sebald's texts demand, in opposition to the rapid linear consumption of the text. And it is, of course, not coincidental that Dyer alludes – albeit fleetingly – to the confluence of digressive narrative and goalless walking.

THE ARCHIVAL TEXT: MODERNITY'S REVENGE

Dyer's comments, which relate boredom to suspended narration and the difficulty of deciding what is significant in *The Rings of Saturn*, suggest that the price one pays for resisting linearity by means of extensive digression is the threat of pointlessness. This threat is even briefly touched upon by the narrator himself when he tells a series of anecdotes about the eccentric and aptly-named major Le Strange, and adds 'To this day I do not know what to make of such stories' (RS 64/83). In other words, the accumulation of micronarratives always has the potential to disorientate or even alienate the reader, who is confronted with the spectre of meaninglessness. The reading of narrative is typically governed by the so-called hermeneutic circle, according to which our interpretation of detail is guided by a provisional conception of the totality, while the conception of the totality is modified on the basis of each detail as it emerges. Such a protocol of reading, however, depends on a text that is fundamentally cohesive, with each event being linked through sequence, logic, entailment or causality to those that precede and follow it within the narrative discourse. The more such cohesiveness disintegrates, the less effective the hermeneutic circle becomes as a mode of cognitively processing the narrative, and the greater the threat of meaninglessness.

The only way in which dilatoriness can be prevented from degenerating into complete incoherence in *The Rings of Saturn* is through the adoption of an archival structure for the text itself. As we saw in the Introduction, one of the characteristics of the archive is equivalence and substitutability, an aspect of Sebald's text to which Claudia Albes has drawn attention. She writes that the episodes that make up the text are 'allegories of a universal history of decline, each of which could be substituted for any of the others' (2002: 288). Commenting on André Breton's *Nadja* – a novel that can be seen as a seminal precursor of Sebald's texts – Peter Bürger remarks that there is no specifically narrative link between the individual events, and no event logically presupposes those that precede it.[18] What links the events, he argues, is structural similarity, which means that paradigmatic rather than syntagmatic relations obtain (1974: 107). Albes makes precisely this point about *The Rings of Saturn* when she claims that every story is a variation on the theme of loss and notes the prevalence of a rich vocabulary of decay: things are shut down, abandoned, extinguished, burned-out, demolished, boarded up, annihilated, rusted and decayed ('stillgelegt', 'erloschen', 'ausgebrannt', 'abgerissen', 'entlassen', 'verschlossen', 'vernichtet', 'verrostet', 'zerfallen') (2002: 286–7). Other critics have echoed her insight. For Pfeiffer, the narrative fragments are variations on the theme of the fragility of human life in history and in nature (2003: 228), while Öhlschläger sees them as variations on the pervasive theme of the alienation or aberration of humankind from what might constitute its true nature (2006b: 201). While they differ on precise emphasis, all these critics employ the metaphor of variations on a theme in order to convey the sense that the structural principle of *The Rings of Saturn* is metaphorical similarity and substitutability. Maier (2006: 113) and Öhlschläger (2006b: 203) stress metonymy as the text's generative principle, and it is certainly true that the distribution of fragments along the narrative syntagma frequently relies on metonymic displacements and substitutions as the narrator moves pace by pace from place to place.[19] But these metonymies are ultimately contained by a pervasive metaphorical similarity that obtains between the various micronarratives. It is this formal aspect of *The Rings of Saturn* that legitimises the list of seemingly unrelated events that occurred on the same date, 13 April, as that on which the text is allegedly completed: the proclamation of the Edict of Nantes, the first performance of Handel's *Messiah*, Warren Hastings' being named governor of Bengal, the foundation of the Prussian Anti-Semitic League, the massacre of Amritsar, the fall of Celle to the advancing Red Army, and the death of the man who, it is implied, is the narrator's father-in-law (RS 294–5/348–9). It legitimises, too, the narrator's assertion that history stumbles blindly from one misfortune to the next (RS 256/305) and consists almost entirely of calamities (RS 295/350). For *The Rings of Saturn* has already demonstrated, within its very fabric, that every event replicates both every other event and the wider process of history, of which the individual event is an epiphenomenon.

And yet the construction of an archival structure in the absence of more cohesive narrative connections is clearly not fully able to dispel the problem that Dyer identifies when he writes that 'any clue as to what was going to make the book work always seemed likely to be hidden in the least interesting passages'. This alerts us to the fact that the archival ordering produces equivalences, not hierarchies, which results in a reduction of qualitative difference to mere quantitative difference and thwarts the attempt to determine which textual events are more important, and which are less. This problem has generated considerable unease among Sebald's critics, particularly in relation to the proximity of a description of the death of millions of herring, and a photograph of Jewish corpses at Buchenwald (RS 56–62/73–80). For Fuchs, the *tertium comparationis* is a utilitarian biopolitics that categorises life according to its usefulness (2006b: 173). Öhlschläger (2006b) notes that the juxtaposition is also sustained by verbal formulations that refer to the herring, but evoke the fate of the Jews, which creates a mysterious or puzzling coincidence. She ultimately sees Sebald's technique, here as elsewhere, in terms of the pre-rational activity of the *bricoleur* that constitutes part of Sebald's critique of rational civilisation. These are certainly apposite comments, but they skirt round what is perhaps the key issue, namely the fact that the text itself offers no criteria according to which either of these events – the killing of the herring for food and the murder of the Jews – can be privileged over the other.

This aspect of *The Rings of Saturn*'s narrative form hints at a profound crisis in the ethics of representation. What Fuchs calls Sebald's 'ethical commitment to the victims of history' (Fuchs 2004a: 39) begins to look like a meaningless gesture in a text that cannot differentiate between the murder of the Jews and industrial trawling for herring. It is this narrative technique of *The Rings of Saturn* that lends the text its particular historical pessimism, prior to and independently of any explicitly articulated metaphysics of history that it may contain, for it demonstrates that history can be understood only in terms of repeating patterns of folly, greed and destruction. This is not, however, the only reason for the text's pessimism. The narrator's repeated attempts to restore semantic density to the spaces he visits go hand in hand with a homogenisation of time produced by constructing equivalences between narrative events, and this technique represents the moment when modernity returns to haunt a text that, in its ambulatory thematics and its digressive poetics, had sought ways of resisting modernity. For as we have seen, both modernity and the archive are dominated by the power to produce equivalences, and equivalence is the structuring principle of *The Rings of Saturn*. It is this, incidentally, that differentiates Sebald's text from other disgressive narratives in the tradition of Laurence Sterne, and from other travel narratives in which the journey itself functions as a thread that unifies otherwise unrelated anecdotes of encounters with the strange or other. What makes *The Rings of Saturn* a specifically modern text is its archival structure, which instals a salient technology of modernity in the very fabric of the narrative.

THE SENSE OF AN ENDING

The narrator's recuperation by modernity can also be witnessed at other levels of the text. The problem is that neither walking nor narrative can go on for ever; they have to end somewhere. *The Rings of Saturn* strives desperately to avoid coming to an end, for even when the narrator reaches the cemetery at Ditchingham, he claims that this was only 'beinahe die letzte Station meiner Reise durch die Grafschaft Suffolk' ('*almost* the last stop on his journey through Suffolk') (RS 361/310),[20] and sets off anew out of Ditchingham towards Norwich, to a pub called The Mermaid. It is from here that he phones the shadowy 'Clara' for a lift home. And while the narrator himself never actually gets 'home', the narrative itself does finally reach a home of sorts, for 'Heimat' is the last word of the German text. It is, admittedly a lost 'Heimat', the one left behind by the departing souls of the dead, and so at the very moment of its ending, the book seeks to figure arrival in terms of a new departure.[21] But the text, like the narrator's walk, ends. Ultimately, then, the digressive narrative, the narrative that entails a 'stepping away from', can only be conceived in relation to that from which it steps away and to which it is therefore inevitably sutured. Digressivity, in other words, can never fully detach itself from linearity.

Likewise, the narrator's leisurely and aimless walking remains reliant upon the very forces of modernity against which it protests. His 'English Pilgrimage' is flanked at both ends by emblematic communications technologies of modernity: he travels from Norwich to Lowestoft in a train, and returns to Norwich after using the telephone to summon a lift home in a car.[22] The train trip to Lowestoft, in particular, foregrounds all the aspects of train travel that makes it quintessentially modern. The train itself is 'grimed with oil and soot up to the windows' with threadbare, mauve-upholstered seats, and is full of silent passengers sitting as far from each other as possible and all facing the direction of travel (RS 29/41). The downhill slope allows the unsteady carriage to freewheel most of the time. 'At intervals, though,' adds the narrator, 'when the gears engaged with a jolt that rocked the entire framework, the grinding of cog wheels could be heard for a while, till, with a more even pounding, the onward roll resumed' (RS 29/41). What follows is an enumeration of the sights visible from the window of the train: backyards, allotment colonies, piles of rubble, storage yards. As the locomotive pulls away after depositing the narrator at his station, it trails a plume of black smoke. This short passage reads like a disenchanted recapitulation of the anxieties surrounding rail travel when it became widespread in the mid-nineteenth century. The industrial nature of railway travel effectively turned passengers into parcels. For decades, first- and second-class carriages were opulently furnished precisely in order to create the illusion that this was not the case. But in Sebald's train, the worn upholstery no longer fulfils this function, and the soot and oil on the windows foreground the industrial nature of the conveyance. This is emphasised, too, by the lack of communication between passengers. Rail travel is anonymous, and the face-to-face layout of railway carriages was recognised at an early stage as an attempt to force passengers into a communicative situation even when they had no social reason to communicate. The experience is fraught, moreover, with danger and shock: the train itself is unstable, and is given to sudden convulsive shudders, jolting the passengers and making them further aware of the machinery that carries them along. In the nineteenth century, trains were regarded by many as pathogenic, causing (amongst other ailments) railway spine and hysterical disorders. Finally, the listing of sights without integrating them into an overall context is typical of the way in which rail travel was deemed to reconfigure the perceptions of the traveller. Railways destroyed the physical contact between traveller and landscape, and reconstituted the former as a distanced spectator. As a result, the landscape itself was no longer perceptible as a totality but became reduced to a series of isolated fragments.

The narrator steps away from this modernity at the beginning of the text when he alights at Somerleyton Hall, and is reabsorbed by it at the end; his resistance remains an interlude. It is, furthermore, an interlude whose structure relies on archival logic and the accumulation of equivalences. Thus both the narrator and his narrative are ultimately beholden to the very forces of modernity that they seek to resist.

These considerations allow us to understand Sebald's melancholy in ways that go beyond merely noting the existence of the 'melancholy mood' that pervades his writings. Firstly, it allows us to historicise this melancholy as arising from the particular conditions of modernity in which any sense of subjective autonomy or authenticity is jeopardised by the technological innovations of modernity symbolised by the train, and the structures of disciplinary power that are so nicely illustrated by the Ordnance Survey map with which I began. While autonomy is asserted by emphasising embodied subjectivity and by rejecting modern modes of transport and itineraries in favour of goalless walking, the narrator calls upon modernity's emblematic communications technologies once his walk is finished. Secondly, my account allows us to locate this melancholy in the very narrative fabric of the text. Digressivity can be prevented from degenerating into complete incoherence only by being organised archivally according to paradigmatic relations of equivalence. Furthermore, it finally has to give way to the need for narrative to have a sense of an ending, to return to the linearity from which it constantly strives to deviate and thereby to align itself with the demands or constraints of cultural order. From the desire to resist modernity and the simultaneous realisation that this desire is destined to be forever unfulfilled – however long the narrator's pilgrimage and narrative digression may defer this acknowledgment – stems the melancholy that constitutes, perhaps, Sebald's most recognisable signature.

NOTES

1. As J. B. Harley points out (1988: 306), the military never specify the criteria according to which installations are omitted from maps. This additional level of secrecy makes the paranoia of Shingle Street residents all the more comprehensible.
2. On the unfalsifiability of conspiracy theories, see Knight 2000.
3. Interestingly, Ordnance Survey maps also reinforce the ascendancy of the car over the train, with roads mapped significantly wider than scale would dictate and in varying colours depending on the quality of the road, while railways are represented by merely a thin black line.
4. Tourism can, of course, be seen as a mode of inefficiency or wastefulness that is both sanctioned and recuperated by capitalism. As we will see, Sebald's narrator seeks to elude even such licensed kinds of inefficiency.
5. Massimo Leone offers a similar argument with regard to the numerous points at which Sebald's narrators and protagonists are overcome by vertigo, and can counteract this sense of disequilibrium only through writing (2004: 91–7).
6. Claudia Öhlschläger notes the context-dependent and provisional nature of knowledge in *The Rings of Saturn*, and relates it to Sebald's critique of post-Enlightenment

civilisation. But she reads the text in terms of a poetics of *bricolage* rather than a concern with the body (2006b: 197).

7. 'The Undiscover'd Country' is the title of one of Sebald's essays on Kafka, in which he traces the motif of death in *The Castle*. See Sebald 1972.

8. These projections of meaning into the ruins of Orfordness have been discussed by Simon Ward 2004: 60–1.

9. Fuchs 2006b: 173; see also Fuchs 2004a: 210–15.

10. A similar point is made by Peter C. Pfeiffer, who is concerned with the opposition of art and science. Both, he argues, erase corporeality, but by representing the destruction of the body, art also makes it visible as the site of individual experience and suffering (2003: 238–9). In his passing reference to modernity, however, Pfeiffer tends to equate it with science, rather than seeing science as one aspect of a wider question concerning the body in modernity.

11. I am, of course, not the first critic to point this out. See, for example, Zilcosky 2004: 104–11 and Albes 2002: 288.

12. Seen in this light, the narrator's walking forms part of a pervasive celebration, in *The Rings of Saturn*, of the anti-disciplinary and unsystematic. In an interview, Sebald contrasts the serendipitous discoveries and unsystematic searching facilitated by walking with the systematic imperatives of academic research (Cuomo 2001). *The Rings of Saturn* evinces an obsession with characters whose labour is totally unproductive in economic terms: Swinburne's reading and writing (RS 165/198), Michael Hamburger's collecting worthless things such as used envelopes and shells (RS 184/219–20), the Ashburys' attempts to run a bed-and-breakfast establishment that fails to attract a customer for a decade (RS 220/262), Edmund Ashbury's building a boat that will never be launched, his sisters' efforts at patchwork that are always unpicked a day or two after completion (RS 211/251–2), and Thomas Abrams' neglect of his farm in favour of modelmaking (RS 244/290). Michael Parkinson is celebrated as a paradigmatic anti-consumer who wears the same clothes for years on end and repairs rather than replaces them (RS 5–6/14–15). Ruth Franklin (2006) has addressed this aspect of Sebald's work, though her analysis is undifferentiated and overstates the case by claiming that *all* of Sebald's works evince an amateur and anti-disciplinary approach to knowledge.

13. It is worth noting that in his book *Loiterature*, Ross Chambers implies that the digressive narrative is fundamentally anti-Cartesian: 'What makes digression a pleasurable experience is the relaxation of vigilance, the abandonment of discipline that becomes associated . . . with the way the body impinges on (or detracts from) the activities of the mind' (1998: 12). This is, of course, fully congruent with the argument offered here.

14. Citing Roman Ingarden, McHale points out the ontological duality on which metaphor relies (1987: 134). *Pace* Jan-Henrik Witthaus' Freudian reading of the sea-monster episode (2006), then, the narrator's experience of the copulating couple is not entirely displaced by the metaphor to which it gives rise. For whether one takes a semantic or cognitive approach, metaphor depends on the perception of both terms of the substitution.

15. For a deconstructive approach to Sebald's poetics of enumeration, see Ceuppens 2006a. Pfeiffer sees inventories and other forms of what he calls 'semantic abundance' as possessing an ethical function in that they represent the physical presence of embodiment within the hybrid text. He notes, too, that they retard the progress of the narrative, but does not say why this might be significant (2003: 239, 231).

16. Santner 2006: 57. Santner talks of 'past suffering', but this seems to me to be too narrow a definition of the presence of the past in the material world that Santner identifies as central to Sebald's work.

17. On these issues, see Huyssen 1988.
18. Markus Nölp sees *The Rings of Saturn* as part of a 'tradition' of photographically illustrated writing, and briefly discusses Breton's text (2001: 132–3). Sebald's relationship to the historical avant-garde remains one of the glaring gaps in Sebald research.
19. As we have seen above, however, metaphor often plays a role here, too.
20. The translation omits the word '*beinahe*' ('nearly'), which I have restored in my paraphrase.
21. As Gregory-Guider has shown, this is a pervasive pattern in Sebald's texts (2005: 446).
22. See Kern 1983: 69–70 and 214–16 for the impact of the telephone and 113–14 for his comments on the automobile. On trains, see Schivelbusch 2004. It may be objected that in our post-modern world of intercontinental air travel, mobile phones, the internet and the slick comfort of the Eurostar, a shoddy diesel train on a rural branch line and a pub telephone are more like quaint relics of a past that already feels distant. Nevertheless, trains and the telephone remain powerful emblems of modernity in the Western cultural imaginary. In particular, railways have been extensively represented in various media that seek to articulate the ambivalences of modernity, including Turner's *Rain, Wind and Speed*, the numerous impressionist canvasses of Parisian stations, commercial art, various strands of photography, cinema and documentary film. In the Conclusion, I address the question of why Sebald foregrounds the persistence of earlier forms of modernity in the contemporary world.

8

THE ARCHIVAL SUBJECT: *AUSTERLITZ*

W. G. Sebald's last completed prose text, *Austerlitz*, contains the author's most extensive exploration of the archive. We have seen in previous chapters how zoos, entomological collections, libraries, maps and various forms of photography are extensively thematised in the text. We have also seen that Sebald is interested in the 'archival consciousness' of the modern subject, and he pursues this investigation to its probable extreme in *Austerlitz*.

On the face of it, *Austerlitz* is a far more conventional text than Sebald's earlier prose works. Reviewers noted that for the first time Sebald had actually written a novel.[1] John Zilcosky argues that *Austerlitz* is more like a 'real novel' because it de-emphasises the confusion of memoir and fiction that had characterised Sebald's earlier prose. Zilcosky reaches this conclusion partly on the basis of the photographs. While these had been mostly authentic in *The Emigrants*, only half of the images in *Austerlitz* testify to the real-life models on whom Austerlitz is based. Furthermore, Zilcosky continues, they are neatly integrated into the novel's fictional framework through the device of having Jacques Austerlitz carry a camera with him, which robs them of their capacity to alienate the reader (2006: 687). This, however, could equally be seen as a profoundly disorientating technique: the photographs, which must have been taken by somebody in the 'real world', are deemed to have been produced by a character who is fictional. The name 'Jacques Austerlitz' has no extra-textual referent, whereas the photographs do, in a double sense: they are indexical traces of both the objects they depict and the hand or apparatus that took them. In this light, the photographs in *Austerlitz* can be seen as contributing to a profound ontological confusion that is only inadequately concealed by the text's narrative devices. The potential for reader alienation that this entails is at least as powerful as in Sebald's earlier prose works. Unlike *Vertigo*, *The Emigrants* and *The Rings of Saturn*, however, *Austerlitz* concentrates largely on the fate of a single character. His biographical trajectory provides the book with a plot which, however fragmentary and however concerned with questions of its own mediation, structures the text almost from beginning to end and renders it more conventionally novelistic. It is on such structural grounds, and not on any putative ontological grounds relating to the 'fictionality' of *Austerlitz* as opposed to the hybrid nature of Sebald's earlier works, that the novelistic qualities of the text rest.

In the course of numerous meetings, which occur by chance as well as by appointment, the narrator of the text slowly learns the history of the eponymous protagonist, Jacques Austerlitz. When the two of them first meet in the *Salle des pas perdus*, the cavernous waiting room of Antwerp Central Station, in June 1967, Austerlitz is an architectural historian working at a university in London and researching the architecture of what he calls the 'capitalist era' (A 44/48) and the 'bourgeois age' (A 197/201) – by which he primarily means the second half of the nineteenth century. As befits a scholar of architecture, his early encounters with the narrator are dominated by his divagations on buildings: Antwerp station (A 8–14/12–18), but also the Palais de Justice in Brussels (A 38–40/42–5), and the various fortresses that are scattered across the Belgian landscape and all over Europe (A 17–23/21–7).

These monologues are signalled by the narrator as particularly unusual. As a seasoned traveller, he has found that:

> solitary travellers, who so often pass days on end in uninterrupted silence, are glad to be spoken to. Now and then they are even ready to open up to a stranger unreservedly on such occasions, although that was not the case with Austerlitz in the *Salle des pas perdus*, nor did he subsequently tell me very much about his origins and his own life. (A 7–8/11–12)

The original German of this passage includes the words 'in der Regel': solitary travellers are, *as a rule*, grateful when you speak to them. This draws attention to what is at stake in this seemingly unobtrusive comment: it establishes a behavioural norm against which Austerlitz's conduct appears slightly peculiar. As Roland Barthes shows in his book *S/Z*, this technique is common in nineteenth-century fiction, particularly the work of Balzac. Barthes reads such aphoristic generalisations as part of what he calls the 'referential code', which consists of a set of assumptions held by the narrator (and by implication also the reader), and which create the illusion, within the text, of reference to external reality

(1970: 211). Maxims or gnomic sayings – supposedly carrying received wisdom – are coined in order to lend plausibility to the psychology and behaviour of characters. It is a device that is seldom used in Sebald's work. One of the few examples, which occurs at the beginning of 'All'estero' in *Vertigo*, offers a particularly transparent illustration of how the device works. To explain his reaction to a series of failed telephone calls, the narrator writes: 'There is something peculiarly dispiriting about the emptiness that wells up when, in a strange city, one dials the same telephone numbers in vain' (V 35/43).[2] The phrase 'the emptiness that wells up when . . .' is the classic formulation, cognates of which can be found everywhere in Balzac. It is so powerful because it presents what is ultimately an arbitrary claim as perfectly natural. If we were to ask 'What emptiness?' the only response would be '*That* emptiness, of course.' By a rhetorical sleight of hand, the structure of the sentence presents its proposition as a presupposition, and in so doing seeks to conceal the ontological gap between the text and the world.

In the case of *Austerlitz*, the function is the same. The assumed norm is gratitude on the part of the traveller towards the person who speaks to him or her, and a willingness to divulge intimate details to a stranger. Austerlitz, on the other hand, does not explicitly demonstrate the former emotion, and fails to conform to the latter expectation. In other words, Austerlitz's behaviour at this point is not entirely comprehensible according to the assumptions of the text. Beyond stressing Austerlitz's atypical nature, then, the passage appears to raise a question that will be the structuring enigma of the narrative: what are the reasons for this atypical behaviour? And will Austerlitz ever 'open up unreservedly' to the narrator, revealing an inner life that is concealed by his refusal to talk about anything other than architecture? The fact that such an opening-up fails to materialise 'subsequently' suggests that these questions will remain unanswered, but we have already learned by this point in the text that Austerlitz and the narrator do meet again in the winter of 1996. This comment, made in a subordinate clause that brackets the time of the Antwerp encounter with 1996 *and* the narrative present, hints towards the chance meeting in the bar of the Great Eastern Hotel that will allow the narrator to renew his acquaintance with Austerlitz after a gap of twenty years, to learn the story of Austerlitz's past and the means by which he was able to reconstruct it. This in turn instals a further expectation that the remainder of the narrative will indeed resolve the enigmas implicitly created by Austerlitz's strange conduct during the early years of his friendship with the narrator. Such structures of enigma and resolution constitute what Barthes terms the 'hermeneutic code' of narrative, and are responsible for guiding the reading of the text through time from beginning to end. They are also the device on which *Austerlitz*'s status as a novelistic text depends. If the tradition of the European novel is sustained by the interplay of psychological and socio-historical factors in the formation of the subject, as Martin

Swales argues (2004: 24), we might also expect the narrative to present the development of Austerlitz as a psychological entity, who reveals a rich inner life that for one reason or another was not communicable at the time of his first meeting with the narrator. In reality, however, the matter is more complex and more ambiguous.

The Archive as Substitute Memory

The foundational moment of Jacques Austerlitz's life-*story* is not the moment of his birth or even that of his separation from his parents, but rather several acts of archival destruction perpetrated by the German Luftwaffe during the Blitz and by Austerlitz's guardian Emyr Elias. Even Austerlitz's revered history teacher, André Hilary, who has published articles in scholarly journals (A 103/107) and is thus likely to have been trained in archival research, is unable to unearth any information about Austerlitz's past. Elias has already sunk into a state of vegetative inanity by the time Austerlitz is enlightened as to his real name, and is therefore unable to respond to his son's questions (A 92/96). Upon his death in 1954, moreover, it emerges that he has obliterated all traces of Austerlitz's origins (A 105/109). Public archives prove equally unhelpful. The Welsh social services and the Foreign Office possess no documentation pertaining to Austerlitz's past, while the Aid Committee responsible for organising the transports of Jewish children from occupied Czechoslovakia lost most of its papers during several evacuations necessitated by the German air-raids on London (A 202/206). The sudden loss of identity that the protagonist experiences when Penrith-Smith invites him into his study and announces to the schoolboy that his real name is not Dafydd Elias but Jacques Austerlitz is figured in the first instance as an archival lack.

This external absence precedes any sense on Austerlitz's part of an internal mnemic void. The way in which Austerlitz seeks to compensate for this void emerges during one of the narrator's visits to Austerlitz's house in Alderney Street, East London. Austerlitz delivers a long monologue in which he links what the narrator calls 'his astonishing professional expertise' (A 8/12) to a strategic attempt to inure himself against things that might remind him of his own past:

> As far as I was concerned, the world ended in the late nineteenth century. I dared go no further than that, although in fact the whole history of the architecture and civilization of the bourgeois age, the subject of my research, pointed in the direction of the catastrophic events already casting their shadow before them at the time. I did not read newspapers because, as I now know, I feared unwelcome revelations, I turned on the radio only at certain hours of the day, I was always refining my defensive reactions, creating a kind of quarantine or immune system which, as I maintained my existence in a smaller and smaller space, protected me

from anything that could be connected in any way, however distant, with my own early history. Moreover, I had constantly been preoccupied by that accumulation of knowledge which I had pursued for decades, and which served as a substitute or compensatory memory. (A 197–8/201–2)

This passage is of vital importance for an understanding of *Austerlitz*. The last sentence, in particular, is much-quoted by Sebald's critics as though it were a kind of key to the psychodrama of the text. It is an admission on Austerlitz's part that he has had no inner life, that his self is composed of nothing but book learning, acquired knowledge that he has accumulated in archival fashion.

Austerlitz's knowledge is archival in several respects. Firstly, it is motivated by a desire for totality and complete systematisation. Such a fantasy of comprehensive knowledge, argues Thomas Richards, was one of the pillars supporting the archival epistemology of the nineteenth century. Knowledge was deemed to be 'singular and not plural, complete and not partial, global and not local, that all knowledges would ultimately turn out to be concordant in one great system of knowledge' (1996: 7). These epistemological assumptions emerge when Austerlitz sets out some of the plans he has for publishing his work, which include a multi-volume systematic-descriptive work, and a series of thematic essays dealing not only with prison architecture and secular temples, but also hydrotherapy, zoos, hygiene and sanitation, arrival and departure, light and shadow, gas and steam, and other things that he does not list but which are 'similar' (A 170/174).[3] Secondly, the way in which the knowledge is arranged stresses the principle of equivalence. In an early description of his studies, Austerlitz speaks of the 'family resemblances' that obtain between the civic buildings that typify the nineteenth-century city: courts and prisons, stations, stock exchanges, opera houses and asylums, and the grid-based housing schemes constructed for industrial workers (A 44/48).[4] 'Resemblance' is the key word, since it establishes metaphorical relations between these various architectural structures. Thirdly, Austerlitz's notes remain in a state of propaedeutic incompletion (cf. Fuchs 2004a: 44). Despite the various forms in which he hopes to cast his study, it never materialises as narrative, exposition or argument. Instead, he is left with piles of notes and box files crammed into his tiny office so that the latter resembles a 'stock-room of books and papers' (A 43/47). As the photograph that accompanies this description shows, Austerlitz's research produces nothing but an archive that awaits in vain its transformation into history.[5] Just as the *The Rings of Saturn* contains a photograph of a maze that the narrator recognises in a dream to be a cross-section through his own brain (RS 173/206), so the image of the office in *Austerlitz* is a spatial analogue for the structure of Austerlitz's mind.

The archive does not, however, only compensate for memory. It also functions as a substitute for the present, as shown by Austerlitz's working methods during his time in Paris in the late 1950s. He would sit in the old Bibliothèque Nationale in the Rue Richelieu and pore over books, pursuing footnoted references to other books, following up the footnotes contained in these books, and so on, in a process of infinite regress that takes him further and further away from the scholarly description of reality into a network of never-ending ramifications (A 363/367). Thus while it is driven by a desire for totality and comprehensiveness – Mary Ann Doane's 'archival desire' of modernity – the archive becomes a self-generating, self-referential system that entails a perpetual deferral of the moment of completion. This in turn has implications for archival temporality. As Derrida notes in *Archive Fever*, the archive is both a recording of the past and a promise of a future (1995: 29). 'If we want to know what [the archive] will have meant,' he writes, 'we will only know in times to come' (36). The archivist merely 'produces more archive, and that is why the archive is never closed. It opens out onto the future' (68).[6] On this reading, the temporal structure of the archive facilitates the elision of all that intervenes between the recorded past and the projected future towards which the archivist is perpetually impelled. In Austerlitz's case, the elision includes the recent past and present of his own life.

It is thus not the case that Austerlitz's project is a fundamentally historicist enterprise that is in thrall to homogeneous empty time and serves to screen the 'differential, discontinuous, and dislocated nature of modernity' by re-establishing 'continuity between past and present in an abstract and chronological form', as Richard Crownshaw argues (2004: 218). It involves, rather, a highly discontinuous mode of temporality that is diametrically opposed to the homogenising impulses that Crownshaw attributes to historicism. Indeed, Austerlitz's substitution of scholarship for memory forms part of his wider efforts to resist the power of linear time by stressing the radically relative nature of temporality.[7] One form this relativism takes is an acknowledgment of various kinds of personal or subjective time, measured by purely internal means rather than the external movements of the clock (A 143/147). Whereas Austerlitz claims that 'a certain degree of personal misfortune is enough to cut us off from the past and future' (A 143/147), however, the past and the future are not really Austerlitz's problem. For his own practice of replacing memory with archival knowledge reveals a structure of temporality in which movement towards the future involves the increasing accumulation of the more distant past, while the present and recent past remain occluded. For Austerlitz, let us recall, the world ends in the late nineteenth century.

Austerlitz's project, then, and the subjectivity that it subtends, are structured around a temporal lacuna in which the truth of Austerlitz's life is assumed to reside. This lacuna also constitutes a textual *Leerstelle*, generating the narrative desire that motivates both the telling and the reading of the tale.[8] The technology by means of which the gap is filled is the confession. This is explicitly signalled when the narrator encounters Austerlitz in the bar of the Great Eastern Hotel in late 1996:

> Oddly enough, said Austerlitz . . . he had been thinking of our encounters in Belgium, so long ago now, and telling himself he must find someone to whom he could relate his own story, a story which he had learned only in the last few years and for which he needed the kind of listener I had once been in Antwerp, Liège and Zeebrugge. (A 59–60/64)

Austerlitz claims that a compelling logic has led the two men to each other again, and singles the narrator out to be the recipient of his tale. As we saw in the Introduction, Foucault sees confession as a fundamental aspect of the production of modern subjectivity and a technology for the enunciation of individual truth. The confessional situation in *Austerlitz*, however, already hints that the power relations inherent in the Foucauldean confession do not fully obtain in this text, for the confessor is placed in that position by the person confessing, rather than occupying a socially or institutionally sanctioned position of hermeneutic authority. The question of individual truth, too, emerges as highly problematic.

AUSTERLITZ'S CONFESSION

When the narrator and Austerlitz meet in the Great Eastern Hotel, Austerlitz makes a few preliminary comments on the tour of the hotel that he has just completed, seeming to fall into precisely the same kind of scholarly monologue that dominated his earlier acquaintance with the narrator. But then he announces that he has found things out about his own life that require narration, and begins his narrative as follows:

> Since my childhood and youth . . . I have never known who I really was. From where I stand now, of course, I can see that my name alone, and the fact that it was kept from me until my fifteenth year, ought to have put me on the track of my origins, but it has also become clear to me of late why an agency greater than or superior to my own capacity for thought, which circumspectly directs operations somewhere in my brain, has always preserved me from my own secret, systematically preventing me from drawing the obvious conclusions and embarking on the inquiries they would have suggested to me. It hasn't been easy to make my way out of my own inhibitions, and it will not be easy now to put the story into anything like proper order. (A 60–1/64–5)

This is a fascinating passage. It ostensibly promises a revelation of all that Austerlitz withheld from the narrator during their earlier friendship, the implication being that Austerlitz *does* now know who he really is because he has undertaken enquiries that have allowed him to trace his origins and uncover his own secret. The passage asks to be read in terms of a Freudian pattern of repression and return, a reading that is supported by Austerlitz's later use of the very same Freudian terminology that we witnessed in 'Max Ferber': the words 'heimsuchen' and 'Zwangsvorstellung' occur in adjacent sentences in *Austerlitz*, though the Freudian allusion is lost in translation, particularly in the case of the latter term, which appears as an 'idea that had obsessed me' rather than a 'compulsive' image or conviction (A 316/320). Furthermore, the notion of a power that functions inside Austerlitz's psyche without his participation or explicit allegiance bears more than a passing resemblance to the Freudian censor, which regulates the traffic of psychical content between the unconscious and conscious.[9]

The suggestion that *Austerlitz* is a novel that dramatises the return of the repressed, however, implies that the past will be brought to light from Austerlitz's unconscious. In other words, traces of the past have been deposited somewhere within the psyche and they can, under propitious circumstances, be recuperated. There are moments in the text where such buried, unconscious memory traces emerge into consciousness. On the cusp of sleep, the young Austerlitz frequently experiences fugitive visions of his mother leaning over him or his father putting on his hat and smiling (A 62/66). He hallucinates images of a bygone age when returning from his nocturnal wanderings through London:

> a squadron of yachts putting out into the shadows over the sea from the glittering Thames estuary in the evening light, a horse-drawn cab in Spitalfields driven by a man in a top hat, a woman wearing the costume of the 1930s and casting her eyes down as she passed me by. (A 180/184)

On two occasions, things that Austerlitz sees during his visit to Prague and on the train journey across Europe suddenly explain certain affective experiences that had hitherto been mysterious. On beholding a vista of windflowers covering the floor of a ravine planted with yew trees, Austerlitz suddenly understands why he had been struck dumb by a similar sight in the grounds of a stately home in Gloucestershire (A 231/235). An analogous moment occurs when the protagonist sees the Mäuseturm emerging from the Rhine, which immediately explains the uncanny impression made on him by the tower in the Vyrnwy reservoir (A 317/321). There are sections detailing Austerlitz's gradual loss and then rapid and almost miraculous rediscovery of his mother tongue. He imagines the slow death of Czech within him, describing its lingering presence as something that has been shut away but nevertheless makes itself felt as a kind of scratching or knocking (A 195/199). At his first meeting with his childhood nanny Vera, though, everything returns and he is able to converse with her fluently in Czech (A 219/223). Since both Vera and Austerlitz are also fluent French speakers, this passage exceeds mere narrative expediency, and implies a purely internal mechanism of memory. Listening to Vera's descriptions of the back yard into which Austerlitz had often gazed as a boy, the latter comments that these images, which had been 'deeply buried and locked away' within him, now came luminously to mind (A 221/225).

The significance of these episodes and the model of memory they imply can be seen with particular clarity in the section of *Austerlitz* that deals with the protagonist's visit to Prague. On returning to the city, walking through the narrow alleyways, and feeling the uneven paving stones underfoot, Austerlitz feels as though he has already walked these streets, his memories revealing themselves to him not through conscious effort, but spontaneously through his reawakening senses (A 212/216). This passage is one of the few genuinely Proustian moments in Sebald's text, and in its explicit contrasting of voluntary and involuntary memory is clearly marked as a kind of Proustian citation. Furthermore, the 'uneven paving' is an allusion to the Venice episode of *Le temps retrouvé*, the final volume of Proust's monumental novel *A la recherche du temps perdu*. As he is entering the Hôtel de Guermantes, Proust's narrator jumps to one side to avoid being hit by a carriage passing through the *porte cochère*. He stumbles, and when he regains his balance, he finds himself standing on uneven paving stones in the courtyard. His bodily pose recalls a similar posture in the Baptistry of San Marco, and his experiences in Venice are immediately rematerialised (Proust 1954: 866–7).[10] The implication of Proust's *mémoire involontaire* is that somatosensory memory is both more powerful and more authentic than voluntary memory, with its reliance on semiosis and all the possibilities of rationalisation, instrumentalisation, and slippage that this entails. The crooked paving stones of Prague emphasise the privileged status of moments of sensory or pre-rational recall that bypass conscious mental efforts at recollection.

Richard Terdiman reads the theory of *mémoire involontaire* as an attempt to restabilise a self that is perceived as compromised and inauthentic:

> Whatever its significance in aesthetic or affective registers may be, 'involuntary memory' is Proust's candidate to serve as the epistemological discovery mechanism that might put a stop to such slippages [as are involved in semiosis], and distinguish the true from the counterfeit. (1993: 209)

The same can be said, of course, of the Freudian unconscious. The entire enterprise of interpreting dreams, Freudian slips, hysterical symptoms and so on, was to reconstruct the truth that was concealed by the insidious ruses of the censor and the conscious mind. Thus despite the significant differences between Freud and Proust's models of memory, there is a sense in which they fulfil the same cultural function. The conspicuous allusions to both writers in *Austerlitz*, furthermore, seem governed by precisely the same desire for the retrieval of an authentic self.

This reading of the text is encouraged by the leitmotif of the false world or false life, which pervades the text. The German terms 'falsche Welt' and 'falsches Leben' are variably translated in the English version of *Austerlitz*. The racoon whose behaviour attracts the narrator's attention in the Antwerp Nocturama is described as having arrived in an 'unreal world' (A 3/7), Vera notes that the Nazi invasion and the sudden decree that all cars should drive on the right plunged the inhabitants of Prague into a 'world turned upside down' (A 243/247), while Austerlitz feels that he has somehow taken a wrong turning and ended up 'living the wrong life' (A 298/302), and hopes that his decision to move to Paris to continue his search for his father will release him from 'the false pretences of his English life' (A 354/357). While each of these translations is possible and plausible in context, it is not only the repetition of the German phrases 'falsche Welt' and 'falsches Leben' that thereby disappears, but also the allusion to section 18 of Theodor W. Adorno's *Minima Moralia*, the closing sentence of which reads: 'Es gibt kein richtiges Leben im falschen' (2003: 43). Adorno's sentence is not unambiguous, but is perhaps best translated as: 'It is impossible to live an authentic life in a world that precludes authenticity'. The word 'falsch' in Sebald's text, then, is concerned less with unreality, pretence and being turned upside-down, than with the possibility of authentic subjectivity. For Adorno, inauthenticity was not a temporary and contingent condition, but rather a permanent state brought about by technological modernity, of which the allied bombings of German cities and the concentration camps were but the instruments. The way in which the terms 'falsche Welt' and 'falsches Leben' are used in *Austerlitz*, on the other hand, ostensibly assumes that the one can find one's way back to a life and a world that are not 'falsch', that inauthenticity is produced by a specific historical or personal caesura which, once identified, can be overcome in a return to the *status quo ante*.

The authenticity that the moments of *mémoire involontaire*, the return of repressed memories, and the notion of the *'falsche Welt'* seem to promise is set up in opposition to the archive. Uncovering the buried past will fill the void produced on the one hand by the destruction of the archives that could have provided information about Austerlitz's childhood, and on the other by Austerlitz's accumulation of archival knowledge, whose temporality, as we have seen, facilitates an elision of the present and recent past. The problem, however, is that the spontaneous emergence of 'internal' memories, discussed above, is so sporadic, and the memories themselves so scanty, that they cannot provide a sufficient resource if Austerlitz is to make good the twofold archival lack that has hitherto constituted his subjectivity. He is thus driven back to precisely the place he seeks to transcend: the archive.

From almost the precise mid-point of *Austerlitz*, the text is structured around a series of visits to archives by means of which Jacques Austerlitz hopes to reconstruct his past and retrieve his putatively buried memories. He experiences an auspicious start to his investigations, for unlike the lost archives in Britain, the Czech state archives contain complete records of the population of Prague between 1934 and 1939 (A 209/213). The archive building itself is reminiscent not only of the prison architecture of Austerlitz's beloved 'bourgeois epoch' (A 204/208) but also of a monastery, a riding school, an opera house and an insane asylum (A 205/209). It is thus a building that presents a syncretic meld of all the disciplinary institutions that have fascinated Austerlitz throughout his academic career, while also being itself a disciplinary apparatus which, as we saw in the case of Theresienstadt, its file room, and its obsessively regular censuses (Chapter 4), facilitated the exercise of power by precisely registering the position of bodies in space.[11] If this kind of archival practice was an enabling condition of genocide, however, it is also the means by which Austerlitz is able to rediscover the residence in which he grew up and in which Vera, his former nanny and present source of information, still resides. What Austerlitz seems to move towards here, then, is a differentiated understanding of the archive that foregrounds its role not as a political and administrative technology but as a historical source and a medium of memory.

After this implausibly easy moment of success, however, the epistemological promise of the archive is repeatedly shown to be illusory. The serendipitous emergence of two stray photographs in the pages of Vera's copy of Balzac's *Le colonel Chabert* demonstrates the capacity of artifacts to elude the usual processes of private and familial archiving which, as we saw in Chapter 6, are a fundamental component of familial identity. But even once they have come to light, the photographs fail to function as bearers of knowledge. Vera initially believes that the two figures pictured in the image of a stage set are Agáta and Maximilian, but soon realises that they are other people (A 257/261). She is able to confirm that the photograph of the young boy is indeed the five-year-old Austerlitz (A 258/262). But far from inspiring a moment of recognition or helping to dredge up buried memories, the image produces nothing but blank incomprehension in Austerlitz. Despite his studying the photograph with the aid of a magnifying glass, and paying considerable attention to the surface detail of the image, it produces no effect beyond dumb incomprehension and, later, a sensation of blind panic (A 259–60/263–4). As Carolin Duttlinger notes, scenarios of wounding or violence are projected into these images, Vera imagining an avalanche tumbling down onto the stage set, and Austerlitz conjecturing that his own arm is broken or in a splint (2004: 163–5). Duttlinger sees this as a displacement of trauma, the photograph of the boy, in particular, dramatising the belatedness characteristic of traumatic recall:

> The traumatic character of the photograph is associated with the conjunction of two temporal structures: first, the irredeemably past character of the photograph which radically separates it from the viewer and his

present context; and secondly, the arrested moment preceding the cata-strophe which will be forever preserved in its anticipation. (165)

The protagonist's alienation, as Duttlinger notes, is tied up with this photo-graphic structure of belatedness. But it is also tied up with the photograph's ineluctable exteriority. Austerlitz's gaze is repeatedly arrested by the surface materiality of the photograph. Unlike the narrator and his interlocutors in *The Emigrants*, he cannot narrativise the image in a way that sutures the external mnemotechnical supplement to the workings of a putatively internal, sponta-neous memory. As has been shown in previous chapters, the photograph's indexical status allows it to function in numerous institutional contexts as the token and proof of identity. But on being presented with the photographic image of himself as the Rose Queen's page, Austerlitz's failure of recognition produces a uniquely powerful sense that he has no place in reality; indeed, that he does not exist (A 261/265).

This process is repeated in Austerlitz's other archival endeavours. His visit to the museum in Theresienstadt, for example, is fraught with an epistemological ambiguity. On the one hand, this visit makes good Austerlitz's previous omis-sions, in the sense that the gaps in his knowledge of European history and geog-raphy are filled in by what he learns about the German Reich and the systematic exploitation and murder of the Jews (A 278–9/282–3). Yet Austerlitz remarks: 'I understood it all now, yet I did not understand it, for every detail that was revealed to me as I went through the museum from room to room and back again, ignorant as I feared I had been through my own fault, far exceeded my comprehension' (A 279/283). When he later reads H. G. Adler's monumental history of the ghetto (Adler 2005), which is itself a quasi-archival account of ghetto life, he notes that despite the vast quantity of empirical detail contained in Adler's report, there is something incomprehensible and unreal about the ghetto system (A 331/335). This is far more than a token deference to the view that despite a huge quantity of historical and philosophical scholarship, the Holocaust will always elude final explanation or comprehension. It also beto-kens the fact that the knowledge Austerlitz desires precludes internalisation, or, to put it another way, Austerlitz will always be shut out from the knowledge he seeks. This is, I think, the meaning of the photographs of the closed doors of Theresienstadt reproduced in *Austerlitz* (A 268–71/272–6). Alexandra Tischel argues that these are part of a topical model of memory that permeates the text, and also represent that which cannot be shown, namely the horrors of the Holocaust (2006: 43). In contrast to the Freudian topical model of the psyche, however, the topoi in *Austerlitz* function less as a metaphor for internal memory than as a substitute for it.

This can be seen in Austerlitz's attempts to trace his mother. Having returned from Prague and Theresienstadt and read H. G. Adler's book, he is still unable to cast his mind back to the ghetto and imagine his mother there, and in order to compensate for this mnemonic and imaginative deficit, he makes considerable efforts to track down a copy of the Theresienstadt film made by the Nazis (A 342/346). As Silke Arnold-de Simine (forthcoming) notes, this film was originally to be titled *Theresienstadt: Ein Dokumentarfilm aus dem jüdischen Siedlungsgebiet* (*Theresienstadt: A Documentary Film from the Jewish Settlement Zone*), rather than *Der Führer schenkt den Juden eine Stadt* (*The Führer Gives a City to the Jews*). As she goes on to argue, the authenticity implied by the notion of a documentary is illusory, since the film was a cynically staged version of ghetto life, whose truth is revealed only once Austerlitz has obtained a slow-motion copy, which exposes the deathly nature of ghetto life. But what Austerlitz seeks in this film is evidence of his mother, which he believes he finds in a section devoted to the musical life of the ghetto. As the camera moves across the audience at a performance of Pavel Haas' *Study for String Orchestra*, he notices a young woman in the background, whom he identifies as his mother on the basis of his 'faint memories' of her (A 351/355). Vera, however, merely shakes her head and puts the image aside when Austerlitz shows it to her (A 353). It is not Agáta after all. Austerlitz's 'faint memories' have proved a chimera, as has his faith in the archival record represented by the film.

The archive is, to a certain extent, redeemed at the text's epiphanic moment, the moment when Austerlitz finally succeeds in discovering his mother's image in the theatrical archives of Prague. But what this episode dramatises once again is Austerlitz's lack of any internal memory. Like the woman in the Theresienstadt film (whom she does not resemble), this woman also seems to tally with Austerlitz's 'dim memory' of his mother. But since these dim memories have already proven entirely illusory, they can possess no authority now. On the contrary, the authority responsible for verifying the referents of the photographs lies with Vera. As Crownshaw (2004: 232) points out, the identity of Austerlitz's mother, like the identity of Chabert in Balzac's story, can be confirmed only by an act of witnessing by a third party. What Austerlitz knows is thus dependent not on what he remembers, but on what he learns from an external source. It is here, however, that the question of authenticity and reliability is destabilised even further, for Vera is herself an unreliable witness. In an earlier episode, Vera tells Austerlitz about her visit to the Reichenberg Diorama. The diorama, perfected by Louis Daguerre in the 1820s, was a mechanical apparatus that generally incorporated an immobile observer sitting on a moving platform that was rotated in order to expose the viewer to a predesigned succession of different scenes and lighting effects (see Crary 1990: 112–13). The diorama is often seen as a precursor of the cinema, but in *Austerlitz*, it comes to function as a representational device that blurs the distinction between memory images and external representations. After describing the idyllic walks that she and Austerlitz undertook before his evacuation (A 223/227), Vera details the wonders of the diorama – the Syrian desert, the Zillertal Alps, Goethe boarding a stagecoach – and then adds that these images are inseparable from the memory of her excursions with Austerlitz (A 224/228). Within the structure of witnessing, Vera is the authority to whom final appeal is made in order to verify Agáta's identity. But her status as witness is undermined by this earlier passage in which she foregrounds the tendency of her own memory images to merge with childhood recollections of visual spectacle. There is, it would appear, no entirely secure refuge from the regime of external mnemonic technologies.

Austerlitz's archival researches repeatedly lead to the same insight: the buried memories that Austerlitz hopes to retrieve fail to materialise. In pursuing himself and his mother through a series of representations – the photograph of the page, the Theresienstadt film, the theatre archive – Austerlitz continues what he has always done, which is to compensate for his lack of memory by substituting the archive for interiority. He is in the most literal sense an archival subject.[12]

The fundamental implication of this is that the boundaries between memory and postmemory become indistinguishable. As we saw in Chapter 6, postmemory occupies the middle ground between documented history on the one hand, and memory, conceived of as a primary, internal and spontaneous mode of recall, on the other. It characterises the experiences of the second and subsequent generations whose lives are dominated by traumatic experiences that preceded their birth. What we find in *Austerlitz*, on the other hand, is a subject whose access to his *own* past is gained almost exclusively by means of the classic modes of postmemorial transmission: photographs, objects, the narratives of others and 'imaginative investment and creation' (Hirsch 1997: 22). This can be seen at several points in the text. We have already seen, for example, that Austerlitz and Vera project fantasies of catastrophe and wounding into the images of the stage set and the Rose Queen's page, and that Austerlitz imagines the childhood view from Vera's flat on the basis of her stories. Such imaginative investment occurs, too, when Austerlitz bribes his way into the auditorium of the Estates Theatre and visualises the orchestra tuning up and a blue sequined shoe peeping out between the curtain and the stage (A 228/232). Far from being a secondary phenomenon that supplements the operation of memory, then, postmemory attains primacy in *Austerlitz*, while memory itself, on the few occasions where it can be said to be present at all, is shown to be largely dependent on typically postmemorial encounters with external representations.

I began this chapter with a discussion of the specifically novelistic features of *Austerlitz*, foremost among them being its greater reliance than Sebald's other texts on structures of enigma and resolution. The question that the text implicitly raises in its opening pages is whether or not the narrator – and the reader – will become privy to details of Austerlitz's inner life which he initially withholds.

The answer must remain strangely ambiguous, for although we learn much about Austerlitz as the dilatory space of the narrative expands, he never materialises as a subject in possession of full interiority. If the past is retrieved, it is retrieved less from previously hidden regions of the protagonist's psyche than from the books, images, documents and narratives that he encounters in the course of his researches. The psychodrama at the heart of *Austerlitz* is a drama of the archive. For this reason, I hesitate to agree with John Zilcosky's claim that the entire text is governed by the logic of lost-and-found and a melodramatic desire to show everything (2006: 694–7). On the contrary, it is the very incompleteness of the archive, the fact that, as we have seen, it is ineluctably orientated towards the future, that full closure and disclosure are impossible. Austerlitz's search for his father is predestined not to be successful, as Zilcosky argues (692–3), but to lead merely further into the eternal incompletion of the archive.

THE ARCHIVE OF SUBJECTIVITY

On this reading, the conversation in which Austerlitz and Henri Lemoine discuss the waning of our ability to remember due to the proliferation of processed data (A 198/400) is merely a nostalgic postlude to what the text has already demonstrated: the subject of modernity is ineluctably dependent on external mnemotechnical prostheses.

In fact, it is possible to read the text of *Austerlitz* as an archive of Austerlitz's subjectivity. There are numerous details, motifs and episodes that are not governed by the unfolding of the plot, nor can they be plausibly reduced to symbols of Austerlitz's psyche.

Austerlitz's Jewishness, for example, is something of which he remains unaware for much of his life, certainly until his real name is divulged, but possibly until much later when he overhears the radio programme about the Kindertransports while browsing in a secondhand bookshop (A 199–200/203–4). This belated revelation is symbolised by the Jewish cemetery, which is next door to the house in which Austerlitz has lived for decades, but which he cannot see from the windows of the house and discovers only a few days before leaving London (A 408/410). But Austerlitz's own childhood enthusiasm for the Bible with which he is presented at school, already suggests a degree of identification with the Jewish people. In his reading of the story of Moses, for example, he is particularly attracted to the perilous moment in which the baby Moses is placed among the reeds and the episode in which the Israelites cross the desert and see nothing but sand and sky for days on end (A 77/81). He also shows the narrator an illustration from the same Welsh children's Bible depicting the children of Israel's camp in the wilderness, and claims to have known that his proper place was among the minute figures populating the image (A 77–80/81–4). It might initially appear that these moments are reducible to symbols of psychological interiority.

The identification with the story of Moses certainly supports such a reading, the biblical narrative providing a transparent metaphor for Austerlitz's own escape from occupied Prague. Once one seeks similar psychological revelations in the image of the Sinai desert camp, however, the issue becomes much more complicated because the image itself and the motivic complex of which it forms a part are highly overdetermined.

Austerlitz notes, for example, the similarity of the mountainous terrain depicted in the Sinai etching to the part of North Wales in which he grows up, and draws attention to what might be railway tracks leading to a quarry. Into the biblical scene, then, is projected Austerlitz's present, for North Wales is well known, among other things, for its slate mines and its narrow-gauge railways. But, of course, the enclosure in the centre of the camp, and the tent from which a plume of smoke rises, also point towards the Holocaust, immediately resemanticising the quarry and railway tracks as signs of forced labour and the mass transportation of European Jews by the Reichsbahn. The Sinai image is also linked to other, similar motifs. So, for example, after playing badminton in Andromeda Lodge, Austerlitz and Adela observe the play of shadows on the wall opposite the windows, and Adela asks, 'Do you see the fronds of the palm trees, do you see the caravan coming through the dunes over there?' (A 158–9/162). Shortly after Austerlitz narrates this section of his biography, he sends the narrator a postcard of a cluster of white tents beneath the Pyramids of Giza – another camp in the Egyptian desert, but this time part of some forgotten military campaign (A 166/170). Austerlitz's father, Maximilian Aychenwald describes a section of *Triumph des Willens*, Leni Riefenstahl's propaganda film about the 1934 Nuremburg rally, in which 'a birds's-eye view showed a city of white tents extending to the horizon, from which as day broke the Germans emerged . . . following, so it seemed, some higher bidding, on their way to the Promised Land at last after years in the wilderness' (A 239–40/243–4). Finally, the readers crouching on low chairs in the vestibule of the new Bibliothèque Nationale strike Austerlitz as nomads who have stopped for the night while crossing the Sahara or the Sinai Peninsula (A 390/392). Far from being reducible to a kind of psychological cipher, these recurring images of tented settlements in the desert represent the key stations and determining factors of Austerlitz's subjectivity – his Jewishness, his escape from Czechoslovakia, the perverted theological framework of the Third Reich, and the annihilation of the Jews to which it led – but in ways that remain purely external.

The same point can be made about Austerlitz's research interests. His fascination with fortress architecture (A 17–23/21–7) and railways (A 44–5/49), for example, initially appears as a displaced memory and a form of transgenerational haunting according to which his mother's past has left traces in her son's psyche.[13] But the star-shape of the fortress at Theresienstadt recurs in the mosaic inset into the floor of Number Twelve Šporkova (A 213/217) and in the stelliform summer residence at Liboc that was beloved of Agáta and Maximilian (A 352/356). Austerlitz encounters railways not only when he turns on the radio and learns that Fred Astaire was actually named Austerlitz and spent his childhood within earshot of the Omaha shunting yards (A 95/99), but also when Austerlitz and André Hilary visit Iver Grove and make the acquaintance of James Mallord Ashman.[14] Ashman shows them round the stately home that he can no longer afford to run, and in the nursery is a train set (A 153/157). In both these cases, what seems to be a metaphor for Austerlitz's memory ultimately becomes a series of externalised and fragmentary allegories of the protagonist's self.

Indeed, the text is strewn with signs of Austerlitz's subjectivity that are not assimilable to a model of psychological interiority. So, for example, one of the items in the Great Eastern Hotel that Austerlitz singles out is a gilded painting of Noah's Ark in the hotel's temple, a photograph of which is reproduced in the text (A 59/63). Noah's Ark then returns in the nursery of James Ashman's house (A 153/157). Emyr Elias' diary, which effectively constitutes his only material legacy, contains a list of all the sermons he preached, including the passage of the Bible on which each sermon was based. Austerlitz quotes from this archival source:

> Under 20 July 1939: The Tabernacle, Llandrillo – *Psalms* CLXVII, 4, 'He telleth the number of the stars: he calleth them all by their names';[15] under 3 August 1941: Chapel Uchaf, Gilboa – *Zephaniah* III, 6, 'I have cut off the nations: their towers are desolate; I made their streets waste, that none passeth by'; and under 21 May 1944: Chapel Bethesda, Corwen – *Isaiah* XLVIII, 18, 'O that thou hadst hearkened to my commandments! Then had thy peace been a river and thy righteousness as the waves of the sea!' (A 66/70)

Given that Elias preached every week, this cannot be regarded as a random sampling of readings, but rather sketches a brief narrative that moves from praise of the Lord to Jewish suffering and an injunction to remain faithful and obedient. During his visit to Marienbad with Marie der Verneuil in the 1970s, Austerlitz claims to have absolutely no memory of having been there before, but he and Marie are given room Number Thirty-Eight – capitalised, lest we fail to notice the allusion to the year of his childhood sojourn at the spa resort with Vera and Agáta (A 293/297). The capital A with which Austerlitz signs his name on a postcard to the narrator (A 166/170) is a single version of the multiple repetitions of the letter A that characterise the paintings of Dachau survivor Gastone Novelli, and which, the narrator claims, represent a long drawn-out scream (A 36/40).

We are once again in the realm of what Frank Kermode would call secrets, and Joseph Frank would call spatial form. The details enumerated above exceed the capacity of the linear unfolding of the narrative to account for them. Taken together, however, they imply that Austerlitz's history and subjectivity are sedimented spatially, in the material world of objects, writing, images and places, which are in turn archived within Sebald's text where they await interpretation and transformation into narrative. Thus the archival nature of the subject is dramatised not only in the story of *Austerlitz*, but in the very fabric of the narrative discourse itself.

NOTES

1. See the discussion of early reviews of the text in Zilcosky 2006: 685–7.
2. Cf. also 'But we never catch the propitious moment' (V 42/51).
3. In the German text, Austerlitz's list ends with the phrase 'und Ähnliches mehr', best translated as 'and other things of a similar kind'.
4. 'Family resemblances' (or, as Anthea Bell translates it, 'family likenesses') are 'Familienähnlichkeiten' – a concept explored by Wittgenstein in his *Philosophical Investigations*. The explicit comparison of Austerlitz and Wittgenstein encourages a Wittgensteinian reading of Austerlitz's family resemblances. In his recent book *Wittgenstein's Novels*, Martin Klebes explores the way in which Sebald establishes links between three entities (normally people) without specifying a criterion of identity that they all share. The perception of likeness, therefore, is dependent not on a metaphysical quality common to all three instances, but on 'a sense for Sebald's use of language and its rhythm as it aligns them into a new word order' (2006b: 109). In the case of the buildings listed by Austerlitz, however, Klebes' Wittgensteinian scheme does not appear to hold because family resemblance is asserted but not demonstrated. If, as I have argued elsewhere (Long 2006a: 224), the buildings are linked by their disciplinary intention, then their resemblance is indeed a function of shared criteria.
5. I am here drawing on the distinction between the archive and history that structures Wolfgang Ernst's *Im Namen von Geschichte* (2003).
6. Derrida sees this orientation towards the future as linked to a 'spectral messianicity' (1995: 36) that is reminiscent of the messianism of Benjamin.
7. This aspect of *Austerlitz* has been much discussed. See in particular Eshel 2003, Fuchs 2004a: 142–6, Gregory-Guider 2005, Restuccia 2005: 307–10.
8. I borrow the term 'narrative desire' from Peter Brooks' book *Reading for the Plot* (1984). Pane (2005) and Whitehead (2004) have applied Brooks' narratology to Sebald's texts, and have sought to relate it to the trauma theory of Cathy Caruth.
9. In German this is an 'in [seinem] Gehirn waltende Instanz' – not merely an agency that directs operations, but a higher authority that rules or reigns over the psyche.
10. Franz Loquai draws attention to this parallel in an essay on 'Max und Marcel' (2005a: 219–20) in the context of a wider discussion in which he argues that Austerlitz's memory basically follows a Proustian model. As we will see, however, this is a simplification and a misrepresentation of Sebald's project.
11. *Austerlitz* also thematises the archival administration of Jewish property by the Nazis. In order to facilitate seizure of her assets, Agáta has to provide an eight-page statement of her bank accounts and securities (A 249/253), and after her deportation to Theresienstadt, every single item of her household, right down to the last teaspoon, is removed for cataloguing and storage (A 255/259). As we have seen, this procedure is explored further in Henri Lemoine's revelations about the new Bibliothèque Nationale. An aspect of *Austerlitz* that has hitherto received little critical attention is the parallel between Czechoslovakia and France, in the sense that

the location at which the Jews of Prague were assembled before their deportation is now the site of an annual trade fair as well as a geological museum and a planetarium (A 254, 352/258, 356). France, clearly, does not have a monopoly on state-sanctioned amnesia.

12. A similar conclusion is reached by Russell Kilbourn on the basis of an investigation of architecture and cinema in Sebald's text: '*Austerlitz* presents not the *production* of an individual subjective interiority, but its ironic *deconstitution*' (2004: 152). Approaching *Austerlitz* from rather different perspectives, Mark Ilsemann (2006) and Michael Niehaus (2006a) also argue that Austerlitz is external to himself. Ilsemann claims that the conditions of trauma, exile and melancholy in Sebald are represented as existential rather than historical, and he thus sees suffering not as psychological but as topographical. Place, not the psyche, is the locus of pain. For Niehaus, the emigrant status of Sebald's protagonists means that institutions can never offer them support or function as guarantors of subjectivity. Austerlitz is external to himself because he is never interpellated or sited by the institutional other that is the necessary third party in a dialogic process of identity formation.

13. I borrow the notion of 'transgenerational haunting' from Abraham 1994.

14. Like the Ashburys from *The Rings of Saturn*, Ashman presides over a crumbling stately home whose decay is sedimented in the first syllable of his name.

15. There are, of course, only 150 Psalms. The Roman numerals should read 'CXLVII'.

9

CONCLUSION

The features of modernity that emerge in Sebald's work originate not in the late twentieth, but in the late nineteenth and early twentieth century. There are no computers, mobile phones, satellite navigation, SUVs, internet connections or iPods in Sebald's work. Air travel is not the intercontinental air travel of today, with its super-jumbo jets and personalised in-flight entertainment. The one transatlantic flight undertaken by the narrator is mentioned in a brief sentence (E 71/103), but on the occasions where flying is thematised more extensively, it is either a question of short-haul flights from provincial airstrips in antiquated machines (E 69, 149–50, 187–8/100–1, 219–21, 279–80), or a leisure pastime for gentleman amateurs (E 92/133; A 164–5/168–9). Sebald's walkers use maps to orientate themselves, not GPS. When his narrators and protagonists travel, they do so by train except in the United States, where the sparse rail network makes driving essential (E 72/104). When they need to communicate, they occasionally use public telephones, but more often than not they write. But they write by hand; there are no word processors, and the narrators of Sebald's texts are frequently represented filling their notebooks with pencil jottings rather than tapping away at a typewriter (let alone a laptop) (V 94–112; E 230–1/345).

This phenomenon has often been explained by the fact that Sebald's work posits the Holocaust and the Second World War either as the *telos* of Western history, as Eshel (2003: 87–9) and Taberner (2004: 190) suggest, or as a caesura that, as Anne Fuchs puts it, divides a pre-war period of historical plenitude from a post-war era of emptiness and amnesia (2004a: 165). Employing remarkably similar terms to Fuchs, Peter Fritzsche offers an even more radical diagnosis of Sebald's philosophy of history. The Second World War separates the plenitude of the past from the historical void of the present, whose emptiness is filled with the remnants of the pre-war era. The absence of the contemporary world from Sebald's texts, Fritzsche argues, ultimately implies that history has ended (2006). A related argument is put forward by Mary Cosgrove. She is critical of trauma theory and its tendency to posit the Holocaust as a founding myth that divides history into 'before' and 'after' the defining catastrophe, and maroons survivors and those born after in the futureless vacuum of the present. Sebald's understanding of history as pure absence, she argues, figures melancholy as an ontological condition, which strands him amid the ruins of the immediate post-war years (2006a: 218–20).

At one level, these arguments are persuasive. Of the numerous episodes in Sebald's work that corroborate Fuchs, Fritzsche and Cosgrove's claims, one might mention the narrator's visit to Somerleyton Hall in *The Rings of Saturn*. The shabby diesel train and the unmanned, desolate station are contrasted with a vision of nineteenth-century bustle and opulence, as the narrator imagines the arrival by train of goods and guests from London (RS 31–2/43–4), while the former glories of the house itself have given way to the property's current run-down condition (RS 36/50). One might also mention the narrator's visit to Bad Kissingen in *The Emigrants*. While Luisa Lanzberg's narrative of bourgeois life in the 1930s is rich in material detail and accompanied by a photograph of an exquisite villa (E 209/313), the narrator finds nothing but a drab and functional municipal building (E 221/332). It is only the Jewish cemetery that hints at the historical plenitude that has now disappeared (E 223–5/334–6).

As I have sought to demonstrate in this study, however, the history of modernity that informs Sebald's work stretches back a good way beyond the Holocaust, and addresses questions of power, knowledge and discipline that continue to produce effects of power and subjectivity in the post-Holocaust era. In the case of zoological display, Sebald's texts suggest that contemporary forms of spectatorship, as represented by television nature documentaries, form part of a much longer history of exhibition whose stages are charted by Thomas Browne's collection, the veterinary museum at Maisons-Alfort, and the collection of the Norwich and Norfolk Hospital. They can be understood on the basis of epistemic shifts and technologies of spectacle and discipline that emerged after the Renaissance. The images of Ambros Adelwarth, the dervish, the interned gypsy women, but also the group photograph of the Stower Grange rugby team and Sebald's own passport mug-shot, testify to a continuous history of disciplinary photography whose capacity to write power on the body extends to the present day. The ways in which the discourses of sexuality and cartography are implicated in structures of social power are likewise shown to be continuous from the nineteenth century to the twenty-first. By juxtaposing the map of Theresienstadt, an image of the Terezin *Registraturkammer*, and a discussion of the new Bibliothèque Nationale, furthermore, the narrator of *Austerlitz* plots a genealogy of biopower that shows the distribution of bodies in space to be a constant and ongoing feature of the disciplinarity that characterises modernity. Austerlitz's discourse on the rationalisation and standardisation of time in the nineteenth century is illustrated in *Vertigo*, where the belated arrival of modernity in the village of W. in the 1950s is thematised in part by references to clocks and watches. One of the thematic constants of Sebald's work is the waning of natural memory and the subject's increasing dependence on extra-individual mnemonic mechanisms. As *Vertigo* shows, this development cannot be seen as a consequence of the Holocaust, nor even as a result of the technical media, but as a development that already inhered in technologies of representation that existed in the early nineteenth century. While *The Emigrants* and *Austerlitz* address the role of mnemotechnical supplements in the service of post-Holocaust remembrance, *Vertigo* shows that it is an ongoing problem that is not limited to the transgenerational transmission of trauma.

Overall, Sebald's work corroborates Austerlitz's comment to the effect that the late nineteenth century is a period that now lies far in the past but continues to dominate and determine our lives (A 9/13). Sebald sees the key to the contemporary world not in the surface phenomena of the immediate present, but in structures and technologies developed a century ago but whose effects continue to be felt. In this sense, Sebald's narrative project borrows from the method of Foucault. Just as Foucault saw the keys to understanding modern society in the developments of the eighteenth and nineteenth centuries, so Sebald writes the history of the present by plotting a genealogy of modernity as an *époque de longue durée*.

In saying this, I do not wish to diminish the central role played by the Holocaust in Sebald's work, nor do I wish to deny that in some respects Sebald does indeed represent the Holocaust as a radical rupture in Western history. My argument in this book is not that the Holocaust is a minor issue or an irrelevance, but that the narrow concentration on post-Holocaust remembrance in a large proportion of criticism on Sebald blinds us to the longer history of modernity with which his texts are also fundamentally concerned. The caesura of the Holocaust has to be thought of not as an absolute, but as a break that exists alongside patterns of continuity that can be traced through European history from the early nineteenth century to the present.

Sebald is interested in the ways in which subjectivity in modernity is formed by archival and representational systems through which various forms of disciplinary power are exercised. He is also concerned with the scope that might exist for eluding disciplinary power or reconfiguring its archival systems in order to assert a degree of subjective autonomy or evade the determinations of power/knowledge. Part I of this study explored these questions with reference primarily to the thematic aspect of Sebald's texts in order to do justice to the high degree of thematic coherence that his work evinces. In Part II, *Vertigo*, *The Emigrants*, *The Rings of Saturn* and *Austerlitz* were subjected to individual analyses. It is not uncommon for Sebald's critics to claim that his texts are all of a piece, a position represented in its most extreme form by Franz Loquai (2005b: 252), who writes that although we can read each individual work on its own terms, it would be better to consider Sebald's output as one single work on which he was engaged throughout his career. My reading of the four major prose narratives, however, suggests that each of them offers a different formal response to the problems of modernity. *Vertigo* constitutes the urban spaces of the contemporary world as sites of wonder, re-injecting magic into the mundanity of a world in which the possibility of subjective authenticity has been hollowed out by the increasing abstraction and mediation of experience and the reliance of memory on external representations. In *The Emigrants*, the failure of the protagonists to narrativise the compulsive visual memories is compensated for by the narrator's reading of the family album. This leads to a rehabilitation of family photography. Furthermore, the extensive patterns of reflexive reference within the text itself create a degree of stability and consistency in the face of entropic decline and historical trauma. The narrator of *The Rings of Saturn* seeks to resist modernity not only by walking, but by employing a poetics of digression. He finds, however, that he is reabsorbed by modernity at the end of the text, just as his narrative itself ends up in thrall to the very structures of linearity and directedness from which it had sought to emancipate itself. In *Austerlitz*, we encounter a protagonist who is in effect external to himself. While ostensibly a psychological drama of repression and return, the novel in fact repeatedly shows that Austerlitz is devoid of stable and authentic subjective interiority. His subjectivity is produced largely by the archive.

What emerges from this reading of Sebald's prose texts is an increasing pessimism concerning the capacity of narrative and artifice to compensate for the dissolution of subjectivity that is dramatised throughout his work. In the Introduction, I drew on Sebald's critical work to show that he was a highly selective, if not tendentious, reader of Foucault. Although he clearly found aspects of Foucault's descriptive analysis of power congenial, his periphrastic allusions to *Discipline and Punish* and Volume 1 of the *History of Sexuality* always stop short of embracing Foucault's account of the formation of the modern subject. Sebald seemed ultimately unwilling to abandon the notion of autonomous subjecthood, and his literary work frequently dramatises a certain excess of subjectivity that is not reducible to determination by disciplinarity and power/knowledge. And yet from *Vertigo* onwards, Sebald shows that autonomous subjectivity is threatened by modernity. Sebald's melancholy, then, is best seen less as an ontological and transhistorical position, as Mary Cosgrove (2006a) argues, than as a response to a profoundly historical understanding of subjectivity in modernity.

This brings us to the question of Sebald's position within literary history. There have been numerous attempts to categorise him as a postmodernist. Anne Fuchs (2004a: 12) argues that his poetics of memory is linked to a postmodern aesthetics of the network, while Stefan Gunther (2006: 285) states that *The Emigrants* 'unambiguously partakes of what could be termed postmodern narrative aesthetics' without, however, saying what postmodern aesthetics might be. Carol Bere (2002: 190) and Arthur Williams (1998) are likewise reticent in spelling out precisely why they see Sebald as a postmodernist. It is certainly possible to find formal features of Sebald's work that tally with this or that definition of postmodernism. The ontological uncertainty produced by all his prose works is a defining feature of postmodernist fiction according to Brian McHale (1987), while the self-reflexive thematisation of history corresponds to Linda Hutcheon's concept of 'historiographic metafiction' (1988). The problem is that as soon as one begins to class Sebald as a postmodernist on the basis of his works' formal features, it emerges that these very features might equally place him in the modernist camp. McCulloh, for example, sees Sebald as a postmodernist on chronological grounds and because he rejects narrative conventions, but the rejection of narrative convention is a fundamental part of the project of modernism itself, as the work of Franz Kafka, James Joyce, André Gide, Alfred Döblin, John Dos Passos, Joseph Conrad and countless others demonstrates. Claudia Albes (2002: 280) argues that *The Rings of Saturn* is postmodern because quotation takes the place of stylistic originality, and because history is presented not as progress but as decay. But Sebald's work is in fact characterised by an immediately recognisable and highly individual style. Quotations are largely subsumed by the stylistic uniformity of Sebald's texts, rather than being juxtaposed in collage-like fashion, as in the work of more genuinely postmodernist writers such as William Burroughs, Heiner Müller, the early Elfriede Jelinek and many others. Sebald's work is also distinct from postmodernist pastiche such as one finds in John Barth. On the contrary, his technique of quotation is fully congruent with the practice of modernists such as T. S. Eliot and Ezra Pound, and makes no attempt to call into question the notion of artistic originality. The argument that modernism involved an ideology of historical progress, meanwhile, may be true of some versions of modernism, but it is certainly not true of the many modernist writers who, like Kafka, saw the dystopian side of modernity.

To understand Sebald's position within literary history, then, it is not enough to list formal features; we need also to consider how his texts respond to the specific historical constellation that I have characterised throughout this study as modernity. David Harvey argues that postmodernity can be distinguished from modernity on the basis of a radicalised experience of time–space compression that is a consequence of a shift from Fordism to flexible accumulation as the principle driving global capitalism (1990: 284–307). The implications of this for a conception of subjectivity are addressed by Fredric Jameson:

> The spatial peculiarities of post-modernism [are] symptoms and expressions of a new and historically original dilemma, one that involves our insertion as individual subjects into a multidimensional set of radically discontinuous realities, whose frames range from the still surviving spaces of bourgeois private life all the way to the unimaginable decentering of global capitalism itself. Not even Einsteinian relativity, or the multiple subjective worlds of the older modernists, is capable of giving any adequate figuration to this process, which in lived experience makes itself felt by the so-called death of the subject, or, more exactly, the fragmented and schizophrenic decentering and dispersion of this last. (cited in Harvey 1990: 305)

Jameson elsewhere talks about this kind of subjectivity in terms of schizophrenia, according to which personal identity and the narratives on which it depends break down, in postmodernity, into a series of unrelated present moments in time (1991: 26–7). While Jameson is generally negative in his evaluation of this 'death of the subject', it has also been celebrated in a ludic acceptance of hybridity, nomadism and decentredness as emancipatory forms of modern subjectivity.

What is notable about Sebald is that the fictional worlds he constructs are not the postmodern spaces of global capital, hyperspace and ever-faster cycles of production, consumption and waste (despite his narrators' occasional visits to McDonalds). His texts do not present unrelated present moments in time, nor do they partake of the waning of history that is frequently noted as a characteristic of the postmodern. Sebald's spaces are those of an earlier modernity that are deeply marked by the traces of history. It is precisely this fact that means that the co-existence of different places and temporalities analysed by Gregory-Guider (2005) and in Chapter 7 of this study does not constitute a 'multidimensional set of radically discontinuous realities', but rather a thoroughly historicised account of modern subjectivity. Subjective dislocation is always perceived not in terms of an emancipatory decentredness, but as a lack. Sebald's texts repeatedly exhibit a desire for autonomous subjectivity even as they acknowledge its erosion under the conditions of modernity, which aligns Sebald thematically, formally and ideologically with modernism.

This is not to suggest, however, that Sebald merely indulges in melancholy and nostalgic brooding over the lost glories of the past. His interest in the past is not purely antiquarian, but forms part of a genealogy of the present. His work suggests that to understand this present, we need to pay attention not to the superficial phenomena of the everyday, but to older structures and practices that continue decisively to shape contemporary life and contemporary subjectivity. We need to see Sebald not only as a chronicler of post-Holocaust trauma but as a historian of the *longue durée* of modernity if we are fully to understand why his work matters.

BIBLIOGRAPHY

Note: The following lists Sebald's major literary works and a selection of his criticism. It also lists secondary literature on Sebald consulted in the preparation of this study and all other references. In general, newspaper reviews of Sebald's texts are not listed. A good, though not exhaustive bibliography of Sebald's literary and critical writings and of secondary sources, including newspaper reviews, is provided by Marcel Atze (2005), 'Personalbibliographie W. G. Sebald', in Marcel Atze and Franz Loquai (eds), *Sebald: Lektüren*, Eggingen: Isele, pp. 260–93.

TEXTS BY W. G. SEBALD

(1969), *Carl Sternheim*: *Kritiker und Opfer der Wilhelminischen Ära*, Stuttgart: Kohlhammer.

(1972), 'The Undiscover'd Country: The Death Motif in Kafka's *Castle*', *Journal of European Studies* 2: 22–34.

(1975), 'Schock und Ästhetik: Über die Romane Döblins', *Orbis Litterarum* 30: 241–50.

(1980), *Der Mythos der Zerstörung im Werk Döblins*, Stuttgart: Klett.

(1982), 'Zwischen Geschichte und Naturgeschichte: Versuch über die literarische Beschreibung totaler Zerstörung mit Anmerkungen zu Kasack, Nossack und Kluge', *Orbis Litterarum* 37: 345–66.

(1985), *Die Beschreibung des Unglücks: Zur österreichischen Literatur von Stifter bis Handke*, Salzburg: Residenz.

(1986), 'Die Zerknirschung des Herzens: Über Erinnerung und Grausamkeit im Werk von Peter Weiss', *Orbis Litterarum* 41: 265–78.

(1988), *Nach der Natur: Ein Elementargedicht*, Nördlingen: Greno.

(1990a), 'Jean Améry und Primo Levi', in Irene Heidelberger-Leonard (ed.), *Über Jean Améry*, Heidelberg: Winter, pp. 115–23.

(1990b), *Schwindel.Gefühle*, Frankfurt am Main: Eichborn.

(1992), 'Damals vor Graz: Randbemerkungen zum Thema Literatur und Heimat', in Rüdiger Görner (ed.), *Heimat im Wort: Zur Problematik eines Begriffs im 19. und 20. Jahrhundert*, Munich: iudicium, pp. 131–9.

[1992] (1993), *Die Ausgewanderten. Vier lange Erzählungen*, Frankfurt am Main: Fischer.

(1995b), *Unheimliche Heimat, Essays zur österreichischen Literatur*, Frankfurt am Main: Fischer.

[1995] (1997), *Die Ringe des Saturn: Eine Englische Wallfahrt*, Frankfurt am Main: Fischer.

(1998), *Logis in einem Landhaus: Über Gottfried Keller, Johann Peter Hebel, Robert Walser und andere*, Munich: Hanser.

(1999), *Luftkrieg und Literatur: Mit einem Essay über Alfred Andersch*, Munich: Hanser.

(2001), *Austerlitz*, Munich: Hanser.

(2003), *Campo Santo*, Munich: Hanser.

and Jan Peter Tripp (2003), *'Unerzählt': 33 Texte und 33 Radierungen*, Munich: Hanser.

(no date), *Verleihung des Heine-Preises 2000 der Landeshauptstadt Düsseldorf an W. G. Sebald*, Düsseldorf: Kulturamt der Landeshauptstadt Düsseldorf.

ENGLISH TRANSLATIONS

(1997), *The Emigrants*, trans. Michael Hulse, London: Harvill.

(1998), *The Rings of Saturn*, trans. Michael Hulse, London: Harvill.

(1999), *Vertigo*, trans. Michael Hulse, London: Harvill.

(2001a), *Austerlitz*, trans. Anthea Bell, London: Hamish Hamilton.

(2001b), *For Years Now*, London: Short Books.

(2003a), *After Nature*, trans. Michael Hamburger, London: Hamish Hamilton.

(2003b), *On the Natural History of Destruction*, trans. Anthea Bell, New York: Random House.

and Jan Peter Tripp (2004), *Unrecounted*, trans. Michael Hamburger, London: Hamish Hamilton.

(2005), *Campo Santo*, ed. Sven Meyer, trans. Anthea Bell, London: Hamish Hamilton.

INTERVIEWS

Alvarez, Maria (2001), 'The Significant Mr Sebald', *Telegraph Magazine*, 22 September, pp. 54–7.

Angier, Carole (1997), 'Wer ist W. G. Sebald? Ein Besuch beim Autor der *Ausgewanderten*', in Franz Loquai (ed.), W. G. Sebald: *Porträt*, Eggingen: Isele, pp. 43–50.

Baker, Kenneth (2001), 'W. G. Sebald – Up against Historical Amnesia', *San Francisco Chronicle*, 7 October.

Balzer, Burkhard (1993), 'Bei den armen Seelen: Ein Gespräch mit W. G. Sebald', *Saarbrücker Zeitung*, 16 March.

Boedecker, Sven (1993), 'Menschen auf der anderen Seite; Gespräch mit W. G. Sebald', *Rheinische Post*, 9 October.

Cuomo, Joe (2001), 'Interview with Joe Cuomo', *New Yorker*, 3 September.

Doerry, Martin and Volker Hage (2001), 'Ich fürchte das Melodramatische' [interview with W. G. Sebald], *Spiegel*, 12 March, pp. 228–34.

Hage, Volker (ed.) (2003), 'Hitlers pyromanische Phantasien', in *Zeugen der Zerstörung: Die Literaten und der Luftkrieg, Essays und Gespräche*, Frankfurt am Main: Fischer, pp. 259–79; also as 'Gespräch mit W. G. Sebald' (2003), *Akzente* 1: 35–50.

Jaggi, Maya (2001a), 'Recovered Memories', *The Guardian*, 22 September.

Jaggi, Maya (2001b), 'The Last Word', *The Guardian*, 21 December.

Just, Renate (1997a), 'Im Zeichen des Saturn', in Franz Loquai (ed.), W. G. *Sebald: Porträt*, Eggingen: Isele, pp. 37–42.

Just, Renate (1997b), 'Stille Katastrophen', in Franz Loquai (ed.), W. G. *Sebald: Porträt*, Eggingen: Isele, pp. 25–30.

Kafatou, Sarah (1998), 'An Interview with W. G. Sebald', *Harvard Review* 15: 31–5.

Köhler, Andrea (1997), 'Katastrophe mit Zuschauer', *Neue Zürcher Zeitung*, 22 November, p. 52.

Löffler, Sigrid (1997a), 'Kopfreisen in die Ferne. Ein Geheimtip: In Norwich, gar nicht hinter dem Mond, lebt und schreibt W. G. Sebald', in Franz Loquai (ed.), *W. G. Sebald: Porträt*, Eggingen: Isele, pp. 32–6.

Löffler, Sigrid (1997b), ' "Wildes Denken": Gespräch mit W. G. Sebald', in Franz Loquai (ed.), *W. G. Sebald: Porträt*, Eggingen: Isele, pp. 131–3.

Lubow, Arthur (2001), 'Preoccupied by Death but Still Funny', *New York Times*, 11 December.

McCrum, Robert (1998), 'Characters, Plot, Dialogue? That's Not Really My Style . . .', *Observer Review*, 7 June.

Pfohlmann, Oliver (1999), 'Ist Bücherschreiben eine Verhaltensstörung?', *Saarbrücker Zeitung*, 6 January.

Poltronieri, Marco (1997), 'Wie kriegen die Deutschen das auf die Reihe? Ein Gespräch mit W. G. Sebald', in Franz Loquai (ed.), *W. G. Sebald: Porträt*, Eggingen: Isele, pp. 133–9.

Pralle, Uwe (2001), 'Mit einem kleinen Strandspaten Abschied von Deutschland nehmen', *Süddeutsche Zeitung*, 22–3 December.

Scholz, Christian (2000), 'Aber das Geschriebene ist ja kein wahres Dokument', *Neue Zürcher Zeitung*, 26–7 February.

Schreck, Denis (1998), 'Leid und Scham und Schweigen und das Loch in der Literatur', *Basler Zeitung*, 6 February.

Siedenberg, Sven (1996), 'Anatomie der Schwermut: Gespräch über sein Schreiben und die Schrecken der Geschichte', in Franz Loquai (ed.), *W. G. Sebald: Porträt*, Eggingen: Isele, pp. 141–3.

Silverblatt, Michael (2001), 'Interview with W. G. Sebald', *Bookworm*, 6 December.

Turner, Gordon (ed.) (2006), 'Introduction and Transcript of an Interview given by Max Sebald [Interviewer: Michaël Zeeman]', in Scott Denham and Mark McCulloh (eds), *W. G. Sebald: Trauma, Memory, History*, Berlin: de Gruyter, pp. 21–9.

Wittmann, Jochen (1997), 'Alles schrumpft: Ein Besuch bei W. G. Sebald, dem deutschen Autor in England', *Stuttgarter Zeitung*, 27 November.

Wood, James (1998), 'An Interview with W. G. Sebald', *Brick* 59: 23–9.

SECONDARY WORKS ON W. G. SEBALD

Aliaga-Buchenau, Ana-Isabel (2006), ' "A Time He Could Not Bear To Say Any More About": Presence and Absence of the Narrator in W. G. Sebald's *The Emigrants*', in Scott Denham and Mark McCulloh (eds), *W. G. Sebald: Trauma, Memory, History*, Berlin: de Gruyter, pp. 141–55.

Albes, Claudia (2002), 'Die Erkundung der Leere: Anmerkungen zu W. G. Sebalds "englisher Wallfahrt" *Die Ringe des Saturn*', *Jahrbuch der deutschen Schillergesellschaft* 46: 279–305.

Albes, Claudia (2006), 'Porträt ohne Modell: Bildbeschreibung und autobiographische Reflexion in W. G. Sebalds "Elementargedicht" *Nach der Natur*', in Michael Niehaus and Claudia Öhlschläger (eds), *W. G. Sebald: Politische Archäologie und melancholische Bastelei*, Berlin: Erich Schmidt, pp. 47–75.

Anderson, Mark M. (2003), 'The Edge of Darkness: On W. G. Sebald', *October* 106: 102–21.

Anderson, Mark M. (2004), 'Introduction', *Germanic Review* 79: 155–61.

Anderson, Mark M. (2006), 'Wo die Schrecken der Kindheit verborgen sind: W. G. Sebalds Dilemma der zwei Väter. Biografische Skizzen zu einem Portrait des Dichters als junger Mann', *Literaturen*, 7 August: 32–9.

Arnold, Heinz Ludwig (ed.) (2003), *W. G. Sebald*, Munich: Text + Kritik.

Arnold-de Simine, Silke (forthcoming), 'The Museum as Memory Site and Memory Medium in W. G. Sebald's *Austerlitz*', in *The Irreducibility of Images: Intermediality in Contemporary Cultural Studies*, Oxford: Lang.

Atlas, James (1999), 'W. G. Sebald: A Profile', *Paris Review* 41:151, 278–95.

Atze, Marcel (1997a), 'Biblioteca Sebaldiana: W. G. Sebald – ein Bibliophile? Eine Spekulation', in Franz Loquai (ed.), *W. G. Sebald: Porträt*, Eggingen: Isele, pp. 218–32.

Atze, Marcel (1997b), 'Koinzidenz und Intertextualität: Der Einsatz von Prätexten in W. G. Sebalds Erzählung "All'estero" ', in Franz Loquai (ed.), *W. G. Sebald: Porträt*, Eggingen: Isele, pp. 146–69.

Atze, Marcel (2004), ' "Wie Adler berichtet": Das Werk H. G. Adlers als Gedächtnisspeicher für Literatur: Heimrad Bäcker, Robert Schindel, W. G. Sebald', *Text + Kritik* 163: 17–30.

Atze, Marcel (2005a), 'Casanova vor der schwarzen Wand: Ein Beispiel intertextueller Repräsentanz des Holocaust in W. G. Sebalds *Austerlitz*', in Marcel Atze and Franz Loquai (eds), *Sebald: Lektüren*, Eggingen: Isele, pp. 228–43.

Atze, Marcel (2005b), 'Die Gesetze von der Wiederkunft der Vergangenheit: W. G. Sebalds Lektüre des Gedächtnistheoretikers Maurice Halbwachs', in Marcel Atze and Franz Loquai (eds), *Sebald: Lektüren*, Eggingen: Isele, pp. 195–211.

Atze, Marcel (2005c), '. . . und wer spricht über Dresden? Der Luftkrieg als öffentliches und literarisches Thema in der Zeit des ersten Frankfurter Auschwitz-Prozesses 1963–1965', in Michael Niehaus and Claudia Öhlschläger (eds), *W. G. Sebald: Politische Archäologie und melancholische Bastelei*, Berlin: Erich Schmidt, pp. 205–17.

Atze, Marcel and Sven Meyer (2005), ' "Unsere Korrespondenz": Zum Briefwechsel zwischen W. G. Sebald and Theodor W. Adorno', in Marcel Atze and Franz Loquai (eds), *Sebald: Lektüren*, Eggingen: Isele, pp. 17–38.

Atze, Marcel and Franz Loquai (eds) (2005), *Sebald: Lektüren*, Eggingen: Isele.

Ayren, Armin (1998), 'Sebald über Canetti', in Gerhard Köpf (ed.), *Mitteilungen über Max: Marginalien zu W. G. Sebald*, Oberhausen: Laufen, pp. 9–20.

Bales, Richard (2003), 'The Loneliness of the Long-Distance Narrator: The Inscription of Travel in Proust and W. G. Sebald', in Jane Conroy (ed.), *Cross-Cultural Travel: Papers from the Royal Irish Academy Symposium on Literature and Travel*, New York: Lang, pp. 507–12.

Barzilai, Maya (2004), 'Facing the Past and the Female Spectre in W. G. Sebald's *The Emigrants*', in J. J. Long and Anne Whitehead (eds), *W. G. Sebald: A Critical Companion*, Edinburgh: Edinburgh University Press, pp. 203–16.

Barzilai, Maya (2006), 'On Exposure: Photography and Uncanny Memory in W. G. Sebald's *Die Ausgewanderten* and *Austerlitz*', in Scott Denham and Mark McCulloh (eds), *W. G. Sebald: Trauma, Memory, History*, Berlin: de Gruyter, pp. 205–18.

Bauer, Karin (2006), 'The Dystopian Entwinement of Histories and Identities in W. G. Sebald's *Austerlitz*', in Scott Denham and Mark McCulloh (eds), *W. G. Sebald: Trauma, Memory, History*, Berlin: de Gruyter, pp. 233–50.

Beck, John (2004), 'Reading Room: Erosion and Sedimentation in Sebald's Suffolk', in J. J. Long and Anne Whitehead (eds), *W. G. Sebald: A Critical Companion*, Edinburgh: Edinburgh University Press, pp. 75–88.

Bere, Carol (2002), 'The Book of Memory: W. G. Sebald's *The Emigrants* and *Austerlitz*', *Literary Review* 46(1): 184–92.

Boehncke, Heiner (2003), 'Clair obscur: W. G. Sebalds Bilder', in Heinz Ludwig Arnold (ed.), *W. G. Sebald*, Munich: Text + Kritik, pp. 43–62.

Bond, Greg (2004), 'On the Misery of Nature and the Nature of Misery: W. G. Sebald's Landscapes', in J. J. Long and Anne Whtehead (eds), *W. G. Sebald: A Critical Companion*, Edinburgh: Edinburgh University Press, pp. 31–44.

Briegleb, Klaus (1992), 'Preisrede auf W. G. Sebald anläßlich der Verleihung des Lyrikpreises "Fedor Malchow" am 17.12.1991 im Hamburger Literaturhaus', *Hamburger Ziegel* 1: 473–83.

Catling, Jo (2003), 'Gratwanderungen bis an den Rand der Natur: W. G. Sebald's Landscapes of Memory', in Rüdiger Görner (ed.), *The Anatomist of Melancholy: Essays in Memory of W. G. Sebald*, Munich: iudicium, pp. 19–50.

Ceuppens, Jan (2002), 'Im zerschundenen Papier herumgeisternde Gesichter: Fragen der Repräsentation in W. G. Sebalds *Die Ausgewanderten*', *Germanistische Mitteilungen* 55: 79–98.

Ceuppens, Jan (2004), 'Seeing Things: Spectres and Angels in W. G. Sebald's Prose Fiction', in J. J. Long and Anne Whitehead (eds), *W. G. Sebald: A Critical Companion*, Edinburgh: Edinburgh University Press, pp. 190–202.

Ceuppens, Jan (2006a), 'Realia: Konstellationen bei Benjamin, Barthes, Lacan – und Sebald', in Michael Niehaus and Claudia Öhlschläger (eds), *W. G. Sebald: Politische Archäologie und melancholische Bastelei*, Berlin: Erich Schmidt, pp. 241–58.

Ceuppens, Jan (2006b), 'Transcripts: An Ethics of Representation in *The Emigrants*', in Scott Denham and Mark McCulloh (eds), *W. G. Sebald: Trauma, Memory, History*, Berlin: de Gruyter, pp. 251–63.

Chandler, James (2003), 'About Loss: W. G. Sebald's Romantic Art of Memory', *South Atlantic Quarterly* 102: 235–62.

Chaplin, Elizabeth (2006), 'The Convention of Captioning: W. G. Sebald and the Release of the Captive Image', *Visual Studies* 21: 42–53.

Cosgrove, Mary (2006a), 'Melancholy Competitions: W. G. Sebald Reads Günter Grass and Wolfgang Hildesheimer', *German Life and Letters* 59: 217–32.

Cosgrove, Mary (2006b), 'The Anxiety of German Influence: Affiliation, Rejection and Jewish Identity in W. G. Sebald's Work', in Anne Fuchs, Mary Cosgrove and Georg Grote (eds), *German Memory Contests: The Quest for Identity in Literature, Film and Discourse since 1990*, Rochester, NY: Camden House, pp. 229–52.

Craven, Peter (1999), 'W. G. Sebald: Anatomy of Faction', *Heat* 13: 212–24.

Crownshaw, Richard (2004), 'Reconsidering Postmemory: Photography, the Archive, and Post-Holocaust Memory in W. G. Sebald's *Austerlitz*', *Mosaic* 37: 215–36.

Darby, David (2006), 'Landscape and Memory: Sebald's Redemption of History', in Scott Denham and Mark McCulloh (eds), *W. G. Sebald: Trauma, Memory, History*, Berlin: de Gruyter, pp. 265–77.

Dean, Tacita (2003), 'W. G. Sebald', *October* 103: 122–36.

Denham, Scott (2006), 'Die englischsprachige Sebald-Rezeption', in Michael Niehaus and Claudia Öhlschläger (eds), *W. G. Sebald: Politische Archäologie und melancholische Bastelei*, Berlin: Erich Schmidt, pp. 259–68.

Denham, Scott and Mark McCulloh (eds) (2006), *W. G. Sebald: Trauma, Memory, History*, Berlin: de Gruyter.

Denneler, Iris (2000), ' "Das Andenken ist ja im Grunde nichts anderes als ein Zitat": Zu Formel und Gedächtnis am Beispiel von W. G. Sebalds *Die Ausgewanderten*', in Iris Denneler (ed.), *Die Formel und das Unverwechselbare: Interdisziplinäre Beiträge zu Topik, Rhetorik, und Individualität*, Frankfurt am Main: Lang, pp. 165–79.

Denneler, Iris (2001), *Von Namen und Dingen: Erkundungen zur Rolle des Ich in der Literatur am Beispiel von Ingeborg Bachmann, Peter Bichsel, Max Frisch, Gottfried Keller, Heinrich von Kleist, Arthur Schnitzler, Frank Wedekind, Vladimir Nabokov und W. G. Sebald*, Würzburg: Königshausen und Neumann.

Detering, Heinrich (1998), 'Schnee und Asche, Flut und Feuer: Über den Elementardichter W. G. Sebald', *Neue Rundschau* 109: 147–58.

Dittberner, Hugo (2003), 'Der Ausführlichste; oder, ein starker Hauch Patina', in Heinz Ludwig Arnold (ed.), *W. G. Sebald*, Munich: Text + Kritik, pp. 6–14.

Dunker, Axel (2003), *Die anwesende Abwesenheit: Literatur im Schatten von Auschwitz*, Munich: Fink.

Duttlinger, Carolin (2004), 'Traumatic Photographs: Remembrance and the Technical Media in W. G. Sebald's *Austerlitz*', in J. J. Long and Anne Whitehead (eds), *W. G. Sebald: A Critical Companion*, Edinburgh: Edinburgh University Press, pp. 155–71.

Dyer, Geoff et al. (2001), 'A Symposium on W. G. Sebald', *Threepenny Review* 89: 18–21.

Ecker, Gisela (2006), ' "Heimat" oder die Grenzen der Bastelei', in Michael Niehaus and Claudia Öhlschläger (eds), *W. G. Sebald: Politische Archäologie und melancholische Bastelei*, Berlin: Erich Schmidt, pp. 77–88.

Elcott, Noam (2004), 'Tattered Snapshots and Castaway Tongues: An Essay at Layout and Translation with W. G. Sebald', *Germanic Review* 79: 203–23.

Eshel, Amir (2003), 'Against the Power of Time: The Poetics of Suspension in W. G. Sebald's *Austerlitz*', *New German Critique* 88: 71–96.

Finke, Susanne (1997), 'W. G. Sebald – der fünfte Ausgewanderte', in Franz Loquai (ed.), *W. G. Sebald: Porträt*, Eggingen: Isele, pp. 205–17.

Franke, Konrad (2002), 'Laudatio auf W. G. Sebald', in *Verleihung des Bremer Literaturpreises 2002: W. G. Sebald, Juli Zeh. Laudationes und Reden*, Bremen: Rudolf-Alexander-Schröder-Stiftung, pp. 13–17.

Franklin, Ruth (2006), 'Sebald's Amateurs', in Scott Denham and Mark McCulloh (eds), *W. G. Sebald: Trauma, Memory, History*, Berlin: de Gruyter, pp. 127–38.

Friedrichsmeyer, Sara (2006), 'Sebald's Elective and other Affinities', in Scott Denham and Mark McCulloh (eds), *W. G. Sebald: Trauma, Memory, History*, Berlin: de Gruyter, pp. 77–99.

Fritzsche, Peter (2006), 'Sebald's Twentieth-Century Histories', in Scott Denham and Mark McCulloh (eds), *W. G. Sebald: Trauma, Memory, History*, Berlin: de Gruyter, pp. 291–9.

Fuchs, Anne (2003), 'Phantomspuren: Zu W. G. Sebalds Poetik der Erinnerung in *Austerlitz*', *German Life and Letters* 56: 281–98.

Fuchs, Anne (2004a), *Die Schmerzensspuren der Geschichte: Zur Poetik der Erinnerung in W. G. Sebalds Prosa*, Cologne: Böhlau.

Fuchs, Anne (2004b), 'Zur Ästhetik der Vernetzung in W. G. Sebalds *Austerlitz*', in Hartmut Boehme, Jürgen Barkhoff and Jeanne Riou (eds), *Netzwerke: Ästhetiken und Techniken der Vernetzung 1800–1900–2000*, Cologen, Weimar, Vienna: Böhlau, pp. 261–78.

Fuchs, Anne (2006a), ' "Ein auffallend geschichtsblindes und traditionsloses Volk": Heimatdiskurs und Ruinenästhetik in W. G. Sebalds Prosa', in Michael Niehaus and Claudia Öhlschläger (eds), *W. G. Sebald: Politische Archäologie und melancholische Bastelei*, Berlin: Erich Schmidt, pp. 89–110.

Fuchs, Anne (2006b), 'W. G. Sebald's Painters: The Function of Fine Art in his Prose Works', *Modern Language Review* 101: 167–83.

Furst, Lilian R. (2006), 'Realism, Photography, and Degrees of Uncertainty', in Scott Denham and Mark McCulloh (eds), *W. G. Sebald: Trauma, Memory, History*, Berlin: de Gruyter, pp. 219–29.

Garloff, Katja (2004), 'The Emigrant as Witness: W. G. Sebald's *Die Ausgewanderten*', *German Quarterly* 77: 76–93.

Garloff, Katja (2006), 'The Task of the Narrator: Moments of Symbolic Investiture in W. G. Sebald's *Austerlitz*', in Scott Denham and Mark McCulloh (eds), *W. G. Sebald: Trauma, Memory, History*, Berlin: de Gruyter, pp. 157–69.

Gasseleder, Klaus (2005), 'Erkundungen zum Prätext der Luisa-Lanzberg-Geschichte aus W. G. Sebalds *Die Ausgewanderten*: Ein Bericht', in Marcel Atze and Franz Loquai (eds), *Sebald: Lektüren*, Eggingen: Isele, pp. 157–75.

Gómez García, Carmen (2005), ' "Ruinen der Gerechtigkeit": Zur Rezeption W. G. Sebalds in Spanien', in Marcel Atze and Franz Loquai (eds), *Sebald: Lektüren*, Eggingen: Isele, pp. 122–32.

Görner, Rüdiger (ed.) (2003), *The Anatomist of Melancholy: Essays in Memory of W. G. Sebald*, Munich: iudicium.

Gregory-Guider, Christopher C. (2005), 'The "Sixth Emigrant": Traveling Places in the Works of W. G. Sebald', *Contemporary Literature* 46: 422–49.

Gunther, Stefan (2006), 'The Holocaust as the Still Point of the World in W. G. Sebald's *The Emigrants*', in Scott Denham and Mark McCulloh (eds), *W. G. Sebald: Trauma, Memory, History*, Berlin: de Gruyter, pp. 279–90.

Hahn, Hans-Joachim (2004), 'Leerstellen in der deutschen Gedenkkultur: Die Streitschriften von W. G. Sebald und Klaus Briegleb', *German Life and Letters* 57: 357–71.

Hall, Katharina (2000), 'Jewish Memory in Exile: The Relation of W. G. Sebald's *Die Ausgewanderten* to the Tradition of the *Yizkor* Books', in Pól O'Dochartaigh (ed.), *Jews in German Literature since 1945: German-Jewish Literature?*, Amsterdam: Rodopi, pp. 153–64.

Harris, Stephanie (2001), 'The Return of the Dead: Memory and Photography in W. G. Sebald's *Die Ausgewanderten*', *German Quarterly* 74: 379–91.

Heidelberger-Leonard, Irene (2001), 'Melancholie als Widerstand', *Akzente* 48(2): 122–30.

Hell, Julia (2003), 'Eyes Wide Shut: German Post-Holocaust Authorship', *New German Critique* 88(4): 9–36.

Hell, Julia (2004), 'The Angel's Enigmatic Eyes, or the Gothic Beauty of Catastrophic History in W. G. Sebald's "Air War and Literature" ', *Criticism* 46: 361–92.

Hellweg, Patricia (1998), 'Lokaltermin Wertach', in Gerhard Köpf (ed.), *Mitteilungen über Max: Marginalien zu W. G. Sebald*, Oberhausen: Laufen, pp. 21–31.

Horstkotte, Silke (2005a), 'Fantastic Gaps: Photography Inserted into Narrative in W. G. Sebald's *Austerlitz*', in Christian Emden and David

Midgley (eds), *Science, Technology, and the German Cultural Imagination*, Oxford: Lang, pp. 269–86.

Horstkotte, Silke (2005b), 'Transgenerationelle Blicke: Fotografie als Medium von Gedächtnisradierung in *Die Ausgewanderten*', in Ruth Vogel-Klein (ed.), *Recherches Germaniques* Revue annuelle hors série: *W. G. Sebald: Erinnerung, Übertragung, Bilder/W. G. Sebald: Mémoire, transferts, images*, Strasbourg: Université Marc Bloch, pp. 47–64.

Hutchinson, Ben (2006), ' "Egg Boxes Stacked in a Crate": Narrative Status and its Implications', in Scott Denham and Mark McCulloh (eds), *W. G. Sebald: Trauma, Memory, History*, Berlin: de Gruyter, pp. 171–82.

Huyssen, Andreas (2001), 'On Rewritings and New Beginnings: W. G. Sebald and the Literature about the *Luftkrieg*', *Zeitschrift für Literaturwissenschaft und Linguistik* 124: 72–90.

Ilsemann, Mark (2006), 'Going Astray: Melancholy, Natural History and the Image of Exile in W. G. Sebald's *Austerlitz*', in Scott Denham and Mark McCulloh (eds), *W. G. Sebald: Trauma, Memory, History*, Berlin: de Gruyter, pp. 303–14.

Jackman, Graham (2004), ' "Gebranntes Kind"? W. G. Sebald's "Metaphysik der Geschichte" ', *German Life and Letters* 57: 456–71.

Jacobs, Carol (2004), 'What Does It Mean to Count? W. G. Sebald's *The Emigrants*', *Modern Language Notes* 119: 905–29.

Jeutter, Ralf (2000), ' "Am Rand der Finsternis": The Jewish Experience in the Context of W. G. Sebald's Poetics', in Pól O'Dochartaigh (ed.), *Jews in German Literature since 1945: German-Jewish Literature?*, Amsterdam: Rodopi, pp. 153–64.

Juhl, Eva (1995), 'Die Wahrheit über das Ungluck: Zu W. G. Sebald *Die Ausgewanderten*', in Anne Fuchs and Theo Harden (eds), *Reisen im Diskurs: Modelle literarischer Fremderfahrung von den Pilgerberichten bis zur Postmoderne*, Heidelberg: Winter, pp. 640–59.

Kastura, Thomas (1996), 'Geheimnisvolle Fähigkeit zur Transmigration: W. G. Sebalds interkulturelle Wallfahrten in die Leere', *Arcadia* 31: 197–216.

Kilbourn, Russell J. A. (2004), 'Architecture and Cinema: The Representation of Memory in W. G. Sebald's *Austerlitz*', in J. J. Long and Anne Whitehead (eds), *W. G. Sebald: A Critical Companion*, Edinburgh: Edinburgh University Press, pp. 140–54.

Kilbourn, Russell J. A. (2006), 'Kafka, Nabokov . . . Sebald: Intertextuality and Narratives of Redemption in *Schwindel. Gefühle* and *The Emigrants*', in Scott Denham and Mark McCulloh (eds), *W. G. Sebald: Trauma, Memory, History*, Berlin: de Gruyter, pp. 33–63.

Klebes, Martin (2004), 'Infinite Journey: From Sebald to Kafka', in J. J. Long and Anne Whitehead (eds), *W. G. Sebald: A Critical Companion*, Edinburgh: Edinburgh University Press, pp. 123–39.

Klebes, Martin (2006a), 'Sebald's Pathographies', in Scott Denham and Mark McCulloh (eds), *W. G. Sebald: Trauma, Memory, History*, Berlin: de Gruyter, pp. 65–75.

Klebes, Martin (2006b), *Wittgenstein's Novels*, New York: Routledge.

Klüger, Ruth (2003), 'Wanderer zwischen falschen Leben: Über W. G. Sebald', in Heinz Ludwig Arnold (ed.), *W. G. Sebald*, Munich: Text + Kritik, pp. 95–102.

Kochhar-Lindgren, Gray (2002), 'Charcoal: The Phantom Traces of W. G. Sebald's Novel-Memoirs', *Monatshefte* 94: 368–80.

Köpf, Gerhard (ed.) (1998), *Mitteilungen über Max: Marginalien zu W. G. Sebald*, Oberhausen: Laufen.

Köpf, Gerhard (1998), 'Das Wertacher Sommerloch', in Gerhard Köpf (ed.), *Mitteilungen über Max: Marginalien zu W. G. Sebald*, Oberhausen: Laufen, pp. 32–48.

Korff, Sigrid (1998), 'Die Treue zum Detail: W. G. Sebalds *Die Ausgewanderten*', in Stephan Braese (ed.), *In der Sprache der Täter: Neue Lektüren deutschsprachiger Nachkriegs- und Gegenwartsliteratur*, Opladen: Westdeutscher Verlag, pp. 167–97.

Körte, Mona (2005), ' "Un petit sac": W. G. Sebalds Figuren zwischen Sammeln und Vernichten', in Marcel Atze and Franz Loquai (eds), *Sebald: Lektüren*, Eggingen: Isele, pp. 176–94.

Kouvaros, George (2005), 'Images that Remember Us: Photography and Memory in *Austerlitz*', *Textual Practice* 19: 173–93.

Lennon, Patrick (2006), 'In the Weaver's Web: An Intertextual Approach to W. G. Sebald and Laurence Sterne', in Scott Denham and Mark McCulloh (eds), *W. G. Sebald: Trauma, Memory, History*, Berlin: de Gruyter, pp. 91–104.

Leone, Massimo (2003), 'Literature, Travel and Vertigo', in Jane Conroy (ed.), *Cross-Cultural Travel: Papers from the Royal Irish Academy Symposium on Literature and Travel*, New York: Lang, pp. 513–22.

Leone, Massimo (2004), 'Textual Wanderings: A Vertiginous Reading of W. G. Sebald', in J. J. Long and Anne Whitehead (eds), *W. G. Sebald: A Critical Companion*, Edinburgh: Edinburgh University Press, pp. 89–101.

Lethen, Helmut (2006), 'Sebalds Raster: Überlegungen zur ontologischen Unruhe in Sebalds *Die Ringe des Saturn*', in Michael Niehaus and Claudia Öhlschläger (eds), *W. G. Sebald: Politische Archäologie und melancholische Bastelei*, Berlin: Erich Schmidt, pp. 13–30.

Lobsien, Verena Olejniczak (2004), 'Herkunft ohne Ankunft: Der Chronotopos der Heimatlosigkeit bei W. G. Sebald', in Barbara Thums et al. (eds), *Herkünfte: Historisch, Ästhetisch, Kulturell: Beiträge zu einer Tagung aus Anlaß des 60. Geburtstags von Bernhard Greiner*, Heidelberg: Winter, pp. 223–48.

Löffler, Sigrid (2003), ' "Melancholie ist eine Form des Widerstands": Über das Saturnische bei W. G. Sebald und seine Aufhebung in der Schrift', in Heinz Ludwig Arnold (ed.), *W. G. Sebald*, Munich: Text + Kritik, pp. 103–11.

Long, J. J. (2003), 'History, Narrative, and Photography in W. G. Sebald's *Die Ausgewanderten*', *Modern Language Review* 98: 118–39.

Long, J. J. (2004), 'Intercultural Identities in Norbert Gstrein's *Die englischen Jahre* and W. G. Sebald's *Die Ausgewanderten*', *Journal of Multilingual and Multicultural Development* 25: 512–28.

Long, J. J. (2006a), 'Disziplin und Geständnis: Ansätze zu einer Foucaultschen Sebald-Lektüre', in Michael Niehaus and Claudia Öhlschläger (eds), *W. G. Sebald: Politische Archäologie und melancholische Bastelei*, Berlin: Erich Schmidt, pp. 219–39.

Loquai, Franz (ed.) (1995), *Far From Home: W. G. Sebald*, Bamberg: Fußnoten zur Literatur.

Loquai, Franz (ed.) (1997), *W. G. Sebald: Porträt*, Eggingen: Isele.

Loquai, Franz (2005a), 'Max und Marcel: Eine Betrachtung über die Erinnerungskünstler Sebald und Proust', in Marcel Atze and Franz Loquai (eds), *Sebald: Lektüren*, Eggingen: Isele, pp. 212–27.

Loquai, Franz (2005b), 'Vom Beinhaus der Geschichte ins wiedergefundene Paradies: Zu Werk und Poetik W. G. Sebalds', in Marcel Atze and Franz Loquai (eds), *Sebald: Lektüren*, Eggingen: Isele, pp. 244–56.

Maier, Anja K. (2006), ' "Der panische Halsknick": Organisches und Anorganisches in W. G. Sebalds Prosa', in Michael Niehaus and Claudia Öhlschläger (eds), *W. G. Sebald: Politische Archäologie und melancholische Bastelei*, Berlin: Erich Schmidt, pp. 111–26.

Meyer, Sven (2003), 'Fragmente zu Mememtos: Imaginierte Konjekturen bei W. G. Sebald', in Heinz Ludwig Arnold (ed.), *W. G. Sebald*, Munich: Text + Kritik, pp. 75–81.

Meyer, Sven (2005), 'Der Kopf, der auftaucht: Zu W. G. Sebalds *Nach der Natur*', in Marcel Atze and Franz Loquai (eds), *Sebald: Lektüren*, Eggingen: Isele, pp. 67–77.

McChesney, Anita (2006), 'On the Repeating History of Destruction: Media and Index in Sebald and Ransmayr', *Modern Language Notes* 121: 699–719.

McCulloh, Mark (2003), *Understanding W. G. Sebald*, Columbia, SC: University of South Carolina Press.

McCulloh, Mark (2006), 'Introduction: Two Languages, Two Audiences: The Tandem Literary Oeuvre of W. G. Sebald', in Scott Denham and Mark McCulloh (eds), *W. G. Sebald: Trauma, Memory, History*, Berlin: de Gruyter, pp. 7–20.

Morgan, Peter (2005), 'The Sign of Saturn: Melancholy, Homelessness and Apocalypse in W. G. Sebald's Prose Narratives', *German Life and Letters* 58: 75–92.

Niehaus, Michael (2006a), 'No Foothold: Institutions and Buildings in W. G. Sebald's Prose', in Scott Denham and Mark McCulloh (eds), *W. G. Sebald: Trauma, Memory, History*, Berlin: de Gruyter, pp. 315–33.

Niehaus, Michael (2006b), 'W. G. Sebalds sentimentalistische Dichtung', in Michael Niehaus and Claudia Öhlschläger (eds), *W. G. Sebald: Politische Archäologie und melancholische Bastelei*, Berlin: Erich Schmidt, pp. 173–87.

Nölp, Markus (2001), 'W. G. Sebalds *Ringe des Saturn* im Kontext photobebilderter Literatur', in Orlando Grossegesse and Erwin Koller (eds), *Literaturtheorie am Ende? 50 Jahre Wolfgang Kaisers 'Sprachliches Kunstwerk'*, Tübingen: Franke, pp. 129–41.

Öhlschläger, Claudia (2006a), *Beschädigtes Leben. Erzählte Risse: W. G. Sebalds poetische Ordnung des Unglücks*, Freiburg in Breisgau: Rombach.

Öhlschläger, Claudia (2006b), 'Der Saturnring oder Etwas vom Eisenbau: W. G. Sebalds poetische Zivilisationskritik', in Michael Niehaus and Claudia Öhlschläger (eds), *W. G. Sebald: Politische Archäologie und melancholische Bastelei*, Berlin: Erich Schmidt, pp. 189–204.

Pane, Samuel (2005), 'Trauma Obscura: Photographic Media in W. G. Sebald's *Austerlitz*', *Mosaic* 38: 37–54.

Parry, Anne (1997), 'Idioms for the Unrepresentable: Post-War Fiction and the Shoah', *Journal of European Studies* 108: 417–32.

Parry, Christoph (2004), 'Die zwei Leben des Herrn Austerlitz: Biographisches Schreiben als nicht-lineare Historiographie bei W. G. Sebald', in Edgar Platen and Martin Todtenhaupt (eds), *Grenzen, Grenzüberschreitungen, Grenzauflösungen: Zur Darstellung von Zeitgeschichte in deutschsprachiger Gegenwartsliteratur*, Munich: iudicium, pp. 113–30.

Pfeiffer, Peter C. (2003), 'Korrespondenz und Wahlverwandtschaft: W. G. Sebalds *Die Ringe des Saturn*', *Gegenwartsliteratur* 2: 226–44.

Prager, Brad (2006), 'Sebald's Kafka', in Scott Denham and Mark McCulloh (eds), *W. G. Sebald: Trauma, Memory, History*, Berlin: de Gruyter, pp. 105–25.

Presner, Todd Samuel (2004), ' "What a Synoptic and Analytic View Reveals": Extreme History and the Modernism of W. G. Sebald's Realism', *Criticism* 46: 341–60.

Reineke, Angela (2003), 'Authenticity, Truth, and the Other in Binjamin Wilkomirski's *Bruchstücke* and W. G. Sebald's *Die Ausgewanderten*', in Eric Caldicott and Anne Fuchs (eds), *Cultural Memory: Essays on European Literature and History*, Oxford: Lang, pp. 85–97.

Restuccia, Frances L. (2005), 'Sebald's Punctum: Awakening to Holocaust Trauma in *Austerlitz*', *European Journal of English Studies* 9: 301–22.

Riordan, Colin (2004), 'Ecocentrism in Sebald's *After Nature*', in J. J. Long and Anne Whitehead (eds), *W. G. Sebald: A Critical Companion*, Edinburgh: Edinburgh University Press, pp. 45–57.

Rovagnati, Gabriella (2005a), 'Canetti, Sebald, und die Quellen des Feuers: Zum apokalyptischen Schluß von W. G. Sebalds Erzählung "Il ritorino in patria"', in Marcel Atze and Franz Loquai (eds), *Sebald: Lektüren*, Eggingen: Isele, pp. 116–21.

Rovagnati, Gabriella (2005b), 'Das unrettbare Venedig des W. G. Sebald', in Marcel Atze and Franz Loquai (eds), *Sebald: Lektüren*, Eggingen: Isele, pp. 143–56.

Santner, Eric (2006), *On Creaturely Life: Rilke, Benjamin, Sebald*, Chicago, IL: University of Chicago Press.

Schedel, Susanne (2004), *'Wer weiß, wie es vor Zeiten wirklich gewesen ist?': Textbeziehungen als Mittel der Geschichtsdarstellung bei W. G. Sebald*, Würzburg: Königshausen und Neumann.

Schlesinger, Philip (2004), 'W. G. Sebald and the Condition of Exile', *Theory, Culture & Society* 21(2): 43–67.

Schlicht, Corinna (1998), 'Einblicke in österreichische Literatur: W. G. Sebalds Essays über Spezifika einer Literatur in Österreich', in Gerhard Köpf (ed.), *Mitteilungen über Max: Marginalien zu W. G. Sebald*, Oberhausen: Laufen, pp. 49–57.

Schlodder, Holger (1997), 'Die Schrecken der Überlebenden: Dialog-Collage über *Die Ausgewanderten* und *Die Ringe des Saturn*', in Franz Loquai (ed.), *W. G. Sebald: Porträt*, Eggingen: Isele, pp. 170–6.

Schuhmacher, Heinz (1998), 'Aufklärung, Auschwitz, Auslöschung: Eine Erinnerung an Paul Bereyter', in Gerhard Köpf (ed.), *Mitteilungen über Max: Marginalien zu W. G. Sebald*, Oberhausen: Laufen, pp. 58–84.

Schulte, Christian (2003), 'Die Naturgeschichte der Zerstörung: W. G. Sebalds Thesen zu "Luftkrieg und Literatur"', in Heinz Ludwig Arnold (ed.), *W. G. Sebald*, Munich: Text + Kritik, pp. 82–94.

Schütte, Uwe (2002), 'Der Hüter der Metaphysik: W. G. Sebalds Essays über die österreichische Literatur', *Manuskripte* 155: 124–8.

Schütte, Uwe (2003), ' "In einer wildfremden Gegend": W. G. Sebalds Essays über die österreichische Literatur', in Rüdiger Görner (ed.), *The Anatomist of Melancholy: Essays in Memory of W. G. Sebald*, Munich: iudicium, pp. 63–74.

Sheppard, Richard (2006), 'Dexter – Sinister: Some Observations on Decrypting the Mors Code in the Work of W. G. Sebald', *Journal of European Studies* 35: 419–63.

Sill, Oliver (1997a), ' "Aus dem Jäger ist ein Schmetterling geworden": Textbeziehungen zwischen Werken von W. G. Sebald, Franz Kafka und Vladimir Nabokov', *Poetica* 29: 596–623.

Sill, Oliver (1997b), 'Migration als Gegenstand der Literatur: W. G. Sebalds *Die Ausgewanderten*', in Armin Nassehi (ed.), *Nation, Ethnie, Minderheit: Beiträge zur Aktualität ethnischer Konflikte*', Vienna: Böhlau, pp. 309–30.

Simon, Ulrich (2005), 'Der Provokateur als Literaturhistoriker: Anmerkungen zu Literaturbegriff und Argumentationsverfahren in W. G. Sebalds essayistischen Schriften', in Marcel Atze and Franz Loquai (eds), *Sebald: Lektüren*, Eggingen: Isele, pp. 78–104.

Steinmann, Holger (2006), 'Zitatruinen unterm Hundsstern. W. G. Sebalds Ansichten von der Nachtseite der Philologie', in Michael Niehaus and Claudia Öhlschläger (eds), *W. G. Sebald: Politische Archäologie und melancholische Bastelei*, Berlin: Erich Schmidt, pp. 145–56.

Summers-Bremner, Eluned (2004), 'Reading, Walking, Mourning: W. G. Sebald's Peripatetic Fictions', *Journal of Narrative Theory* 34: 304–34.

Swales, Martin (2003), 'Intertextuality, Authenticity, Metonymy? On Reading W. G. Sebald', in Rüdiger Görner (ed.), *The Anatomist of Melancholy: Essays in Memory of W. G. Sebald*, Munich: iudicium, pp. 81–7.

Swales, Martin (2004), 'Theoretical Reflections on the Work of W. G. Sebald', in J. J. Long and Anne Whitehead (eds), *W. G. Sebald: A Critical Companion*, Edinburgh: Edinburgh University Press, pp. 23–8.

Szventivanyi, Christina (2006), 'W. G. Sebald and Structures of Testimony and Trauma: There are Spots of Mist That No Eye can Dispel', in Scott Denham and Mark McCulloh (eds), *W. G. Sebald: Trauma, Memory, History*, Berlin: de Gruyter, pp. 351–63.

Taberner, Stuart (2004), 'German Nostalgia? Remembering German-Jewish Life in W. G. Sebald's *Die Ausgewanderten* and *Austerlitz*', *Germanic Review* 79: 181–202.

Theisen, Bianca (2004), 'Prose of the World: W. G. Sebald's Literary Travels', *Germanic Review* 79: 163–79.

Theisen, Bianca (2006), 'A Natural History of Destruction: W. G. Sebald's *The Rings of Saturn*', *Modern Language Notes* 121: 563–81.

Tischel, Alexandra (2006), 'Aus der Dunkelkammer der Geschichte: Zum Zusammenhang von Photographie und Erinnerung in W. G. Sebalds *Austerlitz*', in Michael Niehaus and Claudia Öhlschläger (eds), *W. G. Sebald: Politische Archäologie und melancholische Bastelei*, Berlin: Erich Schmidt, pp. 31–45.

Vees-Gulani, Susanne (2006), 'The Experience of Destruction: W. G. Sebald, the Airwar, and Literature', in Scott Denham and Mark McCulloh (eds), *W. G. Sebald: Trauma, Memory, History*, Berlin: de Gruyter, pp. 335–49.

Veraguth, Hannes (2003), 'W. G. Sebald und die alte Schule: *Schwindel. Gefühle*, *Die Ausgewanderten*, *Die Ringe des Saturn* und *Austerlitz*', in Heinz Ludwig Arnold (ed.), *W. G. Sebald*, Munich: Text + Kritik, pp. 30–42.

Vogel-Klein, Ruth, ' "Stendhal nach Auschwitz": Zur Rezeption W. G. Sebalds in Frankreich', in Marcel Atze and Franz Loquai (eds), *Sebald: Lektüren*, Eggingen: Isele, pp. 133–42.

Ward, Simon (2004), 'Ruins and Poetics in the Works of W. G. Sebald', in J. J. Long and Anne Whitehead (eds), *W. G. Sebald: A Critical Companion*, Edinburgh: Edinburgh University Press, pp. 58–71.

Weber, Markus R. (1993), 'Phantomschmerz Heimweh: Denkfiguren der Erinnerung im literarischen Werk W. G. Sebalds', in Walter Delabar (ed.), *Neue Generation, neues Erzählen; Deutsche Prosaliteratur der Achtziger Jahre*, Opladen: Westdeutscher Verlag, pp. 57–67.

Weber, Markus R. (2001), 'Sechzehn Wege zu Austerlitz', *Neue Deutsche Literatur*: 100–8.

Weber, Markus R. (2003), 'Die fantastische befragt die pedantische Genauigkeit: Zu den Abbildungen in W. G. Sebalds Werken', in Heinz Ludwig Arnold (ed.), *W. G. Sebald*, Munich: Text + Kritik, pp. 63–74.

Williams, Arthur (1998), 'The Elusive First Person Plural: Real Absences in Reiner Kunze, Bernd-Dieter Hüge and W. G. Sebald', in Arthur Williams, Stuart Parkes and Julian Preece (eds), *'Whose Story?': Continuities in Contemporary German-Language Literature*, Bern: Lang, pp. 85–113.

Williams, Arthur (2000), 'W. G. Sebald: A Holistic Approach to Borders, Texts and Perspectives', in A. Williams, S. Parkes and J. Preece (eds), *German-Language Literature Today: International and Popular?*, Oxford: Lang, pp. 99–118.

Williams, Arthur (2001), ' "Das korsakowsche Syndrom": Remembrance and Responsibility in W. G. Sebald', in Helmut Schmitz (ed.), *German Culture and the Uncomfortable Past: Representations of National Socialism in Contemporary Germanic Literature*, Aldershot: Ashgate, pp. 65–86.

Williams, Arthur (2003), 'W. G. Sebald: Weit ausholende Annäherungen an ein problematisches Vaterland', in Volker Wehdeking and Anne-Marie Corbin (eds), *Deutschsprachige Erzählprosa seit 1990 im europäischen Kontext – Interpretationen, Intertextualität, Rezeption*, Trier: Wissenschaftlicher Verlag Trier, pp. 179–97.

Williams, Arthur (2004a), 'W. G. Sebald: Probing the Outer Edges of Nature', in Julian Preece and Osman Durrani (eds), *Cityscapes and Countryside in Contemporary German Literature*, Oxford: Lang, pp. 179–96.

Williams, Arthur (2004b), ' "Immer weiter ostwärts und immer weiter zurück in der Zeit": Exploring the Extended Kith and Kin of W. G. Sebald's *Austerlitz*', in Ian Foster and Juliet Wigmore (eds), *Neighbours and Strangers: Literary and Cultural Relations in Germany, Austria and Central Europe since 1989*, Amsterdam and New York: Rodopi, pp. 121–41.

Wilms, Wilfried (2004), 'Taboo and Repression in W. G. Sebald's *On the Natural History of Destruction*', in J. J. Long and Anne Whitehead (eds),

W. G. Sebald: A Critical Companion, Edinburgh: Edinburgh University Press, pp. 175–89.

Wilms, Wilfried (2006), 'Speak no Evil, Write no Evil: In Search of a Usable Language of Destruction', in Scott Denham and Mark McCulloh (eds), *W. G. Sebald: Trauma, Memory, History*, Berlin: de Gruyter, pp. 183–204.

Wirtz, Thomas (2001), 'Schwarze Zuckerwatte: Anmerkungen zu W. G. Sebald', *Merkur* 6: 530–4.

Witthaus, Jan-Henrik (2006), 'Fehlleistung und Fiktion: Sebaldsche Gedächtnismodelle zwischen Freud und Borges', in Michael Niehaus and Claudia Öhlschläger (eds), *W. G. Sebald: Politische Archäologie und melancholische Bastelei*, Berlin: Erich Schmidt, pp. 157–72.

Wohlleben, Doren (2003), 'Poetik des Schwindelns und Verschwindens bei Hartmut Lange, W. G. Sebald und Horst Stern', in Bettina von Jagow and Florian Steger (eds), *Differenzerfahrung und Selbst: Bewußtsein und Wahrnehmung in Literatur und Geschichte des 20. Jahrhunderts*, Heidelberg: Winter, pp. 333–53.

Wohlleben, Doren (2006), 'Effet de flou: Unschärfe als literarisches Mittel der Bewahrheitung in W. G. Sebalds *Schwindel. Gefühle*', in Michael Niehaus and Claudia Öhlschläger (eds), *W. G. Sebald: Politische Archäologie und melancholische Bastelei*, Berlin: Erich Schmidt, pp. 127–43.

Zilcosky, John (2004), 'Sebald's Uncanny Travels: the Impossibility of Getting Lost', in J. J. Long and Anne Whitehead (eds), *W. G. Sebald: A Critical Companion*, Edinburgh: Edinburgh University Press, pp. 102–20.

Zilcosky, John (2006), 'Lost and Found: Disorientation, Nostalgia and Holocaust Melodrama in Sebald's *Austerlitz*', *Modern Language Notes* 121: 679–98.

OTHER WORKS

Abraham, Nicholas (1994), 'Notes on the Phantom: A Complement to Freud's Metapsychology', in Nicolas Abraham and Maria Torok, *The Shell and the Kernel: Renewals of Psychoanalysis*, ed. and trans. Nicholas T. Rand, Chicago, IL and London: University of Chicago Press, pp. 171–6.

Adler, H. G. [1960] (2005), *Theresienstadt 1941–45: Das Antlitz einer Zwangsgemeinschaft. Geschichte, Soziologie, Psychologie*, 2nd edn, Göttingen: Wallstein.

Adorno, Theodor W. (1974), 'Standort des Erzählers im zeitgenössischen Roman', in *Noten zur Literatur*, Frankfurt am Main: Suhrkamp, pp. 41–8.

Adorno, Theodor W. (2003), *Minima Moralia*, Frankfurt am Main: Suhrkamp.

Adorno, Theodor W. and Max Horkheimer [1947] (1997), *Dialectic of Enlightenment*, trans. John Cumming, London: Verso.

Alloula, Malek [1981] (1986), *The Colonial Harem*, trans. Myrna Godzich and Wlad Godzich, Minneapolis, MN: University of Minnesota Press.

Anderson, Benedict (1991), *Imagined Communities: Reflections on the Origin and Spread of Nationalism*, 2nd edn, London: Verso.

Armstrong, Carol (2001), *Scenes in a Library: Reading the Photograph in the Book*, Cambridge, MA: MIT Press.

Armstrong, Nancy (1999), *Fiction in the Age of Photography: The Legacy of British Realism*, Cambridge, MA: Harvard University Press.

Assmann, Aleida (1999), *Erinnerungsräume: Formen und Wandlungen des kulturellen Gedächtnisses*, Munich: Beck.

Augé, Marc [1992] (1995), *Non-Places: Introduction to an Anthropology of Supermodernity*, trans. John Howe, London: Verso.

Azoulay, Ariella (2001), *Death's Showcase: The Power of the Image in Contemporary Democracy*, trans. by Ruvik Danieli, Cambridge, MA: MIT Press.

Baer, Ulrich (2001), *Spectral Evidence: The Photography of Trauma*, Cambridge, MA: MIT Press.

Bal, Mieke (1994), 'Telling Objects: A Narrative Perspective on Collecting', in John Elsner and Roger Cardinal (eds), *The Cultures of Collecting*, London: Reaktion, pp. 97–115.

Barthes, Roland (1970), *S/Z*, Paris: Seuil.

Barthes, Roland (1977), 'Rhetoric of the Image', in *Image, Music, Text*, trans. Stephen Heath, London: Fontana, pp. 32–52.

Barthes, Roland [1980] (1984), *Camera Lucida*, trans. Richard Howard, London: Flamingo.

Batchen, Geoffrey (2004), *Forget Me Not: Photography and Remembrance*, Princeton, NJ: Princeton Architectural Press.

Bauman, Zygmunt (1994), 'Desert Spectacular', in Keith Tester (ed.), *The Flâneur*, London: Routledge, pp. 138–57.

Bauman, Zygmunt [1989] (2000), *Modernity and the Holocaust*, Cambridge: Polity.

Benjamin, Walter (1973), *Charles Baudelaire: A Lyric Poet in the Era of High Capitalism*, trans. Harry Zohn, London: New Left Books.

Benjamin, Walter (1978), *Reflections*, ed. Peter Demetz, trans. Edmund Jephcott, New York: Harcourt Brace.

Benjamin, Walter (1999), 'The Storyteller', in *Illuminations*, trans. Harry Zohn, London: Pimlico, pp. 83–107.

Bennett, Tony (1995), *The Birth of the Museum: History, Theory, Politics*, London: Routledge.

Berger, John (1980), *About Looking*, New York: Pantheon.

Berman, Marshall [1982] (1998), *All that is Solid Melts into Air: The Experience of Modernity*, New York: Penguin.

Black, Jeremy (1997), *Maps and Politics*, London: Reaktion.

Block, Martin (1936), *Zigeuner: Ihr Leben und ihre Seele*, Leipzig: Bibliographisches Institut.

Blom, Philipp (2003), *To Have and to Hold: An Intimate History of Collectors and Collecting*, Harmondsworth: Penguin.

Boa, Elizabeth and Rachel Palfreyman (2000), *Heimat, A German Dream: Regional Loyalties and National Identity in German Culture 1890–1990*, Oxford: Oxford University Press.

Bopp, Petra (2003), 'Fremde im Visier: Private Fotografien von Wehrmachtsoldaten', in Anton Holzer (ed.), *Mit der Kamera bewaffnet: Krieg und Fotografie*, Marburg: Jonas, pp. 97–117.

Bourdieu, Pierre et al. (1965), *Un art moyen: Essai sur les usages sociaux de la photographie*, Paris: Minuit.

Brecht, Bertolt [1931] (1992), 'Der Dreigroschenprozess: Ein soziologisches Experiment', in Werner Hecht et al. (eds), *Große kommentierte Berliner und Frankfurter Ausgabe*, vol. 21, Frankfurt am Main: Suhrkamp, pp. 448–514.

Brooks, Peter (1984), *Reading for the Plot: Design and Intention in Narrative*, Cambridge, MA: Harvard University Press.

Browne, Sir Thomas (1946), *Musaeum Clausum; or Bibliotheca Abscondita: Containing Some Remarkable Books, Antiquities, Pictures & Rarities of Several Kinds, Scarce or Never Seen by Any Man Now Living*, in Geoffrey Keynes (ed.), *The Miscellaneous Writings of Sir Thomas Browne*, London: Faber, pp. 131–42.

Browne, Sir Thomas [1642] (1977a), *Religio Medici*, in C. A. Patrides (ed.), *The Major Works*, Harmondsworth: Penguin, pp. 57–161.

Browne, Sir Thomas [1658] (1977b), *The Garden of Cyrus; or, the Quincunciall, Lozenge, or Network Plantation of the Ancients, Artificially, Naturally, Mythically Considered*, in C. A. Patrides (ed.), *The Major Works*, Harmondsworth: Penguin, pp. 317–88.

Buck-Morss, Susan (1989), *The Dialectics of Seeing: Walter Benjamin and the Arcades Project*, Cambridge, MA: MIT Press.

Bürger, Peter (1974), *Theorie der Avantgarde*, Frankfurt am Main: Suhrkamp.

Butler, Judith (1990), *Gender Trouble: Feminism and the Subversion of Identity*, London: Routledge.

Cadava, Eduardo (1997), *Words of Light: Theses on the Photography of History*, Princeton, NJ: Princeton University Press.

Cartwright, Lisa (1995), 'Gender Artifacts: Technologies of Bodily Display in Medical Culture', in Lynne Cook and Peter Wollen (eds), *Visual Display: Culture Beyond Appearances*, Seattle, WA: Bay Press, pp. 219–35.

Caruth, Cathy (ed.) (1995), *Trauma: Explorations in Memory*, Baltimore, MD: Johns Hopkins University Press.

Caruth, Cathy (1996), *Unclaimed Experience: Trauma, Narrative, and History*, Baltimore, MD: Johns Hopkins University Press.

Chambers, Ross (1984), *Story and Situation: Narrative Seduction and the Power of Fiction*, Manchester: Manchester University Press.

Chambers, Ross (1998), *Loiterature*, Lincoln, NE: University of Nebraska Press.

Clifford, James (1985), 'Objects and Selves', in George Stocking (ed.), *Objects and Others: Essays on Museums and Material Culture*, Madison, WI: University of Wisconsin Press, pp. 236–46.

Clifford, James (1988), *The Predicament of Culture: Twentieth-Century Ethnography, Literature, and Art*, Cambridge, MA: Harvard University Press.

Comment, Bernard (1999), *The Panorama*, trans. Anne-Marie Glasheen, London: Reaktion.

Conrad, Joseph [1902] (1983), *Heart of Darkness*, ed. Paul O'Prey, Harmondsworth: Penguin.

Crane, Susan A. (2000), *Collecting and Historical Consciousness in Early Nineteenth-Century Germany*, Ithaca, NY: Cornell University Press.

Crary, Jonathan (1990), *Techniques of the Observer: On Vision and Modernity in the Nineteenth Century*, Cambridge, MA: MIT Press.

Crary, Jonathan (1999), *Suspensions of Perception: Attention, Spectacle and Modern Culture*, Cambridge, MA: MIT Press.

Derrida, Jacques (1995), *Archive Fever: A Freudian Impression*, trans. Eric Prenowitz, Chicago, IL: University of Chicago Press.

Descartes, René [1637] (2006), *A Discourse on the Method*, trans. Ian Maclean, Oxford: Oxford University Press.

Didi-Huberman, Georges (2003), *Invention of Hysteria: Charcot and the Photographic Iconography of the Salpêtrière*, trans. Alisa Hartz, Cambridge, MA: MIT Press.

Dillmann, Alfred (ed.) (1905), *Zigeuner-Buch*, Munich: Dr Wild'sche Buchdruckerei.

Doane, Mary Ann (2002), *The Emergence of Cinematic Time: Modernity, Contingency, the Archive*, Cambridge, MA: Harvard University Press.

Dreyfus, Hubert and Paul Rabinow (1983), *Michel Foucault: Beyond Structuralism and Hermeneutics*, 2nd edn, Chicago, IL: University of Chicago Press.

Eagleton, Terry (1981), *Literary Theory*, Oxford: Blackwell.

Ecker, Gisela, Martina Stange and Ulrike Vedder (eds) (2001), *Sammeln, Ausstellen, Wegwerfen*, Königstein: Helmer.

Eckermann, Johann Peter [1835] (1984), *Gespräche mit Goethe in den letzten Jahren seines Lebens*, ed. Regine Otto, Munich: Beck.

Edwards, Elizabeth (2001), *Raw Histories: Photography, Anthropology and Museums*, Oxford: Berg.

Ernst, Wolfgang (2002), *Das Rumoren der Archive*, Berlin: Merve.

Ernst, Wolfgang (2003), *Im Namen von Geschichte: Sammeln, Speichern, Erzählen: Infrastrukturelle Konfigurationen des deutschen Gedächtnisses*, Munich: Fink.

Flusser, Vilém [1983] (2000), *Towards a Philosophy of Photography*, trans. Anthony Mathews, London: Reaktion.

Foucault, Michel (1977), 'Fantasia of the Library', in *Language, Counter-Memory, Practice: Selected Essays and Interviews*, ed. and intr. Donald F. Bouchard, trans. Donald F. Bouchard and Sherry Simon, Oxford: Blackwell, pp. 87–109.

Foucault, Michel [1975] (1979), *Discipline and Punish: The Birth of the Prison*, trans. Alan Sheridan, Harmondsworth: Penguin.

Foucault, Michel (1980), *Power/Knowledge: Selected Interviews and Other Writings 1972–1977*, ed. Colin Gordon, trans. Colin Gordon et al., London: Harvester.

Foucault, Michel [1963] (1986), *Birth of the Clinic: An Archaeology of Medical Perception*, trans. A. M. Sheridan Smith, London: Routledge.

Foucault, Michel [1961] (1989a), *Madness and Civilisation: A History of Insanity in the Age of Reason*, trans. Richard Howard, London: Routledge.

Foucault, Michel [1966] (1989b), *The Order of Things: An Archaeology of the Human Sciences*, London: Routledge.

Foucault, Michel (1990), *The History of Sexuality, Volume 1: An Introduction*, trans. Robert Hurley, New York: Vintage.

Foucault, Michel [1984] (2000), 'Different Spaces', in James Faubion (ed.), *Essential Works of Foucault, Volume 2: Aesthetics, Method, and Epistemology*, trans. Robert Hurley et al., London: Penguin, pp. 175–85.

Foucault, Michel [1969] (2002a), *The Archaeology of Knowledge*, trans. A. M. Sheridan Smith, London: Routledge.

Foucault, Michel [1978] (2002b), 'Governmentality', in James D. Faubion (ed.), *Essential Works of Foucault, Volume 3: Power*, trans. Robert Hurley et al., London: Penguin, pp. 201–22.

Frank, Joseph (1963), 'Spatial Form in Modern Literature', in *The Widening Gyre: Crisis and Mastery in Modern Literature*, New Brunswick: Rutgers University Press, pp. 3–62.

Freud, Sigmund [1920] (1955), *Beyond the Pleasure Principle*, in James Strachey (ed. and trans.), *The Standard Edition of the Complete Psychological Works of Sigmund Freud*, vol. 18, London: Hogarth Press, pp. 1–64.

Freud, Sigmund [1912] (1958a), 'A Note on the Unconscious in Psychoanalysis', in James Strachey (ed. and trans.), *The Standard Edition of the Complete Psychological Works of Sigmund Freud*, vol. 7, London: Hogarth Press, pp. 255–66.

Freud, Sigmund [1914] (1958b), 'Remembering, Repeating and Working Through', in James Strachey (ed. and trans.), *The Standard Edition of the Complete Psychological Works of Sigmund Freud*, vol. 7, London: Hogarth Press, pp. 145–56.

Freud, Sigmund [1939] (1964), *Moses and Monotheism*, in James Strachey (ed. and trans.), *The Standard Edition of the Complete Psychological Works of Sigmund Freud*, vol. 23, London: Hogarth Press, pp. 1–137.

Freud, Sigmund (1989), *Jenseits des Lustprinzips*, in Alexander Mitscherlich, Angela Richards and James Strachey (eds), *Studienausgabe*, vol. 3, Frankfurt am Main: Fischer, pp. 213–72.

Fritzsche, Peter (2004), *Stranded in the Present: Modern Time and the Melancholy of History*, Harvard, MA: Harvard University Press.

Fritzsche, Peter (2005), 'The Archive', *History and Memory* 17: 15–44.

Fuchs, Anne, Mary Cosgrove and Georg Grote (eds) (2006), *German Memory Contests: The Quest for Identity in Literature, Film and Discourse since 1990*, Rochester, NY: Camden House.

Greenblatt, Stephen (1991), *Marvelous Possessions: The Wonder of the New World*, Chicago, IL: University of Chicago Press.

Groys, Boris (1997), *Logik der Sammlung: Am Ende des musealen Zeitalters*, Munich: Hanser.

Gunning, Tom (1995), 'Tracing the Individual Body: Photography, Detection and Early Cinema', in Leo Charney and Vanessa R. Schwartz (eds), *Cinema and the Invention of Modern Life*, Berkeley, CA: University of California Press, pp. 15–45.

Habermas, Jürgen (1988), *Der philosophische Diskurs der Moderne*, Frankfurt am Main: Suhrkamp.

Habermas, Jürgen [1980] (1990), 'Die Moderne: Ein unvollendetes Projekt', in *Die Moderne: Ein unvollendetes Projekt: Philosophisch-politische Aufsätze 1977–1990*, Leipzig: Reclam, pp. 32–54.

Hamilton, Peter and Roger Hargreaves (2001), *The Beautiful and the Damned: The Creation of Identity in Nineteenth-Century Photography*, Aldershot and Burlington: Lund Humphries.

Hansen, Miriam Bratu (1995), 'America, Paris, the Alps: Kracauer (and Benjamin) on Cinema and Modernity', in Leo Charney and Vanessa R. Schwartz (eds), *Cinema and the Invention of Modern Life*, Berkeley, CA: University of California Press, pp. 362–402.

Harley, J. B. (1988), 'Maps, Knowledge and Power', in Denis Cosgrove and Stephen Daniels (eds), *The Iconography of Landscape: Essays on the Symbolic Representation, Design and Use of Past Environments*, Cambridge: Cambridge University Press, pp. 277–312.

Harley, J. B. (1992), 'Deconstructing the Map', in Trevor J. Barnes and James S. Duncan (eds), *Writing Worlds: Discourse, Texts and*

Metaphor in the Representation of Landscape, London: Routledge, pp. 231–47.

Harvey, David (1990), *The Condition of Postmodernity: An Enquiry into the Origins of Cultural Change*, Oxford: Blackwell.

Hauser, Andrea (2001), 'Staunen – Lernen – Erleben: Bedeutungsebenen gesammelter Objekte und ihrer musealen Präsentation im Wandel', in Gisela Ecker, Martina Stange and Ulrike Vedder (eds), *Sammeln, Ausstellen, Wegwerfen*, Königstein: Helmer, pp. 32–48.

Haverty Rugg, Linda (1997), *Picturing Ourselves: Photography and Autobiography*, Chicago, IL: University of Chicago Press.

Hayles, N. Katherine (1998), *How We Became Posthuman: Virtual Bodies in Cybernetics, Literature and Informatics*, Chicago, IL: University of Chicago Press.

Hirsch, Marianne (1997), *Family Frames: Photography, Narrative and Postmemory*, Cambridge, MA: Harvard University Press.

Hirsch, Marianne (1999), 'Projected Memory: Holocaust Photographs in Personal and Public Fantasy', in Mieke Bal, Jonathan Crewe and Leo Spitzer (eds), *Acts of Memory: Cultural Recall in the Present*, Hanover and London: University Press of New England, pp. 3–23.

Hirsch, Marianne (2001), 'Surviving Images: Holocaust Photographs and the Work of Postmemory', in Barbie Zelizer (ed.), *Visual Culture and the Holocaust*, London: Athlone, pp. 215–46.

Hooper-Greenhill, Eilean (1992), *Museums and the Shaping of Knowledge*, London: Routledge.

Hutcheon, Linda (1988), *A Poetics of Postmodernism: History, Theory, Fiction*, London: Routledge.

Huyssen, Andreas (1988), *After the Great Divide: Modernism, Mass Culture, Postmodernism*, London: Macmillan.

Huyssen, Andreas (1995), *Twilight Memories: Marking Time in a Culture of Amnesia*, London: Routledge.

Jahn, Peter and Ulrike Schmiegelt (eds) (2000), *Foto-Feldpost: Geknipste Kriegserlebnisse 1939–1945*, Berlin: Museum Berlin-Karlshorst e. V. and Elephanten Press.

Jameson, Fredric (1983), *The Political Unconscious: Narrative as a Socially Symbolic Act*, London: Routledge.

Jameson, Fredric (1991), *Postmodernism; or, The Cultural Logic of Late Capitalism*, London: Verso.

Kafka, Franz [1926] (1992), *The Castle*, trans. Willa and Edwin Muir, London: Minerva.

Kermode, Frank (1981), 'Secrets and Narrative Sequence', in W. J. T. Mitchell (ed.), *On Narrative*, Chicago, IL: University of Chicago Press, pp. 79–97.

Kern, Stephen (1983), *The Culture of Time and Space 1880–1918*, Cambridge, MA: Harvard University Press.

Kern, Stephen (2004), *A Cultural History of Causality: Science, Murder Novels and Systems of Thought*, Princeton, NJ: Princeton University Press.

Knight, Peter (2000), *Conspiracy Culture: From Kennedy to the X-Files*, London: Routledge.

Koppen, Erwin (1987), *Literatur und Photographie: Über Geschichte und Thematik einer Medienentdeckung*, Stuttgart: Metzler.

Korsmeyer, Carolyn (1989), 'Instruments of the Eye: Shortcuts to Perspective', *Journal of Aesthetics and Art Criticism* 47: 139–46.

Kracauer, Siegfried [1927] (1963), 'Die Photographie', in *Das Ornament der Masse*, Frankfurt am Main: Suhrkamp, pp. 21–39.

LaCapra, Dominick (1994), *Representing the Holocaust: History, Theory, Trauma*, Ithaca, NY: Cornell University Press.

Lalvani, Suren (1996), *Photography, Vision and the Production of Modern Bodies*, Albany, NY: State University of New York Press.

Laub, Dori (1992a), 'Bearing Witness; or, The Vicissitudes of Listening', in Shoshana Felman and Dori Laub, *Testimony: Crises of Witnessing in Literature, Psychoanalysis and History*, London: Routledge, pp. 57–74.

Laub, Dori (1992b), 'An Event without a Witness: Truth, Testimony and Survival', in Shoshana Felman and Dori Laub, *Testimony: Crises of Witnessing in Literature, Psychoanalysis and History*, London: Routledge, pp. 75–92.

Lepenies, Wolf [1969] (1998), *Melancholie und Gesellschaft*, Frankfurt am Main: Suhrkamp.

Liss, Andrea (1998), *Trespassing through Shadows: Memory, Photography and the Holocaust*, Minneapolis, MN: University of Minnesota Press.

Long, J. J. (2006b), 'Monika Maron's *Pawels Briefe*: Photography, Narrative, and the Claims of Postmemory', in Anne Fuchs, Mary Cosgrove and Georg Grote (eds), *German Memory Contests: The Quest for Identity in Literature, Film, and Discourse since 1990*, Rochester, NY: Camden House, pp. 147–65.

Mack, Michael (ed.) (1999), *Reconstructing Space: Architecture in Recent German Photography*, London: Architectural Association.

Maier, Charles S. (1997), *The Unmasterable Past: History, Holocaust, and German National Identity*, 2nd edn, Cambridge, MA: Harvard University Press.

Malamud, Randy (1998), *Reading Zoos: Representations of Animals in Captivity*, Basingstoke: Macmillan.

Marías, Javier (2003), *Dark Back of Time*, trans. Esther Allen, London: Chatto and Windus.

Marx, Karl and Friedrich Engels [1848] (1989), *Manifest der Kommunistischen Partei*, Stuttgart: Reclam.

Maxwell, Anne (1999), *Colonial Photography and Exhibitions: Representations of the 'Native' and the Making of European Identities*, London: Leicester University Press.

McElligott, Anthony (ed.) (2001), *The German Urban Experience 1900–1945: Modernity and Crisis*, London: Routledge.

McGrath, Roberta (2002), *Seeing her Sex: Medical Archives and the Female Body*, Manchester: Manchester University Press.

McHale, Brian (1987), *Postmodernist Fiction*, London: Routledge.

Mitchell, W. J. T. (1986), *Iconology: Image, Text, Ideology*, Chicago, IL: University of Chicago Press.

Mitchell, W. J. T. (1994), *Picture Theory*, Chicago, IL: University of Chicago Press.

Mulvey, Laura (1989), 'Visual Pleasure and Narrative Cinema', in *Visual and Other Pleasures*, Basingstoke: Macmillan, pp. 14–26.

Niederland, William G. (1980), *Folgen der Verfolgung*, Frankfurt am Main: Suhrkamp.

Nietzsche, Friedrich [1874] (1988), *Vom Nutzen und Nachteil der Historie für das Leben*, in *Kritische Studienausgabe*, ed. Giorgio Colli and Mazzino Montinari, Munich: dtv; and Berlin: de Gruyter, vol. 1, pp. 243–334.

Niven, Bill (2002), *Facing the Nazi Past: United Germany and the Legacy of the Third Reich*, London: Routledge.

Patrides, C. A. (1977), 'Above Atlas his Shoulders: An Introduction to Sir Thomas Browne', in C. A. Patrides (ed.), *Sir Thomas Browne: The Major Works*, Harmondsworth: Penguin, pp. 21–52.

Penny, H. Glenn (2002), *Objects of Culture: Ethnology and Ethnographic Museums in Imperial Germany*, Chapel Hill, NC: University of North Carolina Press.

Preziosi, Donald (2003), *Brain of the Earth's Body: Art, Museums, and the Phantasms of Modernity*, Minneapolis, MN: University of Minnesota Press.

Prior, Nick (2002), *Museums and Modernity: Art Galleries and the Making of Modern Culture*, Oxford: Berg.

Proust, Marcel (1954), *A la recherche du temps perdu*, ed. Pierre Clarac and André Ferré, vol. 3, Paris: Pléiade.

Regener, Susanne (1999), *Fotografische Erfassung: Zur Geschichte medialer Konstruktionen des Kriminellen*, Munich: Fink.

Reid, Ian (1992), *Narrative Exchanges*, London: Routledge.

Richards, Thomas (1996), *The Imperial Archive*, London: Verso.

Shields, Rob (1994), 'Fancy Footwork: Walter Benjamin's Notes on *Flânerie*', in Keith Tester (ed.), *The Flâneur*, London: Routledge, pp. 61–80.

Schivelbusch, Wolfgang (2004), *Geschichte der Eisenbahnreise: Zur Industrialisierung von Raum und Zeit im 19. Jahrhundert*, Frankfurt am Main: Fischer.

Schmiegelt, Ulrike (2000), ' "Macht euch um mich keine Sorgen". . .', in Peter Jahn and Ulrike Schmiegelt (eds), *Foto-Feldpost: Geknipste Kriegserlebnisse 1939–1945*, Berlin: Museum Berlin-Karlshorst e. V. and Elephanten Press, pp. 23–31.

Schor, Naomi (1994), 'Collecting Paris', in John Elsner and Roger Cardinal (eds), *The Cultures of Collecting*, London: Reaktion, pp. 252–74.

Sekula, Alan (1992), 'The Body and the Archive', in Richard Bolton (ed.), *The Contest of Meaning: Critical Histories of Photography*, Cambridge, MA: MIT Press, pp. 343–89.

Silverman, Kaja (1996), *The Threshold of the Visible World*, London: Routledge.

Simmel, Georg [1900] (1950), 'The Metropolis and Mental Life', in Kurt H. Wolff (ed. and trans.), *The Sociology of Georg Simmel*, New York: Collier-Macmillan, pp. 409–24.

Simon, Jonathan (2002), 'The Theater of Anatomy: The Anatomical Preparations of Honoré Fragonard', *Eighteenth-Century Studies* 36: 63–79.

Síochláin, Séamus and Michael Sullivan (eds) (2003), *The Eyes of Another Race: Roger Casement's Congo Report and 1903 Diary*, Dublin: University College Dublin Press.

Smith, Shawn Michelle (1999), *American Archives: Gender, Race and Class in Visual Culture*, Princeton, NJ: Princeton University Press.

Solnit, Rebecca (2000), *Wanderlust: A History of Walking*, London: Verso.

Solomon-Godeau, Abigail (1991), *Photography at the Dock: Essays on Photographic History, Institutions, and Practices*, Minneapolis, MN: University of Minnesota Press.

Sontag, Susan (1979), *On Photography*, Harmondsworth: Penguin.

Starl, Timm (1995), *Knipser: Die Bildgeschichte der privaten Fotografie in Deutschland und Österreich von 1880 bis 1980*, Munich: Koehler and Amelang.

Steedman, Carolyn (2001), *Dust*, Manchester: Manchester University Press.

Stewart, Susan (1993), *On Longing: Narratives of the Miniature, the Gigantic, the Souvenir, the Collection*, Durham, NC: Duke University Press.

Stiegler, Bernd (2001), *Philologie des Auges: Die photographische Entdeckung der Welt im 19. Jahrhundert*, Munich: Fink.

Tagg, John (1988), *The Burden of Representation: Essays on Photographies and Histories*, Basingstoke: Macmillan.

Terdiman, Richard (1993), *Present Past: Modernity and the Memory Crisis*, Ithaca, NY: Cornell University Press.

Tester, Keith (ed.) (1994), *The Flâneur*, London: Routledge.

Todorov, Tsvetan [1991] (1999), *Facing the Extreme: Moral Life in the Concentration Camps*, trans. Arthur Denner and Abigail Pollack, London: Weidenfeld and Nicholson.

Torpey, John (2000), *The Invention of the Passport: Surveillance, Citizenship and the State*, Cambridge: Cambridge University Press.

Vidler, Anthony (1990), *Claude-Nicholas Ledoux: Architecture and Social Reform at the End of the Ancien Regime*, Cambridge, MA: MIT Press.

Vietta, Sylvio (1992), *Die literarische Moderne: Eine problemgeschichtliche Darstellung der deutschsprachigen Literatur von Hölderlin bis Thomas Bernhard*, Stuttgart: Metzler.

Whitehead, Anne (2004), *Trauma Fiction*, Edinburgh: Edinburgh University Press.

Williamson, Jack H. (1986), 'The Grid: History, Use and Meaning', *Design Issues*, 3(2): 15–30.

Wimsatt, W. K. and Monroe C. Beardsley (1970), 'The Intentional Fallacy', in *The Verbal Icon: Studies in the Meaning of Poetry*, London: Methuen, pp. 3–18.

INDEX

abnormality, 37
Adler, H. G., 81, 160
administration, 9, 10, 76, 82, 111, 131, 159, 166n
Adorno, Theodor W., 106, 108n, 158
affect, 59, 94, 111, 115, 118, 120, 121, 123, 128n, 140
Albes, Claudia, 137, 142, 172
albums, 11, 57, 65, 66, 68n, 121
    family, 19, 47, 51, 56, 60, 110, 111, 112, 120, 122, 123, 127
alienation, 6, 98, 101, 142, 149, 150, 160
Alloula, Malek, 68n
allusion, 7, 8, 87n, 106
anatomo-politics, 61, 76
anatomy, 30, 34, 36, 73, 135
Anderson, Benedict, 92
Anderson, Mark M., 3, 68n
Angier, Carole, 75
anthropology, 5, 29, 31, 37, 49, 51
archaeology, 29, 82, 83
    of knowledge, 22, 68, 72
    as metaphor in Freud, 4

architecture, 17, 20, 42, 61, 83, 150, 151, 152, 153, 159, 164, 166n
archival consciousness, 65, 93, 95, 99, 100, 107, 149
archive, 4, 8, 9–10, 11–12, 13, 15, 16, 18, 19, 20, 21n, 22n, 27, 35, 37, 49, 65, 68n, 72, 74, 75, 76, 77, 78, 80, 81–3, 85–6, 87n, 93, 99, 100, 106, 107, 110–11, 114, 116, 117, 118, 123, 127, 130, 142, 143, 144, 146, 149, 152–4, 158–63, 165, 166, 170, 171
Armstrong, Nancy, 53
Arnold-de Simine, Silke, 32, 161
Assmann, Aleida, 101, 107n
Astaire, Fred, 165
atlases, 11, 37, 78–80
    anatomical, 80, 135
Atze, Marcel, 101
Auerbach, Frank, 47
Augé, Marc, 101
authenticity, 15, 17, 47, 48, 65, 67, 93, 94, 146, 149, 157–8, 161, 171

202

CPSIA information can be obtained
at www.ICGtesting.com
Printed in the USA
LVHW052156250423
745354LV00007B/268